I am a fleeting moment in time

Kathak Guru **Shovana Narayan**

DR MAYA 'PARIJAT'

Vitasta

Published by
Renu Kaul Verma
Vitasta Publishing Pvt Ltd
4348/4C, Ansari Road, Daryaganj
New Delhi-110 002
info@vitastapublishing.com

ISBN: 978-81-991712-0-6

First Edition 2025
MRP ₹ 750

Edited by Priya Khanna
Cover Design by Smriti Maheshwari
Layout by Shubhpreet Kaur
Printed by Vikas Computer and Printers, New Delhi

Contents

Praise for the Book

Guru Shovana Narayan's creativity is boundless. Beyond being an iconic Kathak dancer, she has crossed many boundaries, interacting with other Indian and western dance forms, using all mediums for expressing her performances, researching its ancient roots as a historian, and deepening our understanding of it as a philosopher. She is a Guru in the true spirit of the word.

Kabir Bedi
Actor

I cannot imagine one book could do justice to the rich and varied life my dear friend Shovana has led. Dancer par excellence, distinguished officer of the IAAS, and devoted wife. The list is too long to mention here. I would recommend this beautifully written story of the life of an extraordinary lady.

Satish Jacob
Journalist BBC (Retired)

I am delighted that a biography of the well-known, highly decorated, and accomplished Kathak exponent Dr Shovana Narayan has been written by Ms Maya, an outstanding author. I have known Shovana for more than forty years and over this period, I have never ceased to be amazed, impressed, and inspired by her energy, dedication, warmth, and commitment to the propagation and promotion of Kathak in India and around the globe. She has beautifully balanced her life as a senior officer in the Government of India, as the wife of a senior and highly successful Austrian diplomat, and of course, as a dancer, performer, guru, choreographer, author, and a loving and caring human being. The current biography will add to a fuller understanding of Shovana's life journey and motivate all readers, particularly young women, on how to achieve success simultaneously in diverse fields and maintain a healthy balance in family and work life. I wish the biography all success.

Ashok Sajjanhar

Former Ambassador to Kazakhstan, Sweden, and Latvia

Smt Shovana Narayan is a dreamer of dreams and has spared no effort to realise those dreams. I am glad that she has not rested on her laurels and continues her journey. May it be meaningful. May success accompany every step that she takes.

Meira Kumar

Former Speaker, Lok Sabha

The biography of the globally acclaimed Kathak maestro-Shovana Narayan is an inspiring document for coming generations and will serve as a reminder of what passion, purpose, and perseverance can achieve. Not just Bihar and the Kayastha community to which she belongs, but the entire nation is proud of Shovana Narayan, daughter of Bihar. She has also served as Director in the Rajya Sabha, exemplifying her remarkable ability to thrive in two demanding arenas. My heartfelt congratulations to Shovana Narayan and also to the author Maya for documenting such an extraordinary journey.

Shatrughan Sinha
MP, Lok Sabha

This biography offers an intimate portrait of Kathak Guru Shovana Narayan, who has redefined centuries-old tradition while remaining deeply rooted in its classical essence. As the wife of former Austrian Ambassador to India, Mr Herbert Traxl, Shovana Narayan has long been woven into the fabric of Austria's cultural and diplomatic presence in India. Through numerous performances, shared initiatives, and a mutual appreciation for the arts, she has become an enduring friend of Austria and a familiar figure within our diplomatic and cultural circles. On a personal note, I am privileged to count her as a cherished friend—her warmth, intellect, and generosity of spirit have been a source of joy and inspiration throughout my tenure in India. This book is more than a chronicle of a remarkable life—it is a tribute to the enduring beauty of classical Indian dance and to the woman who has become one of its most passionate voices.

H E Katharina Wieser
Austrian Ambassador to India, Bhutan,
Bangladesh, Nepal, Sri Lanka and the Maldives

Shovana ji is an enigma and an inspiration. Having worked in the Indian Audit and Accounts Service (IAAS) and achieved the pinnacle in her career, she has reached her greatest heights in Kathak. Her achievements in the field of Kathak can be outlined in a single word 'Guru.' Shovana ji's excellence is reflected in her numerous disciples, which is showcased in the annual Guru Shishya dance festival. The book is a glorious reflection of Shovana ji's commitment in the world of classical dance and music. We wish her all the very best in her future endeavours.

Alok B Shriram
Sr Managing Director and CEO of
DCM Shriram Industries Ltd

Karuna Shriram
Educationist and Social Worker

The biography of Kathak legend Shovana Narayan takes readers on an extraordinary journey, moving beyond the rhythmic beats of the dance to uncover the soul of an art form steeped in cultural history, raw emotion, and timeless storytelling. With remarkable grace, Shovana intertwines centuries of tradition with her own transformative journey through life's trials and triumphs. Far more than a celebration of Kathak, the book is a radiant tribute to the resilience, depth, and splendour of India's artistic spirit and philosophy through the lens of classical music and dance. A must-read for anyone seeking to connect with their core.

Maya Shankar
Art Connoisseur
Former Chairperson SPIC MACAY, Patna Chapter
Professor of History (Retd), Patna University

It is a moment of immense pride for the Kayastha community and Bihar to celebrate Padma Shri Shovana Narayan, an internationally renowned Kathak maestro, whose unparalleled achievements have brought global recognition to our country. As the only Kayastha from Bihar to attain such distinction in this art form, Shovana Narayan is not only a world-class artist but has also been an outstanding civil servant, having served as Director General of Audit. During my tenure as Principal Commissioner of GST and Customs, it was an honour to witness her brilliance and perfect balance of mind and heart, as a bureaucrat. Recognising her contributions to the revival of cultural heritage of India and to the global recognition of Kathak, it is our privilege to have her as a Patron of the Akhil Bhartiya Kayastha Mahasabha. I also commend Maya for the bold and challenging task of documenting the life of Mrs Shovana Narayan in this book, whose achievements transcend words. I wish the book serves as a reminder to our younger generation that they can actually have it all if they pursue their goals in all earnestness with persistence and perseverance.

Dr Anup K Srivastava, IRS (Retd)

President, Akhil Bhartiya Kayastha Mahasabha

It is my proud privilege, indeed, to talk about my association with an international performer of global fame, a bureaucrat with humility and a visionary who has established a fact that dance can be therapeutic for one and all.

I have known Shovana ji for over three decades. Life is all about human relationships and I can talk with pride about the humility of Shovana ji a person who is down to earth.

When I first saw her performance on stage, I could not resist approaching her with my request to train our inclusive team of students with and without disability together on the stage. She took it as a challenge and surprised everyone during the inauguration of International Abilympics. She trained a large group of children with multiple disabilities to perform with the non-disabled. It was an amazing show in front of the Hon'ble Prime Minister of India who inaugurated the sixth International Abilympics hosted by India.

Apart from the applause, there was repeated shouting of having the performance again to understand how inclusion is the ultimate winner. Measuring steps for the visually impaired, preparing visuals for the hearing impaired; repeating steps for the intellectually delayed and keeping accessibility in mind for the orthopaedically challenged was an amazing successful effort.

The relationship continued with the repeated request of sending her disciples to our institute for training so that inclusive performances could be continued.

She succeeded in initiating dance as a therapy for persons with and without disability, which is now a legacy to be followed for years to come. One can easily understand her language spoken through her expressions while dancing on the stage. Through her dance she makes the spirits triumph.

Knitting stories of different themes and putting them together skilfully with a message is her specialty. It used to be a treat when she had her *potato paratha* sitting amongst the children during break time. She picked up sign language also easily when she had to deal with hearing-impaired students.

We always wonder how she could confine her official work, domestic chores and dancing practices in her daily life without feeling exhausted.

As our advisor of Amar Jyoti Charitable Trust, she has been contributing immensely in several ways. Having her gracious presence in our official as well as personal functions has been a source of strength always.

I know, for her age is just a number and she proves it by performing with the same vigour, zeal and passion as she did when she was younger.

We need many avatars of Shovana ji to carry on her legacy of what she has created not only for our country but for the entire universe.

Dr Uma Tuli
Founder & Managing Secretary
Former Chief Commissioner, Disabilities

Dr Shovana Narayan, our veteran Kathak guru-performer-choreographer has made a major contribution to the cultural scene in the Capital over the last several decades. She also completed a career as a government servant in the Indian Audit and Accounts Department till her retirement. She is a scholar and has authored many books. I am happy that her biography is being written which, I am sure, will be most interesting.

Dr Karan Singh
Former Minister of Education and Philosopher

Ich liebe meine Oma so sehr!
Sie ist die tollste tänzerin in der ganzen welt und sie hilft mir immer—sie ist immer für uns da!
Mit viel liebe,

Lyla

Oma tanzt immer für uns—und das liebe ich!
Ihre kleider sind so schön.
Oma, du bist die beste!
Viele bussis,

Suri

I love my grandma so much!
She is the most amazing dancer in the whole world and
she always helps me—
she is always there for us!
With lots of love,

Lyla

Grandma always dances for us—and I love that!
Her dresses are so beautiful.
Grandma, you're the best!
Lots of kisses,

Suri

* Dictated by Suri and written by Lyla, her grandchildren

Ich liebe meine Oma so sehr! ♥
Sie ist die tollste Tänzerin in
der ganzen Welt und sie
hilft mir immer – Sie ist immer
für uns da! ♥
Mit viel Liebe
Lyla

Oma tanzt immer für uns – und
das liebe ich! ♥
ihre Kleider sind so schön ♡
Oma, du bist die Beste! ♥
Viele Bussis
♥ Suri
(dictated by Suri and
written by Lyla)

Ich Liebe ~~meine Oma.~~ Sie
hilft ~~mier immer. Und sie~~
~~Kann sher sher gut Tanzen!~~

Author's Note

As a child, I often gazed at the star-studded skies, enchanted by their timeless brilliance. How were these celestial wonders born? What secret forces sustained their radiant dance? Why did some shine with a commanding brilliance, drawing all eyes, while others shimmered gently in the background, their quiet beauty no less profound?

When I set out to chronicle the life of Padma Shri Guru Shovana Narayan, one of India's most revered Kathak maestros, I felt that same sense of wonder. How does a star like her come into being? How does it forge its unique path amidst a constellation already brimming with brilliance? What keeps its light alive, defying time and challenges?

Shovana Narayan, despite her towering achievements and the reverence she commands, treats any notion of fame with characteristic modesty and humour. Her response to describing her story was delightfully disarming: 'Why on earth would you accept the ordeal of an untimely, unnatural funeral for yourself by taking this up? I'm no Shah Rukh Khan or Madhuri Dixit, you know!'

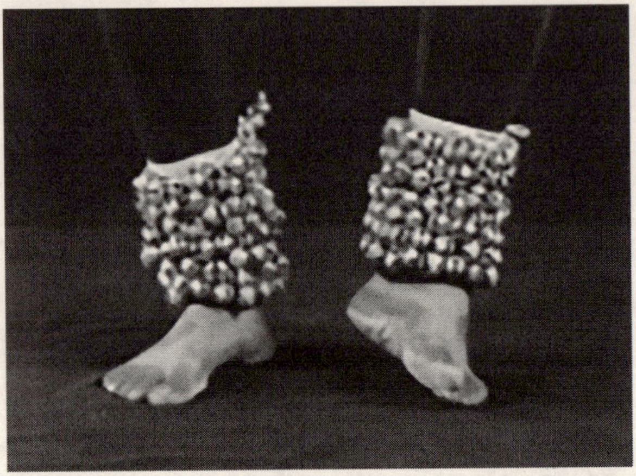

As I delved deeper into this extraordinary star's journey, I saw the process unfold—the raw energy of passion, the magnetic pull of unwavering discipline, and the harmonious fusion of tradition and innovation that fuelled her radiance. Witnessing how Shovana Narayan's light expanded, illuminating not just the world of Kathak but also touching countless hearts across the globe, has been a humbling and inspiring experience.

This journey has been one of discovery—unveiling what it truly takes to achieve greatness and more importantly, to endure.

In sharing her story, I aim to capture not just the ascent of a star but the marvel of its creation, its resilience, and its profound influence on the world it touches.

While many have celebrated her artistry through various expressions, capturing her journey and the essence of her character has been a daunting yet meaningful endeavour. It is in her unassuming nature, her gentle humour, and her unwavering discipline that we see the true spirit of her artistry, and it is this spirit that I hope to honour and preserve in these pages.

Dr Maya 'Parijat'

Foreword

It is difficult for me to be objective about Padma Shri Shovana Narayan. She has been a close and admired friend for so long that the lines blur in my mind when I try to disassociate my personal relationship with her and try to write about her achievements as one of India's most talented Kathak dancers, a person of unbounded creativity transcending being a mere Kathak dancer, and a successful bureaucrat.

But I shall still make the attempt, for the simple reason that she deserves it. I see her multifaceted personality at several levels. First and foremost, is her public image as a much beloved and appreciated *prima donna* of Kathak. I have been a personal witness to the passion, conviction, and sheer hard work she has invested in this arena. Her passion stems from her love—indeed worship—of Kathak, its grandeur, grace, rhythm, and *bhava*. Her conviction is inspired from her belief that to preserve this ancient creative form in all its pristine glory, is her duty. And, both her passion and conviction, have motivated her to master this art form with decades of concentrated *sadhana*, practice, and study, that has few parallels among her peers. I recall that once she told me that prolonged practice has led to hair-line fractures in her feet, but typically, she brushed that aside and reiterated that nothing can come between her and her dance.

In fact, in this process, Shovana has evolved from being merely a Kathak maestro to a creative prodigy. Her ability to see Kathak, not only as technical virtuosity, but as an instrument for a much wider canvas of creative expression, has allowed her to interpret emotion—both modern and ancient—and to adapt, adopt, and modify the genre when the need arises, without the slightest distortion of the sublime spirit animating the original. I have myself been a participant and observer of this remarkable journey. My long poem, *Yudhisthara and Draupadi,* composed in fourteen-line rhymed sonnets and published by Penguin (and later translated into Hindustani by one of India's most celebrated poets, Gulzar), was adapted by her into a dance-theatre performance. Her seemingly effortless ability to convert a somewhat abstruse piece of poetry into one of the most riveting spectacles of dance and theatre (in collaboration with Sunit Tandon), has won accolades, not only in India, but abroad.

I have had the privilege of also knowing Shovana's avatar as a bureaucrat. Indeed, she is my batchmate in service, although we belonged to different services. What is amazing is that her professionalism in dealing with mundane matters of governance did not in any way interfere with her poles-apart world as a Kathak artist. I can say from personal experience that this is not an easy task to achieve. I too have been a full-time diplomat, and later a politician, and simultaneously a writer. Many times, I have been asked how I manage to do both. I now realise that my answers should just have been compressed into one simple sentence: 'I take my inspiration from Shovana.'

At a third level, I have no hesitation in saying that Shovana is one of the most loyal friends to have. She has an ingrained kindness and compassion, that perhaps owes itself to just being a wonderful human being. I have publicly said, and written as well, that I have never seen Shovana back-biting another artist, or speaking an ill word about anybody for that matter. What most people remember about her is her elegance and that ready and full laughter, that literally lights up a room. Ambassador Herbert Traxl, her husband, and she are among the most popular couples in New Delhi's social life, and excellent hosts themselves.

There is another dimension to Shovana too. She has made forays into writing and academics, on Kathak and its history, and in chronicling our civilisational history. I have read her books and have found them always diligently researched and well-written. This is yet another proof that she takes her role as an artist far beyond merely that of a stellar performer, to a serious student of art and heritage.

I am delighted that Maya has brought about this readable and researched biography of my good friend. The book is a labour of love, and I wish Shovana, Maya, and the book all the best.

Pavan K Varma
Former MP (Rajya Sabha)
Former Ambassador of India to Bhutan

Credits:- Indrajeet Singh Grover
Eminent Artist

Cradled in Courage

As the evening sun spread its soft glow over Calcutta, its intensity began to wane as though tired from the day's exertion. The following day promised to be significant, for it would mark the birth of Lord Krishna. All around, preparations for the auspicious day were in full swing. Women hummed softly as they went about their tasks, their voices mingling with the warm hues of the setting sun.

Bhauji cleaned a small *palna* (cradle) for Lord Krishna's *sthapana* (installation). Nearby, Lalita, heavily pregnant, observed the preparations with a serene smile. Noticing her condition, Bhauji remarked that soon she too would be singing lullabies to her little one. She wondered aloud if Lalita's baby would arrive on time, adding with a light laugh that if the baby were born the next day, who knows—it might just be Lord Krishna reincarnated.

Lalita smiled, her heart brimming with prayers for her unborn child. Softly, she sang, '*Adharam madhuram, vadanam madhuram, nayanam madhuram, hasitam madhuram, hridayam madhuram, gamanam madhuram, madhuradhipaterkhilam madhuram*...' She gazed at the evening sun, lost in her devotional chant when she suddenly felt the first pangs of labour.

Feeling a sense of urgency, Lalita called out for Bhauji to summon the midwife quickly. Hearing her cry, Mr and Mrs Gangopadhyaya rushed in to assist. As they awaited the midwife's arrival, Mr Gangopadhyaya, ever the optimist, suggested that Lalita try to hold on until the next day so the baby's birth might coincide with Lord Krishna's.

Lalita's husband, however, was too anxious for such talk. Pacing the floor with frayed nerves, he reminded everyone there was no time to waste, while puffing nervously on his cigarette. The moments stretched unbearably long, but at last, the midwife arrived. Soon after, the tiny wails of the newborn filled the room, breaking the tension. The new father, who had restlessly paced the drawing room, finally sighed in relief.

Inside the bedroom, amidst the flurry of the baby's sudden arrival, Bhauji, in her panic, had forgotten to spread a sheet on which to place the newborn. The tiny infant lay on a newspaper on the floor, a rushed and humble beginning. Lalita, sensing the commotion, asked what had happened. The midwife's reply in Bhojpuri, '*Kuchcho nahin bheel.*' (nothing happened), carried a tone of disappointment.

When Lalita pressed further, she understood the unspoken truth: it was a girl. A sense of social bias crept in—how, for many, the birth of a girl was considered 'nothing.' In a world that often celebrated a son as an heir, a daughter was too often seen as a burden. But Lalita held her newborn daughter close, feeling a deep surge of love and determination. This child, she resolved, would be both a son and a daughter to her. She would not allow her daughter to be regarded as a 'nobody.' She would be the *shobha* (pride) of their home.

Lalita named her daughter 'Shobhana' inspired by her cousin's suggestion. However, due to a small error in spelling, Shobhana soon became 'Shovana.' Her doting parents noticed the mistake but let it be, charmed by the uniqueness of the new spelling.

With unwavering love, they were determined that their little *putul* (doll) would live a life that the world would watch with surprise and in awe. They envisioned a future where their daughter would not just exist, but excel—becoming the pride of their family. *'Meri ichha hai ki jahaan jahaan meri beti ke charan pare, wahaan ki dhool log maathe pe lagaayen....'* (I wish that wherever my daughter walks, becomes sacred dust that people will apply to their forehead in veneration.)

As a restless child, Shovana's boundless energy often left her asking her mother, '*Ma, ab mein kya karun?*' (Mother, what should I do now?). In exasperation, her mother would shrug and say, '*Jao, nacho*!' (Go dance)—a throwaway comment that inadvertently sparked a lifelong passion.

Little did Lalita know that *nach* (dance) would become Shovana's destiny.

Beyond Gharanas

In the sacred silence before dawn, where the veil between reality and the ethereal grows thin, the world of Kathak unveils its myriad faces. Each Gharana, a unique constellation in the grand dance of tradition, sparkles with its narrative, history, and technique. The Jaipur Gharana swirls with the regal elegance of kings, while the Lucknow Gharana narrates tales with delicate grace. The Banaras Gharana pulses with the vigour of ancient rhythms, and the Raigarh Gharana resonates with rhythmic patterns enhanced with imagery. Yet, beyond these storied lineages, there lies an ocean where boundaries dissolve, and the essence of dance transcends specific forms and styles.

In this boundless expanse, the artist's vision emerges as a transcendent force—one that does not merely blend the sacred with the secular but seeks to unite them in a universal expression. The true essence of dance is revealed here amidst the confluence of diverse traditions and the infinite possibilities of the human spirit. For in the artist's embrace of the world's varied rhythms, there is a profound reminder that dance, in its most sublime form, is an unspoken language of unity that speaks to the soul of all humanity.

In the warm, sunlit room, a two-and-a-half-year-old Shovana, with wide, curious eyes, stood before Sadhna Bose, the Kathak guru from Calcutta. Shovana's tiny feet, unsure yet eager, took tentative steps as she faced this great teacher. Lalita, her mother, watched from the side, her heart swelling with quiet pride and a tinge of wonder at the unfolding scene. Though young, Shovana's curiosity and attentive gaze spoke volumes, drawing Sadhna ji in.

At first, Sadhna ji laughed at the idea of teaching such a tiny dancer, but the moment she saw the spark in Shovana's eyes—those talking eyes, full of questions—something stirred within her. A deep and unconditional maternal instinct guided her decision to teach this child.

She led Shovana through the dance basics with infinite patience, teaching her the first step, *ta thai thai tat*, by gently guiding her little feet. After each lesson, the guru would hold Shovana close, cradling her in her lap and feeding her with loving hands. Guru Sadhna was imparting not just her knowledge of dance but creating a bond—a connection that would remain etched in Shovana's heart forever.

Today, as Shovana gazes at the first *lehenga* she wore as a child, now framed and hanging in her living room, her eyes moisten with memories. This lehenga marked the beginning of her dance journey, and though her time with Sadhna ji was brief, her guru's grace, love, and teachings remain with her.

With a voice full of reverence, Shovana speaks about the concept of Gharana, explaining that it comes from the word *ghar*, meaning home. Like a home, each Gharana carries its unique essence, rhythm, and fragrance. Shovana may not know the exact Gharana that her first guru, Sadhna ji, belonged to, but the beauty and influence of those early lessons still echo in her dance, in every graceful step she takes.

When Shovana's father was transferred to Bombay, her journey in Kathak took a significant turn. She began learning from Guru Kundan Lal Sisodia, a respected exponent of the Jaipur Gharana. Under his guidance, she built a strong foundation in Kathak's technical aspects. His teachings rooted her in the intricate rhythms and footwork of the Jaipur tradition. However, Shovana's learning didn't stop there. After her family relocated to Delhi, she became a disciple of the legendary Birju Maharaj ji from the Lucknow Gharana. Under Maharaj ji's tutelage, she was introduced to the aesthetics of movement, grace, and the expressive elements that define the Lucknow style.

While Shovana acknowledges the profound impact of these two great gurus on her dance journey, she also credits two other influential figures for shaping her technique. 'I would credit two more gurus who imparted various technical skills—Naina Devi and my mother,' she reflects.

Naina Devi, a renowned *thumri* singer, was born as Nilina Sen, the granddaughter of the prominent nationalist leader and social reformer Keshub Chandra Sen from the Brahmo Samaj movement. The youngest of three sisters, Nilina was married at sixteen into the Kapurthala royal family, where she became Rani Ripjit Singh. However, in Punjab, she was forbidden to sing. After the death of her husband, she relocated to Delhi, adopted the stage name Naina Devi, and rose to fame as a celebrated thumri singer.

Her mother, Lalita, played a vital role in her Kathak training, nurturing her in ways that went beyond the classroom.

The exposure to the Jaipur and Lucknow Gharanas gave Shovana a unique opportunity to assimilate their distinct styles. This cross-Gharana training deepened her understanding of their specific phrases and differences in expression. For instance, phrases like *dha ta ka thunga* and *tat ta thei* are common to both the Gharanas. However, the Jaipur Gharana employs the *garudh hastak* (hand gesture) while performing *chakkars* (spins), whereas in the Lucknow Gharana, the same movement is executed with open hands.

Shovana also recognises that specific phrases, such as *tram thai thai ta thai*, are more prevalent in the Jaipur Gharana, while they are less common in the Lucknow Gharana. Despite these differences, both traditions emphasise *teyyari ang* or *nritta ang* (rhythmic patterns) and *abhinaya* (expression). However, the Jaipur Gharana focuses more intensely on *kavitt*, expressing it through *bhav* (emotion), highlighting the deep connection between poetry, rhythm, and emotion, whereas the Lucknow Gharana enters the emotional depth of the text with its layers of nuanced interpretations and meanings.

This rich blending of two major Gharanas, combined with the influence of her mother and Naina Devi, allowed Shovana to not only master the technical aspects of Kathak but also to appreciate the beauty and depth of its expressive potential.

For example, in phrases like *Naiyi abla ras bhed na janat, sej chadhi jiya mahe dari, rasa baat kahi tab chaunk padi* or *ek samay ghar su nikasi ali pahan ke cheer kusum ki sari,* there is a distinct emphasis on *bhav* in the Jaipur Gharana. However, if she sings *Sakhi ve mujhse kahkar jate,* the expression of *bhav* shifts, showcasing the Lucknow Gharana's unique approach. Each Gharana brings a different expression to the *kavitt*, (poetry set to rhythm). The Lucknow Gharana emphasises vocal expressions with an aesthetic presentation and sharpness (*tezi*) in *sringara* (romantic expression). With Birju Maharaj, there is still more subtlety and nuance.

The Lucknow Gharana's approach to Kathak presentation

balances *teyyari ang* (technical skill) and *abhinaya* (expressive storytelling). In contrast, the Jaipur Gharana leans more towards showcasing teyyari ang, with abhinaya taking a secondary role. As a result, abhinaya in the Jaipur Gharana is typically limited to kavitt recitations or, at most, a *bhajan* performance.

But when asked, 'Which Gharana does Shovana Narayan come from?' she chooses not to answer. For her, the question holds little significance. The knowledge of a specific Gharana, she believes, matters less than the dance itself—the dance that at its very core must transcend technicality and become a language of the soul.

She reflects, 'I grew up in a time when Gharanas embraced an open and inclusive approach. Today, even the very notion of Gharana lineage is often debated. There is less tolerance and honesty when acknowledging influences or claiming affiliation with a particular Gharana.'

As the final notes of the performance linger in the air, the boundary between performer and audience dissolves into a shared silence brimming with the echoes of countless traditions and the whispers of the cosmos.

The artist stands as a bridge between worlds, where the rich heritage of Gharanas converges into a singular expression of transcendence. The intricate footwork of Jaipur, the delicate gestures of Lucknow, the vibrant rhythms of Banaras, and the rich imagery of Raigarh blend seamlessly as a confluence of styles.

As the final curtain falls and the echoes of the performance slowly fade, one truth remains crystal clear—the art of dance, in its most sublime essence, is a universal celebration of life.

Unfolding Wings

During a visit to her Ma's *mayka* (maternal home), Shovana made many new friends among the neighbourhood children. She noticed the girls practising dance with great dedication for an upcoming competition. Watching them stirred a secret longing in her to join, but she hesitated to express her desire.

She knew her mother's reputation as a strict disciplinarian, and her grand-aunt—whom she fondly called *Phua-nani*, being her mother's father's sister—was even more formidable. Shovana kept her dream quietly tucked away, unsure if she dared to voice it aloud.

Shovana learned about this upcoming All-Bihar dance competition that would take place in a few weeks. She couldn't stop thinking about participating in the competition when she heard about it. Though her heart brimmed with excitement, she remained silent for days.

One day, mustering all her courage and overcoming her habitual fear, she finally approached her mother. Trembling nervously, she tugged at her mother's sari and haltingly voiced her wish to dance in the competition. The words barely left her lips before she buried her flushed face in her mother's *pallu*, overwhelmed by shame and dread. She braced herself for the inevitable reprimand or laughter she thought would follow. And indeed, both came—but they were wrapped in such tenderness and love that they touched her deeply.

Overcome with emotion, Shovana fled from her mother's pallu and sought refuge in the large garden behind the house, tears streaming down her cheeks. She could hear voices calling out to her, but she remained hidden behind a bush, unwilling to emerge. However, the memory of seeing a snake only days earlier near the *shahtoot* (mulberry) tree jolted her into action. She had watched in horror as the snake, pinned under a heavy stone, vomited a frog it had swallowed. The vivid image of that moment sent her scurrying out of her hiding spot, shaken yet determined.

Shovana's mother and phua-nani initially tried to dissuade her from participating in the dance competition, but young Shovana remained resolute. Usually reserved and composed, Shovana was known for her quiet intensity and impeccable behaviour, rarely betraying her emotions.

When her mother finally agreed to enter her in the contest, Shovana's excitement was palpable. However, her phua-nani was far from pleased. She believed that her mother was indulging her daughter unnecessarily. Phua-nani, whose real name was Sharada Devi, was a formidable and principled woman. Widowed at a young age, she channelled her strength into meaningful causes, becoming involved in early political movements and championing women's empowerment. She was among the first three women elected to the Bihar Assembly in 1937, where she served for several years. In 1942, she was imprisoned for her involvement in the freedom movement. She founded *Mahila Darpan*, one of Muzaffarpur's first women's magazines, a bold step in her time. Sharada Devi was a vocal opponent of the *purdah* system and a staunch advocate for women's independence. True to her name, which means 'goddess of learning,' she represented wisdom, courage, and freedom.

The day before the competition, all the participants were called on stage for a rehearsal. As the youngest among them, little Shovana was gripped by an overwhelming stage fright that left her frozen. She refused to move despite repeated efforts to coax her with promises of toffees, chocolates, sweets, and ice cream.

Completely paralysed with fear, she resembled the mythical figure Ahilya, rooted and immobile. Though the desire to dance still burned within her, she could not muster even the faintest smile.

Upon returning home, she faced a severe scolding for the scene she had caused, which embarrassed her mother and her grand-aunt, a highly respected figure in the community.

At just four years old, Shovana felt the full weight of fear and shame. She howled loudly from the confines of the room where she had been locked as punishment. Her cries grew more frantic as the terror of the dark room engulfed her, far surpassing her earlier embarrassment and the rebukes from her elders. The fear was not just about the darkness and being separated from the comforting presence of familiar faces but also about the challenge of expressing herself in front of everyone.

As her mother's words echoed, the little girl felt overwhelmed in a dimly lit room. 'Each of us is a lone traveller,' Ma said, her voice steady and firm. 'You decide, and you must stand by your decision. Don't blame others for your actions.'

Ma's words urged her to confront her fears. 'You wanted to dance in the competition. Why let fear stop you?' She advised the child to overcome her doubts and not to settle for anything less than her best. 'Our support can guide you, but the strength must come from within you.'

As Ma's words sank in, the little girl felt the weight of her decision. 'If you can't overcome your fears, maybe you don't truly love dance,' Ma said. 'If you cannot give it your all, then perhaps it's time to reconsider.'

Desperate to prove herself, the little girl cried, 'No, no! Please don't! I want to dance!'

Her plea marked the beginning of her journey towards becoming one of the most excellent Kathak dancers of her time.

Her mother's warning, '*Tum nautanki band karo varna tumhara dance band ho jayega.*' (Stop your antics, or you won't be allowed to dance), struck fear deeper than the fright itself. The idea of not dancing was unthinkable! Amid her tears, she blurted out in panic, 'Why?'—a dramatic outburst from a child who couldn't imagine life without dance.

Through this trial, she learned a powerful lesson: inner strength and accountability were essential for growth. This resilience, tempered by her mother's wisdom, became a defining character trait.

The incident helped her temper her stubbornness, although a healthy degree of determination remains an essential part of her character. '*Ziddi thi aur hun, aur jab tak jeeungi, ziddi rahungi.*' (I was stubborn and still am. And as long as I live, I will continue to be stubborn.)

She might not have achieved her current success if she had shed her tenacity.

***

Four-year-old Shovana stepped onto the stage the next day, dressed in a cream-coloured khadi kurta-churidar, a Gandhi cap perched neatly on her head. The memory of her stage fright from the previous day had vanished like a fleeting shadow. With the weight of fear lifted, she danced with an untethered spirit. Her tiny feet seemed to glide effortlessly as if carried by an invisible breeze. Each step and gesture became an expression of pure joy, her soul speaking a language only she understood. She was like a bird that had just been freed, soaring high above the world, unafraid and exhilarated by the vastness of the sky.

When her name was announced as the first prize winner, her Guruji scooped her up in jubilation. Yet, Shovana's spirit was still dancing, her joy too boundless to be contained. She wriggled and squirmed, unwilling to be held, as though the act of being grounded might shatter her newfound freedom. Even as the gold medal was pinned to her kurta, she remained lost in the rhythm that still resonated within her, spinning and leaping in her magical world.

Looking into the crowd, she caught sight of phua-nani's radiant smile and her mother's laughter, their faces glowing with pride. But these moments barely registered in her mind—she was still somewhere else, carried by the melody of her heart, dancing in a realm of limitless freedom and unbridled joy.

'Your grandniece danced so beautifully. She is gifted!'

'Didn't she? I am so proud of her. Putul, touch the feet of *Babu* …. or …. *Nani.'* 'Putul, that's me, immediately dived to touch the feet of various *nanas* or nanis, *mausas* or *mausis* for they were all my grand-aunt's colleagues besides the usual crowd of friends and relatives till, at one moment, I turned my back to phua-nani to touch the feet of some elderly person sitting opposite her. As I straightened up, I saw shock and disbelief on her face.'

'*Babuni*, your daughter is impossible. Look at her! Where are her panties?' cried my shocked grandaunt.

My mother quickly gathered me in her arms as I was swept out of sight. Once safely out of phua-nani's sight, she too gave in to peals of laughter.

'Oh Putul...Putul...you are something! What a sight! Dressed in a kurta with a massive gold medal swinging proudly on your chest, a Gandhi cap perched on your head, and below...no pyjamas!' She burst into uncontrollable laughter, tears streaming down her cheeks. (*Meandering Pastures of Memories*)

After the first performance, Shovana remained a constant presence on stage. Her shelves gradually filled with dance awards. Transitioning from a child artist to a serious Kathak dancer, she began to gain recognition in the field. Her guru, Pandit Birju Maharaj began introducing her to discerning art connoisseurs by having her perform a short piece before his full solo performances.

Through the Veil of Time

Shovana Narayan, the celebrated Kathak icon, was born into a family steeped in resilience and history, where ordinary life intertwined with extraordinary influences. She was born in the home of Sarla Devi Chaudhary, a renowned freedom fighter and close associate of Mahatma Gandhi, setting the stage for a life marked by cultural and historical significance.

Yet, beneath the starry legacy she would later carve, Shovana's childhood was filled with the sweet and sour moments that shape every life—bonding with siblings, navigating their contrasting traits, and growing under the watchful eyes of supportive parents. These simple yet profound experiences, set against an environment of tradition and values, quietly nurtured the brilliance that would shine through in her remarkable journey as a dancer.

Shovana had an elder brother who was born in 1948 in Muzaffarpur. Sadly, at that time, her aunt was suffering from smallpox, which the newborn contracted, and he barely survived two months. Shovana was born in 1950, followed by her younger sister, Ranjana, in 1953.

As a child, Shovana was notably serious and kind, seldom smiling, let alone laughing. In contrast, her sister Ranjana was a cheerful child—bubbly and talkative, with a sharp mind. Her love for talking was evident and it seemed almost destined that she would become a lawyer.

'The greatest punishment my parents could give her was to stay quiet for five minutes,' Shovana recalls with a burst of laughter. 'She would immediately plead, "Mom, can I talk? My mouth is itching".'

'Didi was putul—a doll—and I was *mukul*, a flower,' Ranjana grins, reminiscing about their childhood. 'Didi was the quiet one, always so composed like she carried a secret world inside her. And me? I was the complete opposite! A bundle of energy, talking nonstop, and always ready to answer for her if she hesitated.'

Ranjana remembers fondly stepping in whenever her elder sister grew too shy to respond to someone. 'If you asked her a question, she'd pause, thinking, and before she could say a word, I'd blurt out the answer like it was my job! Didi often accepted this sibling dynamic with her usual grace and patience, though a quiet smile would sometimes escape her lips as if to say, "I let you have your fun".'

Shovana bursts into laughter as she recalls her first day at school. 'Oh, what a scene that was! I howled, I kicked, and I clung to my mother as if my life depended on it. My parents still joke that my cries echoed to the next block. It was a full-blown opera of tears and protests.'

Ranjana, sitting beside her, grins mischievously. 'Didi's first day was the talk of the family for years,' she chimes in. 'But mine? Oh, I was the poster child of composure! When my school bus came, I hopped on without a murmur, leaving everyone amazed. No drama, no fuss—just me being my cool, confident self.'

Shovana rolls her eyes playfully. 'Cool and confident, huh? Let's not forget that you were mostly excited about the snacks!'

Ranjana laughs unabashedly. 'Well, you're not wrong! My first school was all about the food. I still remember Mom asking me what I learned, and my only answer was, "I ate!" Then came the convent in Bombay—my first proper school. I was in kindergarten, and while everyone expected tears, I surprised them all. I ran down the stairs, turned around, and chirped, "Bye-bye!"'

'That's because I was already there, and you knew I'd keep an eye on you,' Shovana teases.

'True,' Ranjana admits with a grin. 'Knowing Didi was there made me feel safe. But let's be honest, Didi—the real star of my school debut was my cheerful exit!'

The sisters dissolve into laughter, their contrasting first-day stories capturing the hilarious mix of drama and calm that marked their childhoods.

Shovana and Ranjana briefly attended Hill Grange School in Bombay due to their father's transfer in the middle of the scholastic year. Convent schools in Bombay traditionally start their academic year in January and conclude in December. Since they arrived in October, they were enrolled in Hill Grange School for just two months to bridge this gap.

Reflecting on those days, Shovana recalls, 'Ranjana was still just a little one. After my classes ended, I'd go to pick her up. For her, it was almost like a play school—often overlapping with her nap time. I can still picture myself standing there, wondering, how am I going to get her to the car when I can't carry her, since drivers weren't allowed inside the school.'

'I still chuckle when I think of my pre-primary days. We had a 'sleeping class,' right before school ended, and I would be in the deepest, most blissful slumber. Poor Didi had to come upstairs to wake me and drag me home. Half-asleep and grumpy, I'd reluctantly grab her finger while she carried my bag, tiffin box, and water bottle like a devoted little guardian. Looking back, I must have been quite the pampered package deal!'

Ranjana had a thing for poetry from the start. Their tutor, Anne, was amazed when she told her she had learned many poems on the first day of school. 'Many poems?' Anne asked, clearly surprised. Ranjana had to prove it, so she made up a poem about whatever her eyes landed on—like the clock or the ashtray, stringing together rhymes on the fly. Anne was flabbergasted. How could they teach poems to a kindergartener on the first day? When Anne told her mother about it, Ranjana had forgotten the poems completely. Playfully, Anne grabbed her ear in return for Ranjana pulling her leg. The girl was always full of stories, spinning tales and reciting impromptu verses, much to the amusement (and occasional exasperation) of those around her!

'We were different. Ma's scoldings would silence me, but her mock sternness never fazed Ranjana. Instead, she'd dash around the dining table, singing, "You never caught me!"

'I've looked up to Didi since I was a child—she was like a second mother. As the younger of the two of us, I was always protected and pampered. We were born in Calcutta, where Didi started her schooling before we moved to Bombay. My memories of Calcutta are hazy, but what I do remember is the warmth of our little family bubble—just Papa, Ma, Didi, and me. We had those big, cosy beds, and every night, I'd snuggle up between my parents, feeling completely safe and loved.

'In Bombay, we lived in Shyam Niwas colony and spent hours playing in the park outside our home. I vividly remember my fourth birthday. We hadn't planned a big celebration; Ma told me to invite a few friends from the park. Excited, I ran down and announced, "It's my birthday!" To my surprise, 30 to 40 kids came rushing upstairs to join the fun!

'Our house help was utterly flustered, unsure how to handle the crowd. But Ma, calm as ever, quickly had small *puris* and *sabji* prepared for everyone. It turned out to be the best birthday I've ever had. Holding his half-eaten ice cream, one boy offered it to me as a gift. I accepted it with a cheerful "thank you," and everyone laughed. It was simple, chaotic, and unforgettable—like childhood should be.

'Ranjana's lovely voice was unmistakable. Although trained in music and dance, she had a unique way of showing her preferences. She would often say, "Dance *karne se sar mein dhamaka hota hai*," meaning dancing gave her a headache. Her heart leaned more toward music than dance, yet she was a sharp critic and a gifted writer. Her clever, original four-line poems always earned admiration and appreciation.

'Ranjana and I shared a deep bond growing up. In some ways, we were alike, yet in others, complete opposites. I was more serious and quieter, though I'm much chattier now than I used to be, while she was always lively, bubbling with quick wit and still is. Dance was my passion, but music was hers. She'd often mimic me and try her hand at *abhinaya*. Watching her, Maharaj ji would say, "Ranju does it beautifully. There's a remarkable grace and subtlety in her abhinaya and her dance movements".'

While Shovana often found herself tongue-tied, Ranjana was always forthright in sharing her views. Shovana was passionate about mathematics, while Ranjana was drawn to history and law. Shovana couldn't understand why Ranjana struggled with simple mathematical calculations, just as Ranjana couldn't fathom Shovana's lack of interest in legal cases. Ranjana's aesthetic sensibilities lay on a higher plane, while Shovana felt hers were somewhere below. Ranjana's literary and expressive talents were remarkable—she was a 'natural,' whereas Shovana saw herself as more of a plodder.

Shovana had a legendary sweet tooth, happily devouring any sweets that came her way. Ranjana, on the other hand, had a particular fondness for toffees, especially the J B Mangaram ones that were all the rage in the 1950s. Ranjana often joked with her usual flair for humour, 'I'll marry J B Mangaram's son one day—just think, a lifetime supply of toffees!'

One day, caught up in her playful spirit, she declared, 'From now on, my name is Meethu Lal Patle!' The family laughed, enjoying the absurdity of her self-bestowed title. But the real punchline came later that evening. Their father returned from work with a twinkle in his eye and a story he could barely contain. 'You won't believe this,' he said, trying to stifle his laughter. 'I met someone today—his name was Meethu Lal Patle!'

During their growing years, Shovana was delighted to be the secret cupid among her friends, always ready to help needy sweethearts. Whether it was sneaking love letters across or arranging a covert rendezvous, she played the role with flair. Once, she even hosted a meeting for a couple at their home, with her ever-gracious mother stepping in to ensure everything was perfect.

'Ma, always the epitome of hospitality, asked me, "What should we serve them?" Before I could answer, little Ranjana, all of seven years old, piped up from the corner with the most dramatic menu imaginable: "*Mohabbat ki kheer, prem ke dariya ka pani, and gulab ki khushboo ka pulao*!" Shovana laughs, shaking her head at the memory.

The family burst into laughter at Ranjana's poetic imagination,

Ranjana and Shovana with their parents Lalita Narayan and K D Narayan

and the line became an instant classic in their household. For years afterward, whenever a special guest came over or the family reminisced, someone would inevitably quip, 'Shall we serve mohabbat ki kheer today?' reminding everyone of the playful little sister who always had a way with words.

The Narayan household was a perfect blend of light-hearted moments and profound teachings. Amidst the laughter over playful quips and humorous antics, a strong undercurrent of wisdom and cultural enrichment ran deep. Their home was a vibrant hub where jokes and stories coexisted with meaningful discussions, where joy was celebrated without ever losing sight of values and traditions. Shovana and Ranjana grew up absorbing life lessons not just through words but through the very atmosphere of their home—one that nurtured intellect, creativity, and a sense of responsibility. It was where every laugh carried a lesson, and every moment of learning had a touch of joy.

Hailing from a Kayastha family, Shovana and her sibling were raised in an environment where reverence for all aspects of Goddess Saraswati was deeply ingrained—not only through academic pursuits but also through a dedication to the arts. In Kayastha households, children were taught to balance scholarly subjects with artistic learning. Shovana's mother would sing them verses from the Bhagavad Gita. Even today, Shovana is amazed that she can recite the entire eleventh chapter, where Lord Krishna reveals his *Virat Swaroop*, by heart.

Sthane hrsikesa tava prakirtya
jagat prahrsyaty anurajyate na
raksamsi bhitani diso dravanti
sarve namasyanti ca siddha-sanghah

(O Hrsikesa, the world rejoices upon hearing Your name, and thus everyone is drawn to You. While the perfected beings offer You their respectful homage, the demons become fearful and scatter in all directions. Indeed, all this is as it should be.)

Shovana and Ranjana grew up in an atmosphere of uplifting energy and quiet reverence. Even as children, they could sense a profound divine presence within and around them, though they may not have fully grasped the meaning of the sacred verses they often heard. This spiritual awareness seeped into their subconscious, shaping them into deeply devout individuals committed to living with integrity—never harming anyone in thought, word, or deed: *mansa, vacha, karmana*.

Their upbringing was profoundly influenced by the guidance of their parents, especially their mother, whose nurturing presence brought the timeless teachings of the *Bhagavad Gita* into their everyday lives. From an early age, the scriptures' wisdom became a part of their worldview, woven seamlessly into their thoughts and actions. One teaching left an indelible mark:

Karmanye vadhikaraste ma phaleshu kadachana
Ma karma phala hetur bhur ma te sangostva akarmani.

(You have the right to perform your actions, but not to the fruits of your actions. Let not the results of your work be your motive, nor let your attachment lead you to inaction.)

As they grew, the teachings they absorbed from their mother became a guiding compass through life's challenges. The *Gita* instilled in them ambition without ego, self-awareness, and the courage to rise after every fall. Their mother encouraged responsibility, questioning, and curiosity. These lessons laid the foundation for Shovana's future dance work. Today, as a mentor and teacher, she continues this tradition of meaningful dialogue, guiding her students on the right path.

The Road Less Travelled

For Shovana and her sister Ranjana, childhood was filled with diverse experiences. If, on one side, there were profound verses like Jai Shankar Prasad's *Himadri tung shring se prabuddha shuddha Bharati* or Ramdhari Singh Dinkar's *Vanita ki mamta na hui, sut ka na mujhe kuch moh hua, khyati, suyash, samman, vibhav ka, tyon hi, kabhi na moh hua*, on the other, there were nursery rhymes like Baa baa black sheep and Jack and Jill. Both worlds coexisted harmoniously.

'As we grew up, Mom was the kind of parent who never put limits on our curiosity. Whether we were delving into the

Shakuntala- a dance soliloquy (left); Khalil Gibran- a dance act (right)

Bhagavad Gita or getting lost in the pages of a gripping mystery novel, she encouraged it all. From exploring spiritual teachings to diving into Mr Pink-Whistle's quirky escapades, the Secret Seven's thrilling cases, or the daring adventures of the Famous Five, she enthusiastically supported every interest. It was like having our cake and eating it, too. She encouraged us to follow whatever sparked our curiosity. And funnily enough, that freedom kept us more grounded and disciplined than you'd think. We never had to rebel because we were learning to balance it all.'

The Narayan household was a dynamic space where the air was always buzzing with intellectual conversations and creative energy. Discussions on social work, poetry, literature, and music flowed freely, interspersed with talks about dance, politics, and the arts. The house regularly hosted a vibrant mix of visitors—political figures, musicians, writers, artists, and bureaucrats—each bringing unique perspectives.

Shovana was naturally drawn to these experiences as a child, eagerly accompanying the elders to artistic performances, theatre, seminars, and social gatherings. While she may not have fully understood everything at the time, her mother insisted on her participation, believing that, over time, these experiences would subtly shape her personality.

Living in Bombay, she was further immersed in the vibrant world of art. She attended painting classes, an experience that allowed her to explore yet another dimension of creativity.

The diversity of artistic expressions she encountered during these formative years profoundly influenced her, shaping her appreciation for the richness and variety of the cultural world around her. Through it all, Shovana was like a sponge, absorbing the artistic and intellectual currents that flowed through her home.

Looking back on the influence of her parents, Shovana

reflects, 'The person who truly shaped me was my mother. My father was a man of few words, often speaking no more than twenty a day, but his support for my mother in raising my sister, Ranjana and I, was steadfast. It was my mother who was the true driving force—she had a clear vision.'

Shovana's mother openly allowed her daughters to explore and pursue what resonated with them. She understood that each child would have a path to follow and she encouraged them to choose what they held dear. However, discipline was the cornerstone of this freedom. No matter their chosen art form, she emphasised that there were no shortcuts to mastery.

Though Shovana was trained in both music and dance, and Ranjana had training in music with some exposure to dance, Shovana soon realised that singing wasn't her true passion. Her mother, perceptive as ever, noticed her disinterest and never forced her to practise. Similarly, she recognised that Ranjana's heart lay in music, not dance. The girls knew that any attempt to pretend otherwise or blame external factors for not mastering a particular raga or dance piece would be met with disapproval. A single sharp glance from their mother was enough to remind them that sincerity and dedication were non-negotiable. She maintained a firm hand when needed, always intending to instil honesty, focus, and unwavering commitment to their chosen paths.

'I remember K M Munshi, former minister of Agriculture and Farmers' Welfare in India, and Lilavati Munshi, former member of the Bombay Legislative Assembly, visiting our home. To me, they were just Munshi uncle and Munshi aunty. It was only much later that I realised their prominence. My mother, Lalita Narayan, was the chairman of the A Ward Committee of the Congress in Bombay and served as a moral lecturer at Arthur Road jail. In Calcutta, she was a Reader at Murlidhar Girls'

College, and in Bombay, she taught at Wilson College.'

'My mother came from a progressive family and was highly educated, with a strong passion for social causes,' Ranjana recalls. 'She wrote for newspapers like *Dharm Yug* and *Hindustan Times* and even authored several plays. She worked tirelessly for women's welfare alongside social workers like Lilavati Munshi and Sulochna Modi, never seeking recognition for her efforts. One of her remarkable initiatives was visiting women convicts at Arthur Road jail, listening to their stories, and offering guidance. She realised many were victims of unfortunate circumstances. Her visits were deeply valued.

Those moments left a lasting impression on me. I'd sit and listen intently to her stories, captivated by her accounts. Her empathy and dedication inspired me to choose a career in law. The values I saw in her—compassion and a relentless commitment to making a difference—became my guiding light. They taught me that success in my profession lies in hard work and diligence, as she demonstrated daily.'

'My father, Kamal Dev Narayan, was a typical bureaucrat. My mother would affectionately call him *Narayan sa'ab* and often tease him, saying he looked like a *tabla vadak* in his *dhoti*. She would jokingly say, "*Narayan sa'ab, aap kyun takleef karte hain ghar aane ki, hum vahin khana bhuijva denge.* (Why bother coming home? We'll send food to you there)," because he was always so engrossed in his work.'

Growing up in a socio-political environment left a lasting impression on both Shovana and Ranjana. From a young age, Ranjana naturally gravitated toward humanitarian aid and social work. In school, she founded a 'Cubs' club' with her friends, organising lessons for the children of the neighbourhood staff and providing basic medical aid, like treating minor injuries with tincture iodine. She even launched a magazine called *Teen Era*, showcasing her creativity and drive to make a difference. Shovana has always admired her sister's determination, resourcefulness and deep instinct to help those in need.

At the heart of their values was the quiet yet profound guidance of their mother, Lalita Narayan. She instilled in them the importance of striving for excellence and never doing anything halfway. This principle became their source of strength, shaping their approach to life and work.

Lalita came from a distinguished zamindar family in Muzaffarpur, known for its prominence and respectability. While the family held zamindari status, many members pursued careers as lawyers and owned sugar mills. Shovana's maternal grandfather, Babu Shyama Charan, traced his roots to ancestors who had migrated from Rajasthan, while her grandmother's family hailed from Kashmir. This rich heritage brought a unique diversity to the family, with some members reflecting Kashmiri features and others, distinct Rajasthani features.

K D Narayan and Lalita Narayan

As devotees of Shakti, the family named all their children after the Devi, reflecting their spiritual devotion. They also upheld a strong tradition of excellence in academics, the visual arts, and other creative pursuits, nurturing these values across generations.

Babu Shyama Charan himself was a towering figure in the Independence Movement. In 1919, he became the first person in Bihar to be imprisoned for his involvement in the struggle for freedom. A dedicated Swarajist, he contested and won elections to the Central Assembly in 1922, becoming a member of parliament. His commitment to the cause came at a high cost—despite owning sugar mills, his active role in the freedom struggle drew the ire of the British. After his untimely death in 1930, the mills were seized, leaving the family to face immense hardships, a sacrifice they bore with resilience and pride.

Babu Shyama Charan was the eldest of four siblings, and his family was known for its progressive mindset. His second sister was a writer, while another sister, who became a child widow after marrying young, later returned to live with her parents and brother. She made her mark by founding *Mahila Darpan,* a women's magazine, in 1916 and became one of the first four women elected to the Bihar Assembly in 1937. Though more reserved than Babu Shyama Charan, the youngest brother was actively involved in the Khadi Gram Udyog, contributing to India's self-reliance movement. The family was ahead of its time, rejecting the traditional *pardaa pratha* (veil system) and ensuring that both boys and girls were raised with equal opportunities and freedom.

Shovana's maternal grandfather married Kusum Devi, renowned for her beauty. Together, they had four children. One of their daughters, Shovana's maternal aunt, married Sachidananda Singh, a distinguished judge in Ranchi. They had five children, including Mridula, a celebrated Hindi writer in Jaipur. Mridula's husband, Om Bihari, served as the Additional Chief Secretary of Rajasthan but sadly passed away at a young age.

Shovana's mother was the youngest of her siblings and earned the nickname *jaili beti* because she was born while her father was in prison. Tragically, she lost her mother when she was just nine months old and was lovingly raised by her two grandaunts. Her family history was marked by sacrifice. She had two brothers, Nanku bhaiya and Pyare bhaiya, whom Shovana never had the chance to meet. Both were freedom fighters who died young—one was killed while hoisting the national flag, beaten and trampled by a horse, while the other succumbed to a severe illness.

By 1939-40, all the male members of the family had passed away, leaving a legacy of resilience and dedication. Lalita carved for herself a remarkable path. Highly educated, she earned an MA in Hindi Sahitya Alankar from Banaras Hindu University, where she was awarded a gold medal in 1944. She was a well-known Hindi and Sanskrit scholar. She authored two books, *Seva Mahila Sabha* and *Mukti Path*.

Both Lalita and her sister were deeply passionate about music and social work. Lalita played the Esraj. Both sisters were admired for their vibrant and spirited personalities.

'My mother was deeply committed to social work and incredibly hardworking—she was truly *mehnati*. Our home was always bustling with life, with a constant stream of guests. My parents upheld strong ethical values, and my father often reminded us that honesty wasn't just about telling the truth but about acting with integrity.

'They were a team, always in sync in their parenting. If my father meant to say no to something, he'd direct us to ask our mother, and she would do the same. We often bounced back and forth between them, hoping to get a yes. I remember one time when I had a high fever but still wanted to perform at a show. My father said no. But my mother, understanding how much it meant to me, gave me a subtle signal that I could go, reassuring me that she'd handle my father's temper later. Moments like these made us feel supported.'

The unity and partnership she witnessed in her parents was a powerful model for Shovana's later life. Their teamwork shaped her understanding of marriage, profoundly influencing her relationship with her husband, Herbert, and reflecting the harmony and strength she had always admired in her parents' bond.

The warmth of her family environment shaped her, with dance gradually becoming like a second skin. Shovana was too young to grasp the meaning of fame or the weight of the glowing reviews praising her performance as a child artist. All she knew was that dance was where her heart found its home, and it was in those movements that she truly felt alive.

Shovana smiles gently as she reflects on her childhood curiosity, recalling how every new experience felt like the most crucial thing in the world at that moment. Though there were times when fear tried to hold her back, her curiosity always triumphed, driving her to face each new challenge with open arms. One such memory, deeply etched in her heart, still brings a warm sense of nostalgia.

'I must have been about eight years old, already passionate about dance and recognised as a little Kathak prodigy. I even had a full-page review in *Parag* that read, "*Gudiya jaisi nach rahi Shovana badi chulbulli, bhule chilbille darshak bhi aaj udana khilli.*" My guru, Kundan Lal Sisodia, who often choreographed for Bollywood, invited me to perform at a Filmfare award night at the C J Auditorium in Bombay. My father refused, but my mother secretly sent me with Guruji for the performance.

'I knew Guruji would be performing, and I was set to do my own Kathak piece. When we got to the green room, I noticed two platforms—one covered with protruding nails and the other with swords laid out. Intrigued, I asked Guruji if he planned to dance on them. When he said yes, I pointed to the swords, and to my surprise, he asked if I wanted to try. There were twelve swords laid side by side. He taught me the technique, and though the idea of doing it today would terrify me, my curiosity took over back then.

'I stepped on stage and danced on the swords, fully immersed in the moment. My parents arrived at the auditorium just as I began. Seeing her eight-year-old daughter balancing on swords, my mother fainted. The performance ended with people rushing to embrace me and show me love, but I wasn't spared a severe scolding when I got home!' She laughs, the memory still vivid, her laughter filling the room.

Shovana's father was the youngest of seven brothers, born the same day his second brother got engaged. Interestingly, his brother's wife was the sister of Dr Rajendra Prasad's wife. Shovana recalls that her parents married relatively late for their era—her mother was 24, and her father was 33 at their wedding.

Her father's family, while primarily involved in the legal profession, also held zamindari rights over eight or nine villages. The Narayan family sincerely appreciated the arts, with each member dabbling in creative pursuits. However, while their artistic talents were nurtured and celebrated, none pursued them as a career.

'My father came from a well-respected background and was admired for his integrity. His postings often took us to cities like Bombay, Calcutta, and Delhi. While initially hesitant about Didi's decision to pursue dance, he eventually became her greatest supporter, always seated proudly in the front row at her performances. He had a deep love for music and used to play the flute during his college days. Our home was a vibrant hub, constantly filled with artists, thanks to my father's extensive connections. However, my mother's network was even larger and more meaningful, encompassing well-known litterateurs, artists, politicians, social workers, and others,' Ranjana reminisces.

Shovana often feels a wave of nostalgia wash over her when she reflects on the treasured moments that she shared with some of the legends of the time—moments she was too young to grasp fully as priceless. Looking back, she feels blessed that she and her sister had the opportunity to be part of a world so rich in musical history, surrounded by icons whose influence they could not yet comprehend.

'Music directors like Roshan and S D Burman would invite us whenever they needed chorus singers for their film tracks. This led to a close friendship with Rahul Dev Burman, affectionately known as Pancham Dada. Pancham Dada must have been around twenty at the time, while I was just eight, and my sister was a couple of years younger. We would rehearse in their drawing rooms, learning to sing under S D Dada's careful guidance. Pancham Dada, ever the helpful and patient mentor, would go out of his way to ensure we were practising correctly,' Shovana recalls.

'As a child artist, I sang in films like *Deep Jalta Rahe*, *Kagaz Ke Phool*, and *Chote Nawab*. I was too young to read the lyrics back then, so they would help me memorise the songs. I had a sharp memory. I also enjoyed dance, but dancing never felt like my true passion—singing was always what I loved most,' shares Ranjana.

'Back then, things were so different from today. Artists couldn't record their parts separately at their convenience—everyone had to be together for the rehearsals. It was a world filled with learning and fun. We were just kids, so carefree and innocent that we'd go up to legendary music composers like S D Burman and Rahul Dev Burman, asking them to take us to the loo! We'd sit patiently, and they'd patiently help us memorise songs. Looking back, it feels like we were so fortunate, surrounded by warmth and guidance from these musical giants.'

Shovana holds deep respect for Pancham Dada, not just for his musical genius but also for his down-to-earth nature. 'I must credit him for the kind of person he was—so grounded. He wasn't just a legendary composer but a friend and a mentor. And it was at this time that he had independently composed the music for *Aam Chum Taam Chum* and other songs for the movie *Chote Nawab*.' Her voice softens at the memories.

'Pancham Dada was at the height of his fame, delivering hit after hit, yet he always remembered us. He made time to meet us whenever we visited Bombay, and we always shared either tea, coffee, or a meal,' Shovana recalls. 'The last time we saw him was on 18 December. Then, on 4 or 5 January, while I was in Vienna for Christmas, my sister called from Delhi to inform me that Dada was no longer with us.'

After the family moved to Delhi from Bombay, Ranjana continued her musical journey, learning from Siddheshwari Devi ji for a while and then from Pandit Mani Prasad. She later studied *ghazal gayiki* under Ustad Iqbal Ahmad Khan ji and even sang classical ghazals on the radio for several years.

'Siddheshwari Devi ji taught me at her home in Pataudi House. She would make me sit on her lap and feed me before I sang. I remember her telling me that singing is a *pukar*—a call, a way to connect with the soul. She explained that my voice needed to come from deep within, from the gut, strong enough to reach the furthest person in the audience. While my sister used dance as her form of yoga, singing became mine. I even sang in Farsi! Each language has its nuances, emotions, and flavour. One of my favourites has always been Harivansh Rai Bachchan's *Madhushala*. While my studies nourished my mind, music became the food for my soul. *Swar* means 'self' (*swa*) and 'offering' (*ra*)—it's the offering of oneself. When you give your essence to singing, you become a singer.

'Our home was a vibrant hub of creativity and purpose, where every member found their passion and pursued it wholeheartedly. Ma's songwriting, Didi's devotion to dance, and my immersion in music created an atmosphere buzzing with energy and inspiration.

'Even amid our busy routines, we made time for one another. This nurturing environment shaped our talents and instilled a deep purpose and connection.

'Every summer, our old Fiat would become our chariot to Haridwar, with a stop in Saharanpur along the way. Visiting Har ki Pauri and Lakshman Jhoola became our cherished ritual, a getaway wrapped in simplicity and magic. The journey was as delightful as the destination—we'd stop wherever the whim took us. Didi and I would gather smooth white stones from the river banks, treasures of nature, and tuck them into the car's dickey. Once home, those stones found a new purpose, adorning our plants like little pieces of memory, bringing a touch of Haridwar into our everyday lives.'

Between Verses and Rhymes

Shovana (8-year-old, clutching a book, worried): 'But, Ma, I need to study! The exam is tomorrow! What if I don't finish in time?'

Mother (gently taking the book from her hands): 'Shovana, tell me—what were you just reading?'

Shovana (pausing, fumbling): 'Uh…something about…I can't remember. But I'll try harder!'

Mother (smiling): 'Beta, it's not about trying harder when your mind is elsewhere. You've been staring at this page for an hour. Pretending to study doesn't help anyone—not you, not your exam.'

Shovana (confused): 'So, you're saying I should just stop studying?'

Mother (placing a hand on her shoulder): 'I'm saying you need to study with a clear mind. Go outside, play for a while, and return when ready. It's okay to not do well on an exam, but it's not okay to waste your time pretending to work.'

Shovana (wide-eyed): 'But…won't I fail?'

Mother (softly): 'Even if you do, it's not the end of the world. What matters is learning to use your time wisely and truthfully. Go now, enjoy the fresh air. You'll see how much better you feel.'

Shovana (hesitating, then nodding): 'Okay, Ma.'

(Shovana goes outside, still unsure but obedient. Later, she returns, cheeks flushed from playing, and picks up the book with a renewed focus.)

Shovana (quietly to herself): 'Ma was right…it's easier to concentrate now.'

Though little Shovana didn't fully understand the wisdom of that moment, it became a lesson she carried throughout her life—a fine blend of discipline and compassion, teaching her that genuine productivity comes from honest effort and a balanced mind.

Her father taught her that nothing material stays behind:

Only a sweet and virtuous soul,
Like season'd timber, never gives;
But though the whole world turn to coal,
Then chiefly lives.

Arrogance, beauty, youth, and wealth are transient, powerless against the body's inevitable decline. In the end, you rely on others to carry you to your final resting place, or your body succumbs to decay.

From these teachings, Shovana understood that one's actions should benefit society and foster personal growth. Wealth, symbolised by Laxmi, is fleeting and illusory. In contrast, knowledge, represented by Saraswati, is enduring. Wisdom and self-reflection enable growth and transformation. Rather than blindly following others (*bhed chal*), one should sincerely pursue personal aspirations with values, integrity, and dignity.

She often reflects on a moment from the late 1960s when her family lived at 21 Bharti Nagar, Delhi. Shovana was a teen. Dance carried negative connotations in those days. Concerned neighbours approached her parents, suggesting that as their daughter was growing up, it was time to find her a suitable groom and put an end to her dancing.

Her father remained silent, but her mother responded with grace and determination. She said, 'You are welcome in our home, and we appreciate your advice. However, our children have the freedom to choose their path. It is not the profession that defines a person; it is one's behaviour and values that bring either lustre or disgrace to a profession. You are our guest and have spoken your mind. Any further opinions, however, should be expressed outside this house, not within it.'

Shovana listened closely to the conversation, each word affirming a quiet truth within her. Her path was uniquely hers to shape—a journey guided not by societal expectations but by her vision and inner spirit. She was acutely aware of the restrictive perceptions often surrounding fields like dance, modelling, or acting, particularly for women—professions many deemed risky or unconventional. Yet, her parents' steadfast support shone brightly against the shadows of judgement. Their belief in self-expression and authenticity nurtured her resolve, giving her the confidence to embrace and integrate multiple art forms. For Shovana, this journey was more than a career; it was a calling—a pursuit of something transcendent and divine.

'Our strength always came from home; we never had to struggle for support. The only expectation placed upon us was to uphold our values and remain true to them. While I don't recall my exact thoughts during that incident, reflecting on it fills me with deep gratitude for my parents. Their understanding and refusal to succumb to societal pressures remain a cornerstone of my journey.'

Rooted in the wisdom imparted by her parents, Shovana let

her passion flourish beyond conventional boundaries. She saw herself as a tiny yet vital thread in the vast embroidery of the universe, where all art forms were woven from the same divine source. Believing that dance, like all arts, was a channel for a higher purpose, she allowed her spirit to flow freely, exploring and embracing diverse dance traditions worldwide.

With every step, she sought to create a delicate balance, a graceful interplay between the rhythms and movements of different cultures. Her dance became a canvas where forms, styles, and expressions merged like colours blending in a sunrise—each hue distinct yet together, creating something beyond the sum of its parts.

For Shovana, dance was not just movement but a spiritual journey, a divine alignment that brought together the elements of the universe in a sublime expression of harmony and unity.

'For me, the means of best expressing whatever I feel is dance.' Shovana believed that she could touch the sacred through dance and resonate with the cosmic rhythm. Dance became a harmonious burst of expression through her being.

'Kathak is my breath, my five elements, my energy, and my soul.'

When she says the above, she speaks of a deep, spiritual connection that transcends the physical act of dance. Kathak, for her, is the rhythm of life itself, the heartbeat that syncs with the universe's pulse. It is the air she inhales, filling her with vitality and purpose, and the exhale through which she expresses her innermost being.

Kathak embodies the 'panchabhuta', the five elements—earth, water, fire, air, and ether—that comprise the universe and the human body. In her dance, she becomes one with these elements: her grounded footwork connects her to the earth, while the fluidity of her movements mirror water's grace. The fire within her is reflected in her powerful expressions and intense rhythms, while her swift turns and spins echo the boundless freedom of the air. The ethereal space surrounding her is where the dance breathes, exists, and transcends.

Kathak is her energy—*prana*, the life force that flows through every cell and nerve, igniting her spirit and fuelling her creativity. It is the core that finds expression through the *taal*, *abhinaya*, footwork, and the grace of her every gesture.

Through Kathak, Shovana becomes a medium through which the ancient and the contemporary, the mortal and the eternal, all converse in a silent, sacred dialogue. Her dance, then, is not just a performance but a meditation—a dance of the soul constantly seeking to align with the universe.

Her passion and dedication to dance have made her a respected authority in the field. Her inclination towards experimentation stems from this quest, reflecting her belief in the shared rhythms between Indian and western music. This perspective inspired her to explore and create numerous collaborations in ballet, Flamenco, and tap dancing, drawing parallels between these diverse forms.

Pavan Varma, an accomplished Indian diplomat, politician, and author who served as India's ambassador to Bhutan and Cyprus, has enjoyed a long-standing friendship with Shovana. Their connection dates to their time in the Indian Administrative Service (IAS), where they were batchmates and met during the foundation course in Mussoorie. When Shovana was in the audits and accounts service, and Pavan was in the foreign service, their bond grew more assertive.

Shovana is recognised by Pavan as an exceptionally talented and committed Kathak dancer whose artistry transcends technical mastery. Her hallmark as an artist has been her imagination, innovation, and willingness to experiment with dance and ideas.

He describes her as a scholar of Kathak, a fact underscored by her published works on the subject.

Interestingly, Shovana and Pavan share cultural roots, both coming from a similar cultural belt near Bihar. This shared heritage, combined with their professional camaraderie and mutual admiration, cemented their friendship.

'One of my notable works is a long poem written in fourteen-line rhymed sonnets titled *Yudhisthir and Draupadi*. Shovana and I discussed the possibility of adapting it for dance and theatre. I must admit, she brought it to life in a way that exceeded all expectations. Her adaptation was a remarkable achievement, turning the poem into a stunning success.'

Shovana also worked with Sunit Tandon, a seasoned theatre artist. His interactions with her primarily revolved around her stage work. These shared interests led to numerous collaborations over the years.

Sunit has had an impressive and diverse career. He has been a banker, held a position in government service, served as the director of film festivals, and worked as the director-general of the Indian Institute of Mass Communication. He was the chief executive of Loksabha TV, a television channel he helped establish and lead. Additionally, he is well-known for his television work, particularly as an anchor for national news and current affairs. He is currently the director of the India Habitat Centre (IHC). Sunit has also directed a prominent theatre group called Yatrik and is the president of the Delhi Music Society, reflecting his involvement in western classical music.

Sunit and Shovana's association spans over three decades. Sunit first saw her dance while in college, and they later collaborated on dance productions based on poetry. One notable project was

Yudhishthir Draupadi by Pavan Varma.

Together, they created a brilliant production that seamlessly blended dance, music, theatre, and storytelling. While the poem had previously been staged at Prithvi Theatre in Mumbai, their interpretation elevated it further, with performances in Delhi drawing packed audiences, multiple times. The adaptation also toured extensively across India, and internationally, receiving widespread acclaim.

This experience highlighted Shovana's exceptional ability to use Kathak as an interpretative medium. Her creativity combined the traditional art form with theatrical elements and narrative depth, transforming the poem into a mesmerising dance drama that resonated deeply with audiences everywhere.

Pavan deeply admires Shovana's unwavering commitment to her art, which is evident in her constant stream of new productions. Her ability to remain creatively vibrant and consistently deliver compelling works reflects her dedication and passion for aesthetics.

Shovana has worked on several dance productions that explore the poetry of Mirza Ghalib, including *Chiragh-i-Dair*, blending his profound verses with the expressive power of Kathak. Through her performances, she brings to life the emotional depth, philosophical reflections, and complex layers of Ghalib's ghazals. In these productions, she masterfully uses Kathak to interpret the essence of his poetry, focusing on themes such as love, loss, longing, and the existential questions that pervade his work. Her approach is not merely to recite the verses, but to weave them into a visual narrative that amplifies their emotional resonance. The rhythm of Kathak, combined with the lyrical beauty of Ghalib's words, allows her to express both the pain and beauty his poetry evokes. Her deep understanding of Ghalib's literary world and Kathak's storytelling tradition enables her to connect with audiences profoundly. She collaborates with renowned vocalists or musicians to create a holistic experience where dance and music work together to celebrate the legacy of the artist.

Pavan believes that true artists must remain open-minded, but he also emphasises that artistic expression is deeply personal and should remain an individual pursuit. He is not a proponent of blending different art forms.

'Even when collaborating, the differences between traditions are apparent. For instance, a western classical musician typically sits on a stool with notations in front of them. In contrast, an Indian artist sits on the floor, taking up space without the aid of notations, relying on the musicians. Despite these contrasting approaches, both traditions share the same *sapt swara* (seven notes). Understanding music comes with exposure—the more you listen, the deeper your appreciation of its subtleties. To me, art is universal, but traditions should remain distinct, and they must be preserved in their unique forms.

'I have some reservations about the fusion elements within classical traditions. However, I acknowledge that collaborations can be remarkable when executed by highly talented artists. Shovana, of course, is one such artist. Similarly, Malavika Sarukkai, one of India's leading Bharatnatyam dancers, can seamlessly adapt a Bharatnatyam performance to a thumri from Varanasi—something not everyone can do.'

In Pavan's view, the risk with fusion lies in the potential to mishandle traditions, creating something that neither fully respects one nor fully embodies the other.

'Fusion is a delicate endeavour, and while I can praise certain artists for their successful collaborations, I can also be critical when it falls short. It takes a maestro to blend two evolved traditions effectively.'

Shovana is a dancer who moves with the wisdom of one who understands that every step carries the weight of a story. The power of her art lies in her mastery of nuance—the knowledge that a single misplaced word can shift the narrative, altering the essence of the message. When asked—'You have blended Kathak with many other dance forms; don't you think it mars the sanctity of your art form?'—her response is measured and deliberate: 'I have never blended Kathak with other dance forms or violated its purity. The right way to put this is to say that I have collaborated with other dance forms. We come together to create something special, like two hands joining in the *namaskar* mudra, symbolising respect, gratitude, and the joy of working together. It's like fitting jigsaw pieces to form a complete picture or serving a plate filled with a variety of delicious dishes, where each part adds its flavour to the whole experience. This collaboration is about enhancing what we create and celebrating our teamwork.'

Shovana has a deep reverence for the purity of her craft. Her collaborations have never compromised Kathak's integrity; they have embraced other mediums. Her pursuit is not of perfection, which she believes is a misnomer, but of excellence. Her dedication demands clarity, ensuring the essence of her work remains untarnished. Although Shovana is a purist, deeply rooted in the art form she has devoted her life to mastering, her passion and curiosity have led her to explore other dance traditions with remarkable depth and sensitivity. Through her nuanced approach, she has sought to uncover the intricate threads of similarity and the defining contrasts that connect and distinguish various dance forms.

She has brought a unique blend of Kathak to various artistic collaborations, one of the most notable being her interpretation of

Claude Debussy's piano piece *Clair de Lune*. In this performance, she seamlessly integrated Kathak's lyrical movements and softness with the delicate nuances of the piano composition, creating an exceptional fusion that captivates audiences.

Beyond this, Shovana has also danced alongside a ballet dancer, a Flamenco dancer, and a tap dancer, showcasing her versatility and willingness to explore different dance forms.

She respects the traditional foundations of Kathak and has consistently worked to preserve its core integrity. With an unwavering dedication to her foundational training (*taiyari*), she emphasises the seamless blend of *nritta* (pure dance), *nritya* (expressive dance), and *bhav* (emotional expression) to deliver authentic performances.

Shovana has continuously innovated even within Kathak's framework. Her innate curiosity drives her to delve into the rich heritage of Kathak, exploring its roots in various villages known for this art form. Her intensive study spans multiple disciplines, from the ancient caves of Ajanta to classical paintings, mythology, literature, music, and dance. This extensive research allows her to weave a comprehensive narrative that connects all these elements into an organic whole.

At her core, she is a scholar, passionate about deeply understanding the subjects she holds dear, reflected in her teaching and performances. Her approach not only enriches her artistry but also inspires her students to appreciate the depth and beauty of Kathak.

Her passion for dance drives her to challenge herself, constantly sparking an internal dialogue of curiosity: 'Can I do this? Is this possible?'

This self-reflective questioning propels her to push beyond her limits and experiment with new ideas and styles.

For Shovana, every performance is an opportunity to discover a new dimension of artistry as she embraces the spirit of innovation. Her relentless pursuit of challenge has been the strongest motivation behind her artistic endeavours, allowing her to continuously evolve as a dancer and creator.

In her book, *Meandering Pastures of Memories,* she shares her reflections and insights on Flamenco, offering a fresh perspective on its essence:

> As Kathak, Flamenco, too, is intensely earthy and gravity-bound with the dancer bearing a natural vertical stance. As in Kathak, exaggerated body bends and hip distortions were part of their dynamic movements and did not freeze to become identifiable characteristic features of the form. Kathak and Flamenco seem to share the same spirit of the dance—a very personal experience, a celebration of life, and a manifestation of inner joys, sorrows, and yearnings. But the more self-assertive, arrogant, and uninhibited attitude of Flamenco finds a counterpart in the more contained, refined, and formalised attitude of Kathak.
>
> What strikes one immediately is the footwork *zapateado* in Flamenco, an integral part of Kathak and known as the *tatkar*. The ankle bells or *ghunghroos* amplify the foot sounds in Kathak, whereas the boots perform a similar function in Flamenco. Rhythm in Kathak is provided by percussion instruments such as the tabla and the pakhawaj whereas in Flamenco, this is provided by the clapping of hands. The guitar virtually performs the same function as that of our harmonium and the sitar. Both dance forms share the latent belief that mood is to be expressed through every part of the body, whether through the degree of tautness of the body and the hands or the varying force of the striking heel and toe. Their rhythmic structures also are in cycles of seven, eight, nine, ten, or twelve beats,

with the patterns going into fractions of a beat. However, in our Indian scenario, the rhythmic patterns and rhythmic cycles are highly developed and complex. In Kathak, in the pure rhythmic display, the intricacies of the rhythmic patterns are discernible when the dancer articulates the patterns while highlighting the importance of the *lehera*—the rhythmic cycle given by the accompanying string or wind instruments.

Our rhythmic mnemonics have developed a vocabulary based on the sounds of the feet, dance, various percussion and musical instruments, as well as the sounds of nature such as *ta-thai, na-dhin, diga-diga, dhumakita-kran, tigda, tharikita, dhitam, takita-taka, naggi-tharri,* and *kukku, jhanaka,* to name a few. The Flamenco dancers seem to articulate rhythmic syllables with a simple *tak-ta-tak-ta-tak*. On the issue of the patterns that Dario Arboleda, the Spanish Flamenco dancer, was dancing, I had no difficulty, as they were traditionally taught as part of training for our budding artists. In the execution of footwork, the swishing and swirling of the women Flamenco dancers' long skirts impart a sensuality different from the comparatively grave mood of a Kathak dancer. In both forms, one aspect is common, namely that women dancers have perforce to raise their long ankle-length skirts in order to facilitate the display of their footwork without the sound being hindered and muffled by their long skirts.

On the abhinaya front, without which no discussion on Indian dance can be complete, I found that the Flamenco dances are divided into two strains of dance, namely *cantes chicos* and the *cantes jondos,* the former expressing joy, laughter, love, birth, marriage or success and the latter being mournful dances with themes of death, torture, lost love, imprisonment, breach of trust, among others. The large number of cantes chicos include tango, rumba, alegria, buleria and fandango. However, in their delineation, there is a heavy emphasis on body language alone.

In Kathak, the various abhinaya pieces employ several *hasta-mudras* or hand gestures and *mukha*-abhinaya or facial expressions, besides body language. There is also a well-developed storyline and interpretation of the song's words while expressing the associated mood in Kathak. In Flamenco, it is predominantly the mood that the artist is dancing out. Further, in Kathak, the abhinaya items are distinct from the rhythmic items, but this distinction is not in Flamenco. Besides, Kathak's strongly traditional religious base is not discernible in Flamenco.

The musicians in Flamenco consist of the guitarists and the singers who clap out the beats. In contrast, in Kathak, the four or five musicians would include one or two percussionists (on the tabla and/or pakhawaj), a vocalist on the harmonium, and one or two instrumentalists on the sitar or sarod, flute, and so on.

Interestingly, even though gravity bound like Kathak, the usage of pirouettes in Flamenco is limited. In Kathak, pirouettes are a part of its feature as they are philosophically linked with the visual interpretation of the cycle of life and death. In this respect, Christian Rovny, the ballet dancer, and I had much in common.

Traditionally, both Flamenco and Kathak were handed down from generation to generation. But today, in addition to the *Gitanos* (gypsies), there are the *payos* (non-gypsies) who dance the Flamenco. The same is true of our system, too, where the number of *non-gharanedar Kathaks* perhaps may equal, if not outnumber, the *gharanedar Kathaks*.

For Shovana, art is not merely a discipline but a way of life—a path that nurtures the soul and shapes the spirit. Her journey as an artist has been in seeking *wisdom* and embodying *compassion*, qualities that define her approach to her craft and interactions with the world.

Through decades of devotion to her art form, she has gained profound insights that transcend technique, embracing the universal language of expression in dance and other art forms. This openness has allowed her to connect deeply with artists and traditions across the globe, fostering a sense of unity and shared humanity.

Pavan argues the idea of artists being global citizens, saying he is not particularly fond of the term. He believes you can be a global citizen while deeply connected to your culture and roots. If your cultural understanding is shallow, it may seem more straightforward to adopt the label of a global citizen, but that is ultimately a superficial approach. A genuine embrace of other cultures must come with discernment, as it can quickly turn rash, condescending, or overly accommodating.

'One must know where to set boundaries. Cultures are inherently unique. For instance, the Indian tradition of touching the feet of elders as a mark of reverence is a deeply aligned concept within our culture, but it may seem foreign to someone from a different background. Many customs that are second nature to us may appear strange or incomprehensible in a globalised world. Every culture has its uniqueness, and it is essential not to sacrifice it for the allure of global citizenship. Attempting to homogenise cultures leads to unnecessary challenges and dilutes authenticity. After all, no one respects photocopies; they serve a purpose, but they're not the original.' Pavan, a connoisseur of the arts and a scholar—deeply immersed in the study of Hindu civilisation—has extensively explored its expressions across art forms, scriptures, the Vedas, and the broader framework of the *purusharthas.*

To quote him from his book, *The Great Hindu Civilisation*, 'The Hindu Civilisation has not become a historical relic, an antiquary of the past, but has survived as an unbroken continuum to the present.'

Shovana deeply comprehends this unbroken continuum, dedicating herself to bridging generations across time and space while preserving its essence. She skilfully maintains the delicate balance required to merge traditions seamlessly, while retaining their distinct, unblemished identity. In her hands, art becomes a spiritual journey—one that continually enriches her understanding of the world and deepens her empathy for all those who walk the creative path. While her art celebrates a universal essence, she remains deeply rooted in her cultural heritage. Her ability to bridge traditions is not about dilution but dialogue—a meaningful exchange where each culture retains its integrity while finding resonance with others.

This duality allows her to honour the specificity of Kathak while inviting broader conversations that transcend boundaries. Her artistry demonstrates that embracing the global does not require abandoning the local; instead, it is about finding harmony where the two coexist.

In her evocative production, *Wisdom and Compassion: The Way of Buddha*, performed in 2001, Shovana once again showcased her unique approach to dance. Staged at Ravindra Bharathi, this performance exemplified her renowned eclectic style, seamlessly blending the intricate *tatkars* of her dance troupe with the serene chants of Buddhist monks. The production, divided into five acts, drew heavily from the teachings of Buddha, and created a mesmerising experience that transported the audience into a realm of profound beauty and spirituality.

The music, lighting, and harmonious chants from the Tashi Dargye monastery created an atmosphere that left some audience members in tears, particularly during the poignant depiction of Emperor Ashoka's disillusionment with the devastation of war. The performance concluded with a meditation segment led by the monks.

In one of Shovana's heartfelt letters to her son, Ishan, she tenderly expresses the emotions the performance stirred within her, 'I almost forgot to tell you that what I had been dreaming of since I heard the chants of the Buddhist monks in Bhutan, namely, to dance to Buddhist chanting, finally materialised in October this year. This was performed to the chanting of the monks from the Tashi Dargye monastery from Karnataka.

'The story was woven around Amrapali and Buddha and the effect of Buddhism on Emperor Ashoka, an emperor whose empire ranged from the middle of Afghanistan up to Burma and further. He was so ambitious that he spread bloodshed and terror all around in expanding the boundaries of his kingdom till one day, he stood in the middle of the battlefield at Kalinga among the hordes of dead bodies, and the realisation of the hollow victory hit him. It was then that he converted to Buddha's teachings of following a peaceful path and the renunciation of violence. What stupendous lighting effect was provided by R K Dhingra! Wow! Buddhist shlokas' powerful, deep, and base chanting created a mesmerising ambience.

'I collaborated with the monks of the Tashi Dargye monastery at Delhi, Hyderabad and in Vishakhapatnam under the guidance of Lama Duboom Tulku Rinpoche.

'Then later, I also did a collaboration with the Grammy Award winner monks of the Palpung Sherabling monastery under the guidance of Guru Vajradhara Chamgon, the twelfth Kenting Tai Situpa.

'I am a seeker. That will continue till my last breath,' says the Kathak maestro.

A true seeker in any art form carries the weight of tradition while daring to expand its horizons. They honour the essence distilled through generations, yet their journey is incomplete without infusing it with their personal experiences—the sum of their joys, struggles, and revelations. This inner urge compels them to explore uncharted paths, to stray from rigid conventions, and to reinterpret the rules through a fresh lens. Such artists are not content with preservation alone; they are driven to add their voice to the ongoing narrative, creating something timeless yet deeply personal.

'Classical dance was evolving in the sixties, bringing a new awareness to its standards. One key change was the focus on stylisation, including precise rules like how much to smile during *shringar* and not showing teeth while emoting.

'The prevailing view was that maintaining the *maryada* of performance meant sticking strictly to traditional rules. Adaptations for different characters, venues, or audiences were discouraged, leaving little scope for personal expression or flexibility.

"But you are young. Remember, these are your yardsticks!" we were reminded.

"But what if I, as Radha, wanted to fly into Krishna's arms?"

"No, no—she has to be restrained."

"But what if Radha, in her dreams, imagines herself acting wantonly? Dreams can depict the impossible, and behaviours in dreams often differ greatly from those in reality," we questioned.

"No, no...that would be a sin," came the stern warning.'

A Dialogue Within

'Restraint is beauty,' the voice declares,
'Tradition is the anchor you must bear.
Radha is coy, her steps refined,
Her love is subtle, her gaze aligned.'
But in my heart, a tempest brews,
A yearning for colours, for bolder hues.
What if Radha breaks free one day,
And leaps to Krishna in wild disarray?'

'No, no,' they warn, 'She must remain,
Bound by decorum, untouched by disdain.
Her dreams, too, must bow to the mould,
For maryada's grace is worth more than gold.'

Yet I wonder, can love be contained?
In measured steps, in smiles restrained?
'What if her dreams, untamed and vast,
Reveal a passion too fierce to cast?'

'Sin!' they cry, 'An unforgivable plight!
Radha is pure; her path is right.
Do not disturb what time has sealed,
Let her remain in a world concealed.'

But I am Radha; I feel her fire,
A longing, a pulse, an unquenched desire.
To dance her truth, raw and divine,
Beyond the boundaries of the sacred line.

'Dare you defy?' the voice persists,
'Tradition holds; it must not twist.'
But art, I reply, is ever anew,
Its essence grows as we dare to pursue.

So, I weave her story in my way,
A Radha who dreams, who loves, who sways.
For the heart of dance is the soul's release,
A timeless love, a boundless peace.

In the rigid framework of artistic standards, Shovana found herself constrained, her creativity often measured by stringent yardsticks that left scant room for the spontaneous bursts of passion that truly inspired her. The boundaries set by conventional norms stifled the full range of her artistic expression. She felt a deep, persistent longing to transcend these limitations and celebrate the essence of her craft through diverse modes of expression.

With reverence for the mythological tales she portrayed, she sought to bring a fresh perspective to these ancient narratives. She pondered why Radha, bound by tradition, was always portrayed as coy and reserved. Why, Shovana wondered, could Radha not sometimes express her passionate love for Krishna with the same fervour that made her heart race? She envisioned a dance transcending conventional portrayal, allowing Radha to embody a more dynamic and multifaceted expression of love.

Shovana sought to explore and celebrate the more profound, unspoken dimensions of these timeless stories, enriching them with new layers of beauty.

'The important learning that maintaining the *atma,* (essence) of stage technique, and deep internalisation, was essential and that the *maryada* of the stage and the *maryada* of the form were complementary. The true success in performance lay in balancing innovation with the *samarpan* (dedicated devotion) to the dance's spirit, ultimately captivating both connoisseurs and newcomers,' Shovana sums up in her book, *Meandering Pastures of Memories.*

When the Flame Fades

Shovana was thrilled about her first posting as Assistant Accountant General (AAG) in the Accountant General's (AG's) office in Jaipur. Apart from her training stints in Mussoorie and Simla, this would be her first experience managing a household independently. Until now, she had been sheltered under the comforting care of her parents.

However, she couldn't shake off a sense of foreboding, as Diwali at home in 1977 had been unusually subdued and lacking in its usual cheer.

Arriving in Jaipur on a crisp mid-November morning that year and later meeting Shri K C Das, the AG, felt almost surreal to her. The weeks seemed to pass in a blur.

On 22 November she received a call from her father, who was in Jaipur for a meeting and wished to spend some time with her.

Shovana promptly approached the Senior Deputy Accountant General (DAG), who graciously granted her leave after lunch.

She rushed to her father's hotel, only to find he was still in a meeting. The meeting ran longer than anticipated, pushing back his departure to Delhi. With no available flights, he chose to take the midnight *Ahmedabad Mail* train instead. The unexpected delay allowed them more time together, providing an opportunity to talk and reconnect.

'Ma had a habit of calling the railway station or the airport to find out whether the train or the plane was arriving as scheduled. In keeping with her habit, she called the railways to inquire about the scheduled arrival of the *Ahmedabad Mail*. A brusque voice first said, "The train is late," which he quickly amended to "The train is derailed." That got her nervous. Further inquiries revealed that there were quite a few casualties. Hoping against hope that Papa hadn't been a passenger on that ill-fated train, she had called me up in Jaipur. But my reply gave her further cause for worry. She told me to find out more details at my end while she did the same in Delhi.'

Shovana vividly remembers someone telling her, 'I remember your father well—he was the last to board the train. He was about to leave when I called him back, saying a first-class air-conditioned (AC) berth had just become available due to a cancellation.'

When she pressed for more information, the person advised her to go to Alwar and wait for the relief train there. He quietly mentioned that the first few coaches had been severely damaged, and the first AC coach, where her father was, was the fifth from the engine. Her heart sank upon hearing this. Following his guidance, she took a taxi to Alwar after informing the AG and Senior DAG. As she made her way there, her mind raced, trying to process the details. Could the fifth coach have sustained such severe damage in the derailment? She clung to hope yet braced herself for the worst.

After what felt like an eternity of agonising waiting at Alwar, the relief train finally crawled into the station, its slow approach seeming almost cruel, as if mocking her anxiety. Her heart pounded as her eyes scanned the crowd with frantic hope, yearning to catch sight of him.

For a brief, electrifying moment, she thought she saw him. She darted toward the figure, only for her hope to shatter—it wasn't her father. Again and again, she repeated the mistake, clinging more tightly to the fragile reassurance she whispered to herself: 'Nothing has happened to Papa.'

Amid her frantic search, a voice called out sharply, 'What are you doing here? Go to the accident site!' Overwhelmed, she cried back, 'But where is it?'

She and the cab driver set off into the night with only vague directions to guide them. Sensing her distress, the driver remained silent, offering his sympathy without words. As the car wound its way through the dark and unfamiliar roads, she wrestled with the storm of emotions threatening to consume her—worry, desperation, and fear, each wave more overpowering than the last. A hollow emptiness washed over her at moments, leaving her numb and unsure of what lay ahead. Yet, despite the crushing weight of uncertainty, she held herself together, her composure masking the ache that gripped her heart.

'By the time I reached Rewari, it was nearly 4 pm, and every second felt like a lifetime. I moved worriedly between the civil hospital and the railway hospital, my every step driven by a single, desperate need: to find my father. I lost count of how many times I scanned the lists of the dead and injured, each name blurring into the next. My mind couldn't process the endless faces, the haunting silence of the rooms. I walked past every bed, everybody lying on the ground, hoping, praying that one of them would be him. But there was no sign of him.

'Then, with no more strength to hold back, I pushed myself into the postmortem room. The air was thick with the unbearable smell of antiseptic and death. The room was stark and cold, its walls echoing with the weight of the tragedy it held. The bodies—too many to count—were lined up, covered with white sheets that seemed to mock me with their quiet finality. I felt my legs tremble as I approached each one, my eyes searching desperately for a sign, a clue, anything.

'When I didn't find my father there, a sharp wave of relief hit me, almost knocking me off my feet. For a fleeting moment, I thought he might be safe. But it was short-lived. The relief quickly dissolved into a more profound, gnawing fear. If he wasn't here, then where could he be? The uncertainty was suffocating, and I couldn't shake the image of everybody lying cold, knowing my father might be among them somewhere.'

She stood outside the postmortem room, lost and desperate, her sorrow hanging heavy in the cold, open space. In the distance, a truck loomed, its presence both ominous and inevitable. Clinging to a fragile hope, she described her father to a worker nearby.

'That matches a body on the truck that hasn't been unloaded yet,' he said quietly.

The words hit her like a blow, stealing the breath from her lungs.

Stunned and unwilling to believe, she watched strangers form a makeshift ladder with their hands, urging her upward. With trembling steps, she climbed onto the towering truck, her heart pounding in disbelief. Carefully, she stepped over the rows of neatly lined bodies until she found him—her father.

'He's just sleeping; he can't be dead,' she thought as she looked at him. She bent down and touched his face—it was cold. The reality of the loss hit her like a wave. But she didn't cry. There was only numbness and disbelief, a refusal to accept the unbearable truth.

As she climbed down from the truck, she stood motionless, paralysed by the weight of what she had just seen. Her mind was blank, overwhelmed, and numb from the sheer shock.

'The postmortem will have to be done,' someone said.

Almost instinctively, she found herself following as they carried her father's body toward the postmortem room.

'How long will it take? Can I call my mother in Delhi?' she asked, her voice trembling.

'The market is just around the corner. And get a white sheet,' a voice suggested.

She wandered into a shop in a haze and purchased a white sheet. Her hands trembled as she arranged for a trunk call to her mother in Delhi. Each passing moment felt unbearably long—fifteen, perhaps twenty minutes—before the call finally connected, stretching her agony to its limit.

Travelling back to Delhi in a taxi with her father's postmortem body, Shovana felt a profound mix of disbelief and sorrow. Just the day before, she had shared a vibrant, heartfelt conversation with him, filled with hope and familial duties. He had entrusted her with responsibilities traditionally reserved for sons, a gesture of his deep faith in her. Now, barely twenty-four hours later, she was grappling with the heavy reality of carrying out these very duties in the wake of his sudden passing.

The transition from their lively meeting to the sombre task of transporting his body felt jarring and surreal. Every mile she travelled was a stark reminder of the unanticipated flip in her life—from a moment of familial connection to a day defined by grief and responsibility. As she sat in the taxi, the burden of her new role weighed heavily on her, intertwining with the searing ache of her loss.

The next day, the question of who would light her father's

pyre arose. For Lalita, it seemed natural that one of her daughters should perform the ritual. The loss was theirs—deeply personal, intimate, and irreplaceable. No one else could share their grief.

However, some mourners voiced objections, insisting it was not appropriate for a daughter to perform the *mukhagni*, the sacred act of lighting the pyre, claiming it might hinder the soul from finding peace.

Lalita listened to the murmurs in silence before speaking with unwavering resolve. She declared that her daughters had always been both sons and daughters to their family. One would light the pyre, and the other would immerse the ashes in Haridwar. She firmly stated that true peace for her husband's soul would come from rites performed with genuine love and devotion, not from blind adherence to tradition.

With the support of Mrs Indira Gandhi, Mrs Mukul Banerji, Mrityunjaya Prasad, son of Dr Rajendra Prasad, and other eminent personalities known to the family, Lalita stood her ground. The mourners had not anticipated such unshakable strength from the Narayan women.

Stepping forward with quiet courage, Shovana performed the last rites, lighting her father's pyre and severing the final earthly bond with him. Later, her sister Ranjana carried their father's ashes to Haridwar, performing the immersion rites with heartfelt love and dignity, honouring his memory in the truest sense.

Attachment and detachment shape your journey as you navigate the tension between clinging to the transient world and letting go. You often find comfort in attachments, but they are fleeting, clouding your understanding of impermanence. The scriptures speak of *moh*, the illusion binding you, and true wisdom lies in transcending it.

The shift from being a *karta*, deeply involved in outcomes, to a *sakshi*, a detached observer, requires balance. The Bhagavad Gita guides you toward *sthit pragya*, steady wisdom that keeps you grounded, unaffected by the vicissitudes of life.

True detachment doesn't mean renouncing the world, but embracing its fleeting nature with peace, accepting both attachments and losses without being overwhelmed. This is the path to finding inner calm amid life's turbulence.

Vividha vachanani tu ya: sthita prajna nishthita: |
ya: sada moksha-siddhi: Sankhya-Yoga-nishthita ||

(He who is steadfast in wisdom and firmly rooted in knowledge, and who is always engaged in the pursuit of liberation through the path of Sankhya and Yoga, is the one who attains the highest state of realisation.)

Shovana Narayan with her father K D Narayan

Dancing to My Beat

Shovana's life was defined by a strict routine and a sense of discipline instilled in her early on. Her typical school day would start early in the morning with a revision of the subjects she had to tackle, setting a focused tone even before she stepped out of the house. After school, she finished her homework before allowing herself the joy of playing with her friends. This rhythm of work and play taught her the importance of balance—ensuring that she could dedicate herself fully to her studies and passion without compromising.

Dance was woven into the fabric of her daily life as seamlessly as academics. Three to four times a week, she attended dance classes with Guru Kundan Lal ji, pouring her heart into each session and relishing every moment despite the physical effort. These sessions were more than practice—lessons in focus, perseverance, and the joy of hard work. She fondly recalls days when, while playing with friends, she'd spot Guruji approaching. Unlike the other girls who would scatter and hide, she would happily turn back, eager to tie her ghunghroos and join the class.

Her love for dance, combined with the discipline of her routine,

Shovana Narayan with Pandit Birju Maharaj ji

nurtured a dedication that shaped her approach to life. This early foundation in discipline and time management became her strength, enabling her to juggle multiple roles and responsibilities with poise. Whether excelling in academics, immersing herself in dance, or stepping up after her father's passing, she adapted and thrived. The structure and values instilled in her formative years taught her the art of balance—much like in Kathak, where every graceful move is rooted in equilibrium and strength.

'Ma was searching for a guru for Didi when, upon seeing Birju Maharaj ji, she felt he was *sakshat* Krishna (Lord Krishna incarnate). Maharaj ji's mastery extended beyond the technical brilliance of Kathak to the emotive art of abhinaya,' shares Ranjana.

However, when Birju Maharaj first saw Shovana, he was not particularly impressed. He often remarked that she seemed timid and reserved, her demeanour serious and scholarly, and this reflected in her posture and expression. Yet, he was deeply drawn to her parents, especially her mother, Lalita, who soon became affectionately known as *Amma* within the Kathak group at Bharatiya Kala Kendra, later known as Kathak Kendra. She believed her mother's influence led Maharaj ji to accept her as a disciple.

Her initiation ceremony into Maharaj ji's tutelage was a memorable one. He meticulously explained the meaning behind every aspect of the ritual, and she was now old enough to appreciate its significance fully. Until that day, her wardrobe had consisted of frocks, skirt-and-blouse ensembles, and occasionally *churidar-kurta* or *salwar-kameez*. But with this new chapter, she was instructed to wear only saris, with churidar-kurta permitted reluctantly. On the day of her initiation, dressed in thc latter, she sat before Maharaj ji, ready to embrace her new identity as his disciple.

In front of her lay a large silver tray laden with offerings—sweets, fruits, her revered ghunghroos, an oil lamp, incense sticks, small bowls of curd, *roli*, *mauli* thread, rice, betel leaves, *supari* nuts, jaggery, and roasted gram—all lovingly prepared by her mother. Beneath the tray were photographs of Maharaj ji's ancestors, legendary maestros whose presence added a profound reverence to the occasion. The *puja* began, following a familiar Hindu ritual often seen at festivals, though without a *havan*.

Maharaj ji blessed her ghunghroos and instructed her to eat some roasted gram followed by jaggery. As the ritual unfolded, he explained the meaning behind each act. Speaking of the *chana* and *gur*, he said that just as chewing the tough gram is challenging, so is the rigorous journey of learning dance. But once mastered, dance becomes internalised, bringing joy and ecstasy, symbolised by the sweetness of the jaggery.

Initially, Maharaj ji entrusted one of his senior students, Pradeep Shankar, with her training. However, as he observed her dedication and passion for Kathak, his perception of her shifted. Gradually, his interest in her progress deepened. He soon took over her training, visiting her home daily to provide additional lessons alongside her regular classes at Kathak Kendra. He refined every movement and stance with meticulous care and patience, ensuring she achieved perfection.

'Birju Maharaj ji began teaching Didi and continued for eight years at Bharti Nagar, never charging any fee. Didi would return home from Delhi University around 7 pm, often skipping meals to devote herself entirely to her dance practice. I would sit on the bed in the room where Maharaj ji conducted her lessons, watching intently and absorbing every detail. Later, when Didi practised independently, I occasionally pointed out corrections in her steps, as I remembered everything vividly. Didi embraced his teachings with dedication.

'Didi, later, a full-time officer working nine to five, infused our home on Pandara Road with vibrant energy when she returned in the evenings. The atmosphere would buzz with lively discussions about politics, art, and literature. *Chai* was always simmering on the stove, and extra food was prepared to welcome unexpected guests. Our home in Bharti Nagar, a government accommodation, frequently became a haven for artists, some of whom stayed with us for months.'

Lalita, always present during these sessions, would later guide Shovana, pointing out areas where she had faltered and reinforcing Maharaj ji's teachings. On holidays, Maharaj ji would arrive at 10 am, and the practice sessions would extend well into the evening, often leaving her physically drained. For over a year, she wrestled with mastering just a few *toras* and *parans*, as Maharaj ji insisted she hadn't perfected them to his high standards. Only when he was satisfied with her progress did he introduce new material.

During this period, she faced numerous moments of despair. For years, Maharaj ji prohibited her from performing publicly, believing she should only step onto the stage after achieving something truly meaningful. Her parents wholeheartedly supported his decision, and together, they agreed that she should only make her debut when she was genuinely 'ready.'

Since Maharaj ji never charged for her lessons, her parents often wondered how to express gratitude. Aware of his love for *paan* and *rabari*, they ensured these treats were served daily. After each dance session, Maharaj ji would sit with her mother, listening intently as she shared nostalgic stories about dancers and performances from bygone days.

Shovana's journey was marked by her unwavering commitment to whatever she believed in, regardless of the judgement she received from others. While her well-wishers and self-appointed commentators were quick to applaud her academic achievements in mathematics and physics, they were less enthusiastic about her passion for dance. Accepting her academic ambitions came easily to them, but her dedication to Kathak left them perplexed. 'How will she manage both?' they wondered, their approval faltering at the apparent incongruity of her pursuits.

As a middle school student, she often heard cautionary voices: 'It's easy to balance studies and dance now but wait until the pressure increases in higher classes.' Yet, when she progressed to higher grades, the scepticism didn't fade. Well-meaning advisers suggested she opt for 'soft' subjects like literature or arts to make room for her dance. She boldly chose physics, chemistry, and mathematics to defy these expectations. Her decision stunned her critics, who were convinced she couldn't handle the demands of science and dance—two pursuits they believed to be worlds apart.

Shovana and her sister continued to excel, consistently securing top academic positions while equally dedicating themselves to music and dance. The doubts, however, only grew louder when Shovana pursued a BSc Honours and a master's degree in physics from Delhi University, all while gaining recognition for her Kathak performances among critics and connoisseurs. Her days, often stretching to nineteen or twenty hours, became the norm as she skilfully balanced the rigorous demands of her academic and artistic pursuits.

She remains deeply grateful to Birju Maharaj ji, not just for teaching her the intricate art of Kathak, but for his dedication in guiding her to emerge as a true dancer. In the rich tradition of the *guru-shishya parampara*, where the relationship between guru and disciple is sacred and transformative, Maharaj ji embodied the very essence of this wisdom. A guru, he believed, seeks the *suyogya patra*—the exemplary disciple, ready to receive and honour the knowledge imparted to them.

Maharaj ji understood that Shovana's passion for dance had to coexist with her commitment to her studies, particularly her pursuit of a master's degree in physics. Recognising that her time during the day was limited, he would often bend the rules of time itself, adjusting his schedule to accommodate hers. Every evening, he made the extra effort to visit her home for two-hour lessons, ensuring she could nurture her academic and artistic aspirations with equal devotion.

In doing so, he not only taught her Kathak but also imparted the deeper wisdom of the guru-shishya parampara: that a true guru shapes their disciple's path, not just through technical teaching, but by being a constant presence, adjusting to the needs of the disciple's journey.

Tad viddhi praṇipātena paripraśnena sevayā,
Upadekṣyanti te jñānaṁ jñāninastattvadarśinaḥ.
— *Bhagavad Gita*, 4.34

(Know that by surrendering to the guru, through humble inquiry and service, those who are wise and knowledgeable will impart to you the knowledge of the truth.)

This lesson learned through the years of her training became the cornerstone of Shovana's approach as a guru today. She goes beyond the rigid structure of time and technique, understanding that the true teaching spirit lies in moulding herself to meet her students' needs, just as her guru did for her.

After years of rigorous training, Maharaj ji believed Shovana was finally ready for the stage. To start, he arranged for her to perform for half an hour before his programmes, allowing her to capture the attention of critics and connoisseurs.

Her debut performance occurred at the prestigious Sapru House auditorium, though she had not fully established herself as an independent artist. Nevertheless, these early performances were pivotal in building her confidence, strength, and stage presence, with Maharaj ji's tabla accompaniment being a constant source of support and assurance.

The actual test of her abilities came in 1971 at Shanmukhananda Hall in Bombay, where she performed solo for a full hour without Maharaj ji by her side. Though eager to prove herself, she soon discovered the stark contrast between theory and practice. After a promising start, with the audience showing appreciation for the first twenty minutes, restlessness set in. Her extended focus on the *thaat ang,* an older dance style, began to lose the audience's engagement.

As panic gripped her and her family's anxious faces loomed from the wings, she was on the verge of abandoning the stage. But in that fleeting moment, something within her stirred—a quiet shift. With a determined pirouette, she reclaimed her resolve and pressed on. The audience, once restless, fell into a hushed stillness, drawn in by the transformation unfolding before them. What began as a struggle with panic soon gave way to a fluid, effortless grace. Once rigid and strained, her movements began to flow naturally, as if the dance had finally found its true home within her. The fears that had once held her captive dissolved into the rhythm of the performance. She was no longer bound by anxiety; she was one with the art.

In that moment, she transcended the mechanics of performance and embraced the dance as an extension of her soul. It was not just technique but a visceral understanding of her art. The lesson was profound, not through formal instruction but through the raw, unrelenting pressure of fear. She had conquered it—her audience, too, had been conquered.

And in that moment of profound release, she was once again the four-year-old Putul who had danced with wild abandon after a day of self-doubt and quiet probing. She had questioned whether dance was meant for her and whether she was meant for dance. The answer had come from deep within: 'Yes.' And in that very instant, she had become dance—both then and now.

This transformation illustrates a fundamental truth about any art form: only by internalising it do artists become natural in their expression. When artists reach this stage, they are no longer constrained by doubt or fear. Instead, they embody the art, shaking off anxieties and finding a deeper connection with the audience. For Shovana, that performance became a turning point, not only in technique but in mastering the self-assurance that comes with artistic maturity.

In 1975, her decision to sit for the civil services examination instead of completing her PhD in physics raised many eyebrows. Yet, Shovana never looked back with regret. Her choices were deliberate, guided by passion rather than societal expectations.

For her, life was never about conforming to a predefined mould but embracing diverse pursuits with conviction. She found fulfilment in harmonising intellect with art, seamlessly weaving the two into her journey. Unfazed by how unconventional her path appeared to others, she walked it with courage and purpose, staying true to herself at every step.

Shovana completed her MSc in 1972 and began pursuing a PhD, supported by a Council of Scientific and Industrial Research (CSIR) junior fellowship. Unlike the conventional route of taking the civil services exam immediately after completing her BSc, she chose a different path. It wasn't until 1975 that she appeared for the exam, joining the 1976 batch. By then, she had already gained recognition as a professional and acclaimed solo Kathak dancer, having established herself on the stage by 1970–71.

Determined not to abandon dance, Shovana consciously decided to join the Audit and Accounts Service. This career choice allowed her to maintain a harmonious balance between her artistic pursuits and professional responsibilities.

'I have often found myself judged through the narrow lens of deep-seated biases—people find it hard to believe that a person can be both a dedicated Kathak dancer and a committed government officer. When I started my career in public service, my colleagues initially had no idea that the person they saw on stage in elaborate Kathak costumes and makeup was the same individual working alongside them.

Over time, as they connected the dots, new challenges

emerged. While I was respected as an artist in the dance world, my role as a public servant altered their perceptions. Suddenly, securing performances became more complex; organisers found it hard to reconcile with my dual identity, clinging to the notion that an artist must remain solely an artist. I had to prove myself repeatedly. Meanwhile, in my professional life, there were assumptions to overcome as well. Some colleagues, once they learned of my dance career, viewed me through a different lens, questioning my commitment or capability. However, those who worked closely with me recognised my sincerity and skills and could vouch for my dedication in both fields. I have learned to navigate these worlds without letting biases define me. Whether on stage or in the office, my work has always been my answer to any scepticism. Those who truly know me understand that both roles are integral to my identity. I've continued to thrive in both, letting my passion and hard work speak for themselves.'

Ranjana adds: 'With her strong educational background and spiritual inclination, Didi began delving into the works of various poets and writers, broadening her creative horizons. Our family shared a deep bond, supporting one another in every endeavour. I wrote the first ballet, *Dishantar,* for her, including some lyrics, a title that signifies a shift in direction. The music was composed by Jwala Prasad ji, and the production was staged in the open air. I've had the privilege of serving as anchor and narrator for many of her past performances—and what an incredible journey it has been!

'Didi took on the central role of Vasudha, a representation of the Earth. The performance was groundbreaking for its time, addressing environmental themes well before the enactment of the Environment Protection Act. The narrative revolved around Vasudha's loss of her child to a famine caused by deforestation.

Resolute in her grief, she inspired the villagers to plant trees, ushering in rain and prosperity.

'The production was layered with powerful metaphors. For example, Holi symbolised equality, joy, the cyclical rhythm of nature, and collective happiness. Through its profound themes and innovative storytelling, *Dishantar* resonated deeply, leaving an indelible mark on the audience.'.

Shovana's home was always a hub of warmth and activity, whether in the modest house on Pandara Road or a grand embassy setting. Regardless of the surroundings, her essence remained constant—she valued and respected people of all backgrounds, faiths, and cultures. Her home was a sanctuary where every visitor was greeted with a meal and genuine hospitality.

'After her marriage, when Herbert arrived in Delhi as the Austrian ambassador, Shovana suddenly stepped into the role of Mrs Ambassador. While she retained her flat on Pandara Road as a government officer, she also took on the responsibility of hosting events at the Austrian Embassy. But when Shovana was the hostess, it felt less like an embassy and more like home. We spent much time there, treating the embassy as our retreat. After the formal parties, a close-knit group of four or five of us would return for these intimate, warm after-parties. We'd rehearse, play the piano, and unwind. However, after Herbert's term ended and a new ambassador took over, the atmosphere changed. The embassy returned to being a more formal space for us, but those memories of it being a cosy, welcoming haven remain unforgettable,' Sunit Tandon shares.

Deep, meaningful conversations with intellectuals enriched her perspective as she eagerly absorbed their insights and experiences. Their mother, Lalita, played a pivotal role in shaping Shovana's and Ranjana's artistic journeys. She contributed significantly, including writing half the dialogues for *Dishantar* and other productions and actively supporting and enriching her daughters' creative expressions.

Shovana created numerous ballets highlighting pressing social issues. Among them was *Mukti Lekha*, a powerful production centred on human rights and deeply rooted in the philosophy of non-violence. This impactful piece was broadcast multiple times on Doordarshan. Each of her productions seamlessly merged art with activism, offering thought-provoking narratives that resonated with audiences.

'An artist is a *sutradhar*, a storyteller connecting the past, present, and future,' Ranjana explains. 'Bhava is eternal, transcending boundaries.'

Shovana's engagement with the professional art world grew steadily in the 1970s. She staged operas like *Ghalib ki Dilli*, where she first performed to the verses of the eighteenth-century Urdu poet Mir Taqi Mir. On her guru Sadhana Bose's first death anniversary, she performed *Omar Khayyam*, *Nartaki*, and *The Street Beggar* at a Calcutta festival. Reflecting on life's transience, these pieces deeply resonated with her and profoundly influenced her artistic journey.

Omar Khayyam blended theatre and dance, pushing Shovana beyond her shyness with specific costumes. The piece meditated on time, indulgence, and the balance between the physical and the profound, embodying Khayyam's reflections on savouring life's fleeting beauty.

Nartaki delves into the struggles of ageing, particularly for dancers confronting the loss of youth and fame. Through her portrayal of an ageing performer, Shovana highlights the fleeting nature of accolades while delivering a powerful message of resilience, leaving audiences with a lasting impression of beauty and truth.

The Street Beggar gives voice to society's marginalised members, reflecting the inner struggles and desires of those often overlooked. Shovana highlights social attitudes and the universal human experience of longing and aspiration through this performance.

Shovana's choice to perform these pieces goes beyond honouring her guru, Sadhana Bose. They reflect her deep engagement with life's fleeting nature, a central theme for any artist. Through these works, she confronts impermanence, recognising that an artist's role is to immortalise moments of truth, beauty, and emotion.

An artist's drive to leave a lasting mark in a transient world is at the heart of these performances. Aware of life's impermanence, artists capture and preserve the essence of human experience, seeking immortality through their work. In doing so, they ensure their spirit, thoughts, and emotions endure, transcending time and lcaving a legacy.

When Lalita sensed Shovana's growing maturity in dance, she took her to Ramdhari Singh Dinkar, the eminent Hindi poet and laureate. He patiently explained *Urvashi* to her, a poem that remains a landmark in Hindi literature. He expressed his desire to see her translate *Kurukshetra* into dance and personally marked passages in the book he handed her. Similarly, Dharamvir Bharati, another renowned Hindi dramatist and writer, envisioned parts of *Andha Yug* to be enacted through dance. She fulfilled the dreams of these two literary giants, but unfortunately, it was long after they had passed away—a regret she carries within.

During this time, Rashtrapati Bhawan hosted grand banquets for visiting heads of states and governments, featuring classical performances. Shovana had the honour of dancing before numerous dignitaries, including Prince Charles, the late Lord Mountbatten, President Daoud of Afghanistan, Zayed bin Sultan al Nahyan of the UAE, Kenneth Kaunda of Zambia, King Jigme Singye Wangchuck of Bhutan, President Carter of the USA, His Excellency Ashraf Pahlavi of Iran, and the President of Nigeria. She fondly remembers Prince Charles's genuine interest in her dance, asking thoughtful questions that reflected his deep appreciation for her art.

In 1982, during Indira Gandhi's state visit to the USSR, Shovana had the rare honour of performing in the majestic Tchaikovsky Auditorium before her and President Brezhnev. In an unexpected and moving gesture, a member of the audience broke through security to shower her feet with flowers in appreciation, prompting a standing ovation. Upon returning from the tour, her mother beamed with pride, showing her the newspaper articles celebrating her performance in the Indian press.

Looking back, Shovana's mother had once expressed a heartfelt wish: '*Meri beti jahan jahan bhi jaye, log uske pairon ki dhool mathe par lagayen*' (Wherever my daughter goes, may people place the dust of her feet on their foreheads). This prayer, born of a mother's love, came to life in ways beyond imagination as Shovana found herself receiving the admiration and respect of a world that had once dismissed her as 'nothing' simply for being a girl.

A decade later, during Rajiv Gandhi's tenure as Prime Minister, Shovana performed for Yasser Arafat of Palestine, President José Eduardo dos Santos of Angola, and the President of Nicaragua. During the presidency of Shri Venkataraman, she had the honour of performing before President Dr Censu Tabone of Malta. At the Icelandic festival, she danced for President Ms Vigdís Finnbogadóttir, and in Vienna, she had the pleasure of performing several times in front of President Rudolf Kirchschläger of Austria.

By the late seventies, Shovana's performances were in full bloom, with invitations flooding in from prominent festivals both in India and abroad. Her reputation as a dancer soared, and her growing inner maturity was gracefully reflected in the depth and evolution of her dance.

Shovana's growing passion for Hindi and Sanskrit literature, nurtured by her mother, began to shape her abhinaya compositions. She became increasingly captivated by the philosophical nuances of romance, favouring it over more conventional portrayals. This shift sparked her exploration of Kathak's literary heritage beyond the traditional verses.

'I realised that I was growing increasingly dissatisfied with the mundane portrayals of romance and found the philosophical nuances of romance far more compelling. I also wanted to delve deeper into the world of Sahitya, which is Kathak's legacy beyond the verses I had been taught. Gradually, the thumris of Bindadin Maharaj gave way to lesser known yet traditional thumris, as well as the verses of Kalidas, Bihari, Surdas, Padmakar, Ratnakar, Swami Haridas, Dinkar, Mahadevi Verma, Harivanshrai Bachchan, and Maithili Sharan Gupt, among others. Naina Aunty introduced me to the beauty of Sufism, the ghazals of Ghalib, Mir, and Zauq, and the connection between Sufism and Vaishnavism, which I brought to life in the piece *Bansuri*, which premiered in 1979. Rumi's *ney* spoke of the eternal sound of the flute that lingers long after we are gone, carrying us into a divine trance. We seek this purity of sound and feel its absence as pain. This parallelism with Vaishnav philosophy, where the flute of Lord Krishna aims to elevate the soul, cleansing it and transporting it into a sublime state, was deeply profound.'

Rumi's ney and Sarojini Naidu's poem, 'The Flute Player of Brindaban' reflect the soul's deep longing to connect with the divine. In Rumi's poem, the ney—a reed flute—cries out, mourning its separation from the reed bed, symbolising the soul's yearning to return to its source, the divine. Its music speaks of love, loss, and the desire for reunion, capturing the essence of Sufi spirituality, where love is the path to God.

In Naidu's poem, Krishna's *bansuri* (flute) becomes the call of higher consciousness, urging the devotee to cast aside worldly attachments and follow the divine melody.

Still, must I like a homeless bird
Wander, forsaking all
he earthly loves and worldly lures
That held my life in thrall,
And follow, follow, answering
Thy magical flute-call.

India Habitat Centre, AUM Ballet

Pic Credits:- Saurabh Siddharth

Shovana brings out the soul's deep yearning for union with the Divine through her dance, drawing from both Sufi and Bhakti traditions. While emerging from different cultures, these two spiritual paths share a belief in a higher reality and the idea of moving beyond worldly attachments to achieve ultimate liberation.

In blending these mystic traditions, she highlights universal themes of love, longing, and surrender in a way that transcends cultural boundaries, bringing out the beauty of humanity's shared spiritual quest. Her unique productions connect audiences with these timeless messages of unity and peace.

Her journey as a dancer is one of profound self-expression, where she moves to the rhythm of her soul, carving a path uniquely her own.

Dohari Zindagi
A Dual Life

'People have always been a mix of intrigued and incredulous when they discovered my *dohari zindagi*—balancing life as a senior bureaucrat and a celebrated Kathak dancer. Their reactions were priceless. "Wait, you manage files 'and' footwork? How does that even work?" one person exclaimed, clearly trying to picture me signing memos mid-spin. Another asked, "Do you ever show up to meetings in a lehenga and ghunghroos by mistake?" My personal favourite: "Do your staff clap in 'tala' patterns when you enter the office?"

'I'd laugh and assure them that my worlds don't overlap in quite those ways. And, of course, the ever-recurring question: "Doesn't your dance interfere with your work?" or "Surely, your work cuts into your dance rehearsals?" My answer is always the same—a firm 'no.' With discipline and good time management, I've kept both sides of my life flourishing. Though, I must admit, the idea of conducting a meeting with rhythmic tatkar in the background does sound tempting!' Shovana exclaims.

Balancing two seemingly unrelated careers was not without its challenges, but it was also deeply rewarding. Each role enriched the other in surprising ways. What truly stood out was Shovana's ability to find parallels: both dance and administration demanded impeccable timing, adaptability, and the ability to handle unexpected challenges with grace. Dance brought creativity, poise, and emotional depth to her administrative work. At the same time, her professional responsibilities honed her analytical thinking, decision-making skills, and resilience—qualities that fed back into her art. It wasn't about dividing time equally between her passions but finding a synergy that allowed both to coexist and thrive.

Throughout her thirty-four years of service, since joining the 1976 batch, her postings were demanding yet enriching. As Under Secretary and later Deputy Financial Advisor in the Ministry of Water Resources, she dealt with complex irrigation projects. She learned extensively about marine life, power generation, and human psychology. As Senior DAG, she managed the administration and conducted detailed audits for the Comptroller and Auditor General's (CAG's) report. Her time at the Rajya Sabha secretariat involved handling parliamentary duties, including the Question Hour and servicing committees, which

Sunit Tandon with Shovana Narayan

provided her invaluable experience. Later, as Joint Controller General of Accounts (CGA) in the Ministry of Finance, she further deepened her understanding of government accounts.

Shovana fully embraced the challenges and opportunities for growth in every role she undertook, skilfully balancing her responsibilities while ensuring they never overshadowed her unwavering passion for dance.

She maintained a sense of humour and ease, as evidenced by her playful conversations with colleagues, highlighting her ability to balance her professional duties with her identity as a dancer. Humour was her secret weapon to diffuse scepticism about her dual life as a civil servant and a celebrated dancer. When colleagues expressed disbelief that she could seamlessly navigate two vastly different worlds, she would quip, 'I've been practising double roles since childhood—academics by day, Kathak by night! It's my *dohari zindagi,* and I've memorised the steps for both stages.' She once joked during an intense meeting, 'If I can keep a sixteen-beat cycle in my head while spinning, managing government files feels like choreography of a different kind.'

Sunit Tandon acknowledges that he never saw any conflict in Shovana's dual career, as he himself navigated a similar balance between artistic pursuits and professional responsibilities. Their offices were in the same building in Khan Market—and they often met for tea or coffee, sharing a mutual understanding of balancing both creative and professional lives.

Sunit admires Shovana's unwavering positivity, which she radiates effortlessly. Their friendship, spanning over three decades, has been shaped by shared travel, rehearsals, laughter, and countless memories. Even now, they continue to meet at social gatherings, preserving their connection, grounded in mutual respect and understanding.

'When Shovana first stepped into an administrative role, she faced two significant biases. As an accomplished dancer, many presumed her artistic pursuits would hinder her dedication to administrative responsibilities. Consequently, she was initially entrusted with less complex tasks. However, she swiftly demonstrated her competence and reliability, earning the trust and confidence of her superiors. Additionally, doubts arose regarding her ability to manage male subordinates as a female administrator. Through unwavering determination and professionalism, Shovana silenced these doubts, gaining recognition and respect in her bureaucratic and artistic career,' shares Dr Anjan Banerjee, who was three years senior to Shovana. Although their paths rarely crossed professionally, they briefly worked in the same office at the CAG, albeit in different roles.

'Shovana joined the administrative services in the 1976 batch as a young officer, and our friendship dates to that time. Whenever I'm in Delhi or she's in Lucknow, we always make it a point to meet and share a meal. We have many fond memories together. I recall an impromptu event where I sang, and she danced. Over the years, we've seen each other grow personally and professionally. She has built valuable connections and gained rich experiences, always handling complex situations with grace. Coming from an aristocratic family—she learned early on how to assert her authority with refinement and subtlety. While jealousy and bitterness are common in any field, Shovana rose above it all, thanks to the strong values instilled in her by her upbringing,' Dr Banerjee adds.

Shovana firmly believes that the idea of being unable to handle two careers is a self-imposed myth. 'Life,' she often said, 'constantly demands multitasking, and as we navigate through it, we each learn to embody our own *virat roop*—our vast, multifaceted selves.' She frequently draws inspiration from Ma Durga, the goddess who epitomises this duality, embodying both the gentle *shail-putri* and the fierce, indomitable Mahakali.

She sees Kathak as a powerful metaphor for womanhood—a perfect union of grace and resilience. Outwardly, Kathak embodies softness and elegance, its movements fluid and delicate. Yet beneath that gentle exterior lies an unshakable core of strength, as unyielding as steel. It takes a lot of strength to be soft, to maintain grace while holding onto a core of unwavering strength. To her, being a dancer is not just about mastering the art form but also about understanding these profound metaphors. Kathak is an expression of life's duality—of being soft like a whisper and strong like a storm.

'As I reflect on Shovana's remarkable journey, I marvel at how she managed far more than just her dual roles as a senior officer and a celebrated artist,' shares Ashok Sajjanhar. 'Her work hours were anything but typical—often stretching from nine to nine, with weekends as busy as weekdays. Yet, despite this relentless schedule, she brought elegance and poise to everything she did. What amazed me most was how, amidst all this, she could host grand dinners and lavish parties, taking care of every detail from soup to nuts with effortless finesse. She balanced it all—her career, her art, and her social commitments—with a grace that was truly extraordinary.'

Ashok Sajjanhar is a distinguished member of the Indian Diplomatic Service, which he joined in 1978. Earlier, he was a banker. An alumnus of St Stephen's college, Delhi, he has served as India's ambassador to Kazakhstan, Sweden, and Latvia. In addition, he has held senior roles in Indian embassies across Belgium, Geneva, Washington D C, Moscow, Tehran, and Dhaka, as well as at the Ministry of External Affairs headquarters.

After retiring from the diplomatic service, Ashok took on the role of heading the National Foundation for Communal Harmony. During this time, he and Shovana collaborated on impactful initiatives, a partnership that continues to thrive.

'My first interaction with Shovana dates to the late 1970s when we both applied for membership at the Delhi Gymkhana club. At the time, I was a junior officer in the diplomatic service, while she was already a well-established figure and a senior officer in the Audit and Accounts Service. Despite her accomplishments, she was incredibly humble and warm, and from that point on, our friendship grew. Our connection has gone far beyond her roles as an artist or an officer. It is her essence as a human being that has left an indelible impression on me. She has a persona that feels larger than life. When she walks into a room, she doesn't need to raise her voice to command attention—the brightness in her expression and the warmth of her smile light up the entire space. Her genuine care for people is evident in her interactions. I've seen her at gatherings where, even from across the room, she would wave with a warmth that made you feel instantly welcomed.'

Ashok frequently invited Shovana and her troupe to perform at various locations where he was posted. Deeply devoted to India—its ethos, culture, philosophy, and ideology—Shovana tirelessly championed its heritage both at home and on global platforms. On occasions such as the Austrian National Day hosted by Herbert as the ambassador, she graced the events in traditional Austrian dirndl as the hostess. The rest of the time, in any national day not hosted by Herbert, she wore a sari, thus carrying the essence of India in her heart and showcasing it with pride. Adapting to a new role is often more straightforward for male diplomats, as their offices are typically prepared with support staff. However, for the lady of the house, the responsibility is different—she must not only manage but also infuse her unique character to transform the house into a home. Shovana accomplished that to the fullest extent of her ability.

Shovana and Herbert have always been exceptionally supportive of one another, a dynamic that has not only sustained their relationship but allowed it to blossom. They have had a dream run, as many would say.

'I had the privilege of visiting her home several times during her years in service. She was remarkably gracious and generous as a host, always opening her home and heart to everyone. Our families have shared an incredible bond over the years and her husband, Herbert, has been a dear friend. We spent considerable time together when Herbert was the Austrian ambassador in Bangkok, and I was posted there. Those moments were enriched by Shovana's presence, with numerous programmes and performances where she brought her artistry to life.

'She carried herself with grace, warmth, and a deep commitment to cultural excellence. As ambassadors, organising events and programmes was demanding, requiring significant effort. Moreover, she managed the Asavari school, rehearsed, choreographed, travelled, and performed. *Is sabke bavzood, Shovana ke mathe par kabhi shikan nahin thi* (Despite everything, there wasn't a single wrinkle of worry on her forehead). Her energy levels were remarkable, and even now, she easily outshines people half her age,' Ashok shares.

Shovana has a rare gift for building meaningful relationships across diverse walks of life. She is deliberate in choosing her friends, valuing depth over numbers. But once someone becomes part of her circle, she gives her whole heart, going above and beyond to bring joy to their lives. Shovana's friendships are warm, generous, and genuine, whether through thoughtful gestures, uplifting words, or an unwavering presence in times of need.

'My association with Shovana dates back more than four decades, when I first met her as a guru while seeking to enrol my eight-year-old daughter, Divya, in her Kathak dance classes. She was already a highly respected figure in the field. That first meeting began a long and pleasant relationship, which has only grown stronger over the years,' says Dr Jyotsna Suri, chairperson and managing director, The Lalit Suri Hospitality Group, India's leading privately owned domestic hotel brand focusing on luxury.

Jyotsna draws inspiration from Shovana in many aspects of her life and work. Reflecting on her multifaceted journey, she remarks, 'Beyond her artistic achievements, she also excelled as a bureaucrat, carving out a distinct space for herself. She is a devoted wife who has upheld her marriage in truly extraordinary ways. While her husband served as an ambassador, she forged her path as an accomplished dancer and a distinguished bureaucrat. Seamlessly transitioning from a brilliant performer to an equally brilliant teacher, she carried forward the legacy of creativity she inherited from her strong-willed mother. Women often find themselves balancing two worlds—household responsibilities and a professional life—but Shovana managed to navigate three. It's hard to say whether bureaucracy or dance took precedence, as she pursued both with equal dedication and nurtured lifelong friendships. Excelling in every sphere, she emerged with flying colours.'

After completing school, Jyotsna's daughter, Divya, went abroad for college, which led to a break in her connection with dance. However, Jyotsna's bond with Shovana remained intact, and she made it a point to attend her performances whenever possible.

'I have watched her perform countless times, yet she brings

a fresh burst of truly infectious energy each time. She has an incredible ability to command the entire space with her dynamic presence. Beyond being an extraordinary performer, she is a dedicated mentor who has built a legacy of her own—Shovana Narayan is not just a name; she is a brand in her own right.'

'Shovana's connections run deep, thanks to her role as a senior Indian government administrator. She balances both worlds beautifully, deeply rooted in the cultural realm, while managing her professional responsibilities with remarkable skill. I witnessed firsthand how she interacted with her staff during my visits to her office in Noida. She genuinely cares about the esteem of those around her, fostering a sense of camaraderie and respect. Although I was a complete outsider in her office, I felt welcomed and accepted as a part of her workspace dynamic. Shovana's amiable nature makes everyone feel included, bridging the gap between her cultural commitments and administrative duties effortlessly,' shares Vinod Pandey, a highly experienced film and television professional with a strong background in both corporate and creative media.

He had moved from Bombay to London as an immigrant for work. It was in London that he first met Shovana, who was there on a concert tour with her troupe.

Vinod wasn't particularly into performing arts, but this was the first time he had watched a full performance at the Royal Festival Hall.

'I first met Shovana in 1976, and she immediately made an impression on me. Young, beautiful, and full of energy, she had a dynamic presence that was impossible to ignore. Her dance performance that evening was unforgettable—graceful and intense, deeply rooted in Indian culture. After the show, I felt an instant connection and suggested we share a meal. Our conversation flowed effortlessly, and we quickly struck a chord.

Drawn by her talent and the depth of emotion she brought to classical dance; I began attending more of her performances. Our friendship grew with each meeting. At the time, I was navigating a challenging phase in my personal and professional life, and Shovana's empathy and kindness as a friend were a source of great comfort. With my sister living in Delhi, I had more opportunities to meet her, often at cultural events or at her performances. She lived in a government apartment then, and her home always felt warm and inviting. Her mother was just as hospitable and gracious. I also had the privilege of observing Shovana as a teacher—always guiding her students with gentle guidance and a nurturing spirit.'

When asked what her friends think of Shovana, the most common response is that they perceive her as warm and compassionate. She likely has a way of making people feel welcome and supported, creating a positive and uplifting atmosphere wherever she goes.

The only time Shovana ever had to step away from her unwavering commitments to the world of art was when duty called her to Vienna—not for a performance, but for something far more personal. On the afternoon of 25 April 2023, around 4 pm, she was deeply engrossed in rehearsals with her students when her phone rang. It was Ishan. His voice carried the weight of devastating news—Herbert had slipped into a coma. What was meant to be a temporary pause stretched into an emotionally turbulent nine to ten months, where she devoted herself entirely to his care. For someone who had always prioritised her art and her audience, this was the rare moment when love and duty took precedence over everything else.

It was also a silent yet profound response to those who often murmured that Shovana had sacrificed her family life for her art.

'Whenever my wife and I talk about Shovana, we can't help but smile—it's the warm and radiant aura she exudes that we visualise. Delhi, being a vibrant city, has countless events, making it hard for people to attend them all. Yet, when it comes to her programmes, the auditoriums are always packed. She invites with such genuine warmth that it's impossible to decline. The Lalit Arpan programme, annually held in Delhi, is her initiative. I recall one particular year she was in Vienna with her husband, and the annual Lalit Arpan programme still took place. Remarkably, the hall was full—a heartfelt tribute to her. Even in her absence, people rallied around to support her initiative. Shovana has given so much to the world, bringing joy to countless people through the sheer beauty and elegance of her performances,' Ashok shares.

'Shovana started the Lalit Arpan festival, which she has curated for over twenty years and is continuing to do so. I have supported her in this endeavour, where she brings together Kathak dancers and artists from various genres, making each edition unique. The festival was initiated in honour of my husband, Lalit Suri. His name became an integral part of it, and even after his passing, it has continued as a tribute to him. Lalit had a great love for the performing arts and music. Over the years, we have celebrated various artistic expressions—dance, visual arts, instrumental music, and more. She presents the festival remarkably, drawing an engaged and appreciative audience,' Jyotsna shares.

Shovana faced one of the most testing periods of her life when Herbert fell ill. For Jyotsna, this was a defining moment of resilience—being in India while he was in Vienna, separated by distance yet bound by love and worry. Jyotsna made it a point to check in with her regularly, offering comfort over the phone and reminding her that she was handling everything with remarkable strength.

'But it was undeniably a difficult time for her,' Jyotsna reflects. 'Her endurance was put to the ultimate test. When she finally flew to Vienna, she had little support, yet with the unwavering dedication of her son and daughter-in-law, she cared for Herbert with immense devotion. And despite it all, she returned not broken but renewed—taking to the stage again with an even greater intensity.'

Jyotsna remains in awe of Shovana's unwavering spirit and her ability to rise from personal hardships and transform pain into purpose. She steps onto the stage, not as someone weighed down by sorrow, but as a reminder that life is too fleeting for regret.

'As I have supported her, she has always been there for me. When I lost Lalit, she was a pillar of emotional strength, always present whenever I needed her. A simple connection through my daughter's Kathak classes became a lifelong bond. Friendships don't always form just because you know someone—she was once just an acquaintance. But we connected, and our journey has been extraordinary ever since.'

Behind the scenes, Shovana's life is a whirlwind of meticulous planning and relentless dedication. On performance days, she packs her dance costumes, makeup, and instruments in her car before heading to the office. She ensures she can leave directly for the venue, airport, or railway station afterward. Her schedule is nothing short of remarkable; for out-of-town shows, she often arrives just hours before the performance, dazzles the audience with her art, and heads back to Delhi immediately afterward—all to ensure she is back in time for her official duties. Balancing these dual careers requires constant movement, unwavering discipline, and extraordinary commitment.

It is this tireless dedication that allows her to touch lives, inspire audiences, and keep both her artistic and professional worlds thriving in perfect harmony.

'The first word that comes to mind when I think of her as an artist is industriousness. Shovana inspires anyone pursuing the arts, not just in cultural fields like classical dance but in any domain. She takes all significant challenges on her chin. I've subconsciously adopted traits from her, such as industriousness and a go-getter attitude, which have helped me navigate the tougher periods in my life. I developed a never-say-die mentality, managing to get my films released despite the obstacles I faced as someone without formal qualifications in filmmaking. The impressions she left on me weren't explicitly taught; instead, they seeped into me through osmosis. Her stoicism profoundly influences me—I've never seen her shed a tear, and she always appears in control. My sensitivity allows me to perceive what lies beneath her calmness, composure, and quiet strength. You'd marvel at how she brushes off tough situations, treating them as if they were merely fleeting roles she was performing—just like she does on stage,' Vinod adds.

Vinod returned to Bombay to record songs for his movie *Ek Baar Phir*. He was a young adventurist trying to build something in life. He found a kindred spirit in Shovana, who was empathetic to his experiences. The two stayed in touch consistently. The movie became Vinod's ticket back to India, where it was warmly received. His film premiered in both Bombay and Delhi, with the Delhi screening held in a government hall. During the event, he, Shovana, and her sister, Ranjana, formed a small host community, welcoming guests and celebrating the occasion together.

Dr Banerjee often ponders whether anyone can remain unruffled, never allowing anger to take over, no matter what happens. Shifting the equation from, *Albert Pinto ko gussa kyon aata hai*? (Why does Albert Pinto get angry?), perhaps the real question he would like to ask is, *Shovana Narayan ko gussa kyon nahin aata hai?* (Why doesn't Shovana get angry?)

'I've known her since 1976, and I've never heard her speak ill of anyone. She inherited excellent people skills, always staying calm, even when most would lose their temper. Instead of engaging in conflicts, she would gracefully withdraw. If pressed for an opinion, she would tactfully avoid criticising others. Her composure reflects a lack of insecurity, which many others can't claim. However, she is firm in her principles, displaying quiet strength without verbal clashes. People often explode in anger over trivial matters, and I've seen that happen with many. *Paan par choona thoda idhar se udhur ho gaya, toh vo admi gusse se fat gaya.* Shovana, however, is different—clear, direct, and without ambiguity. She says what she means and means what she says. I once heard of an incident where a renowned performing artist publicly snubbed a high-ranking official for trying to leave during their performance. It was improper of the official, an insult not only to the artist but also to the art they were representing, and the artist's reaction was equally inappropriate. Even in such a situation, I can claim that Shovana would have stayed calm. That's the essence of Shovana—composure in all circumstances.'

In a letter to her son Ishan, Shovana recalls a dangerous situation during a performance abroad when the stage was littered with glass shards. Mid-performance, she calmly removed a large shard embedded in her foot, showed it to the audience, and handed it to a prominent official present. The incident passed with a meek apology and little acknowledgment, yet her grace and professionalism shone through as she refused to let it disrupt her performance.

Dr Banerjee recalls another incident where anyone in

Shovana's position might have lost their cool, but she remained calm. 'Shovana was performing with her troupe while I anchored the show. Due to back-to-back events, we were under time pressure. For artists, time often seems to disappear during a performance, but I had to keep things moving as the anchor. As Shovana came dancing toward the wing, I gestured for her to wrap up, and she acknowledged it. However, as time passed, I began thanking her and the troupe. Shovana gently stopped me with a smile, asking if she could introduce her dancers. She then held my hand and took the time to introduce each of her artists personally, ensuring they received the recognition they deserved before I moved on to the next segment.'

This admiration for Shovana's unparalleled ability to seamlessly balance dual careers with such grace and composure is not limited to her friends and colleagues alone. Her brilliance transcends professional boundaries, earning her profound respect in the broader dance fraternity. Esteemed classical dancers from diverse forms also hold her in the highest regard, acknowledging her as a true luminary whose name commands reverence across the artistic world.

'Shovana ji is genuinely one of a kind—a remarkable individual who embodies warmth, friendliness, and an ever-helpful, cheerful disposition. Beyond her incredible persona, she is an awe-inspiring artist whose talent leaves a lasting impression. A true all-rounder, she excels in every endeavour, making it challenging to encapsulate her multifaceted brilliance in words.

'As a professional, Shovana ji was an efficient officer whose contributions left a positive and enduring imprint. Admired and loved by many, she is spoken of in the most endearing terms. Her artistic journey began as a young disciple of the legendary Padma Vibhushan Pandit Birju Maharaj ji, from whom she imbibed a deep understanding of Kathak. Equally influential were the values she inherited from her family, especially her mother, Lalita—a brilliant intellectual who surrounded herself with artists, played an active role in politics, and dedicated herself to social work. This culturally and intellectually rich family environment, combined with the mentorship of a Kathak maestro, has shaped Shovana ji into a multi-dimensional personality.

'Her legacy as a teacher is unparalleled. Unlike top-tier artists who refrain from teaching and thus fail to pass on their knowledge, Shovana ji has tirelessly trained numerous students, many of whom have become exceptional artists. Her dedication to sharing her art ensures that her legacy continues to thrive. She is never idle; every day, she seems to have more than twenty-four hours in her world. Her boundless energy is unmatched, and I often call her the *Ashta Bhujā Durga* for her incredible efficiency and grace in managing her responsibilities.

'Shovana ji's life is marked by her unique ability to lead a *dohari zindagi*—effortlessly balancing her roles as the wife of an ambassador, a homemaker, a writer, and a consummate artist. She remains the same vibrant, petite, and charming individual, radiating positivity and inspiration. Words fall short when trying to describe her. She is, quite simply, extraordinary. To conclude, where I began—Shovana ji is genuinely one of a kind,' Sonal Mansingh shares.

Sonal Mansingh is a distinguished Indian classical dancer and guru renowned for her mastery of Bharatnatyam and Odissi. Nominated to the Rajya Sabha by the President of India (2018-24), she has been recognised with numerous accolades, including the prestigious Padma Vibhushan in 2003. Known for her magnetic stage presence, eloquence, intellect, and profound sensitivity, she is celebrated globally as a veteran artist. Revered among the elite of the artistic world, Sonal Mansingh continues to inspire admiration and respect from her family, friends, and the worldwide artistic community.

Ravi Shankar Prasad, a renowned politician, shares a close friendship with Shovana Narayan, which began at a function in Delhi and grew stronger through his wife, Maya Shankar's involvement in cultural activities.

He admires Shovana for her exceptional ability to balance two demanding careers: as a distinguished civil servant and a celebrated Kathak dancer. 'It's not easy to combine both, but she excelled in each, leaving a significant mark. Shovana has nurtured many students into accomplished dancers while maintaining her professional integrity. She never allowed her passion for dance to hinder her career as a civil servant and vice versa. Achieving this balance required immense dedication and hard work.'

Their bond is further strengthened by their shared roots in Bihar and their connection through the Bhojpuri language. He quips, '*Bahut achcha kalakar bani aur bahut achcha officer bani. Theek baa*?' Ravi acknowledges the scepticism Shovana faced for pursuing dual careers but credits her diligence and determination for silencing critics.

Highlighting her remarkable achievements, Ravi remarks that coming from Bihar, a state better known for Madhubani paintings and folk singing than classical arts, and gaining global acclaim as a Kathak dancer is extraordinary. While middle-class Bihari families traditionally focus on education, stable careers, and family life, Shovana went beyond these expectations to shine professionally.

Ravi also emphasises India's unique strength in its soft power—its culture and spirituality. 'Despite centuries of subjugation, India's culture and soul remain unbroken. Indian classical music and dance are timeless, deeply impacting the soul. They act as tranquillisers, showcasing India's rich heritage to the world.' He sees Shovana as a shining example of this enduring cultural legacy.

Shovana's remarkable ability to juggle dual careers while maintaining her composure has consistently amazed people while presenting her with unexpected situations. Yet, she often laughs at these situations, using humour to navigate life's quirks. Fuelled by her passion and dedication to her art and profession, this balancing act frequently results in tight schedules and a fair share of light-hearted moments:

Bhed Chal

Due to her dual career, Shovana has often found herself in situations where after finishing her office work, she had to take the last available mode of transportation to reach performance venues and return the same way.

In 1993, Shovana was booked to perform at the Meera Festival in Chittor. The night before, however, she had a performance at Kamani Auditorium in Delhi. While most of her musicians left by the only direct train to Chittor at 2 pm, her pakhawaj player, Tulsi, and she, herself, set out after their performance. They took an overnight air-conditioned bus to Jaipur, planning to switch to a supposedly deluxe bus heading somewhere en route to Chittor. From there, they had no choice but to board a local bus.

'I found myself literally in a *bhed chal*—my travel companions were none other than sheep and goats! At the Chittor bus stand, as I carefully disembarked among my special four-legged friends, I noticed a policeman staring at me, bewildered. The next adventure was finding our way to the hotel, given that our organisers had no idea when we would arrive. Tulsi suggested we head to the police station to ask for directions and inform the organisers. On reaching the station, the constables could hardly believe their eyes. "She's the famous dancer everyone's been waiting for?" their expressions seemed to shout. "How could a renowned dancer be travelling with goats and sheep?" they must have thought. I was breaking all the rules of the classic *bhed chal*.'

As if that wasn't enough, Shovana's silver medals and other mementos, which she had entrusted to someone to carry for her, were stolen by that very person. She later had to write a note to the organisers apologising for the incident, and they sent her a miniature replica of the same as a replacement.

The Costume That Found Me

Another incident from 1979 brings a smile to Shovana's face as she recalls it. They were scheduled to perform in Dehradun, but performances didn't pay much back then, and the troupe had to travel by local bus. Exhausted, they had all dozed off, only to be jolted awake by the bus conductor shouting, 'Dehradun, Dehradun!'

'Life has always felt like a mystery novel where I am both the protagonist and the detective, piecing together the twists and turns as they unfold. One such moment came during a performance trip that started quite dramatically. I vividly remember opening my bag and realising—much to my horror—that all my belongings were missing. All I had were my ghunghroos, tucked neatly in my makeup bag. No toothbrush, no clothes, no dance costume, and certainly no jewellery. For a moment, I stood there, utterly at a loss, wondering how I had ended up in such a scene. But then, as I often do, I adjusted to the moment. I dashed to the market and bought whatever I could—a bit of makeup and a change of clothes to get by. Just as I mentally rehearsed how to spin this situation into some semblance of normalcy, help arrived in the form of Pushp Mala Jain, the secretary of Sangeetanjali, the cultural society that had invited us. Like a *deus ex machina* from a well-plotted story, she came to my rescue, sorting things out just in time.

'I couldn't help but marvel later at how life always seemed to drop me into these curious situations, only for solutions to appear, almost magically, when I needed them the most. It's all part of the intrigue, I suppose—a never-ending plotline where I'm just trying to keep up with the turns!' Shovana laughs.

Nirmala Joshi, the founder of Sangeet Natak Academy, had a niece named Pramila, also a dancer. By a stroke of luck, Pramila's costume was a perfect fit for Shovana.

Now in her nineties, Pushp Mala Jain finds joy in exploring the memory, cherishing each moment from the day with a touch of wistful reflection:

'During the 1960s and 1970s, music and dance were often seen as unconventional and ungraceful career choices, particularly in more traditional or orthodox families. At that time, we formed a cultural society named Sangeetanjali to promote classical dance, music, and theatre. I served as the secretary, and Vasudev Deshpandey, a singer from Dehradun, was one of the founding members. We regularly organised performances like *Ramlila, Krishna Leela*, and various dramas, but we lacked the resources to host artists in hotels or provide substantial fees. All we could offer them was our love, hospitality, and a small token of appreciation. Selected dance events were held at the Ram Dev Mission Hall, while most musical events were held in my home due to lack of funds. Coming from a conservative family where my father strongly opposed music and dance, I was often made to withdraw from such pursuits whenever I showed interest. My marriage brought me into another orthodox family that also looked down upon these art forms. However, my husband, a freedom fighter, and a forward-thinking patron of the arts, supported me in pursuing my passion. I attended every cultural event, often pulling all-nighters to enjoy them. Our home became a frequent venue, with its large dining hall accommodating sixty to seventy people. We would clear out the dining table, spread carpets on the floor, and transform the space for the programmes. It was around this time that I first encountered Shovana Narayan, who we had invited as a young artist to perform. Our house couldn't accommodate her performance, so we booked the hall. Unfortunately, her suitcase was stolen shortly after she arrived, but Shovana seemed to have a remarkable knack for handling setbacks with grace and a smile. Instead of being upset, she seemed genuinely intrigued by this unexpected turn of events. She graciously agreed to wear Pramila's costume for her performance. During her stay with us, I found her exceptionally humble and down-to-earth, always smiling, and radiating grace.'

***

A Slip-up in the Red-Light District

On one occasion, Shovana Narayan was invited to deliver a lecture-demonstration at the Mussoorie Academy. Given that it was winter, the event was scheduled for 3 pm. Typically, she would have preferred to travel to Mussoorie the evening before. However, due to a performance in Delhi, she had no choice but to set off by road early the following day, aiming to reach Mussoorie by noon. The plan was to depart by 5 am, with the musicians gathering at her residence by 4.15 am to account for any possible delays. Everything went according to schedule—except for one musician who did not show up. Since the instrument this musician played was crucial, a frantic search began at that ungodly hour to find a replacement. Eventually, one of the musicians suggested, 'Didi, I know where X lives. Let's drive to his place and wake him up. He won't refuse to help us.'

They all squeezed into the car and drove to X's residence through the cold, dark morning. Upon arrival, Shovana stayed in the car with one musician and the driver while another went down a narrow lane. The lane was barely visible under the dim streetlight, and a policeman could be seen huddled under a blanket on a makeshift seat in the shadows. The stillness was palpable—nothing moved, not even a stray dog. A thin layer of fog drifted around them, occasionally wrapping them in its cold embrace. She wasn't sure how long they had been waiting. She had dozed off. She was startled awake by Lakhan speaking to her through the window, asking for her identity card. The senior civil servant found herself in a rather unusual situation.

Soon, she was approached by a thickly muffled police officer. The officer, suspicious about their presence at such an hour, demanded to see her identity card. Lakhan, her Pakhawaj artiste, speaking to her through her window, asking for her identity card. tried to assure the officer of her official status, saying, '*Bhaisaheb,* she is a senior civil servant.' But the officer wasn't convinced. 'If she is a civil servant, then why is she here?' he questioned, his tone becoming increasingly suspicious.

Lakhan, determined to clear up the confusion, explained that she was also a reputed dancer waiting for a replacement musician. The driver chimed in, pointing out that the missing musician had gone into a nearby alley, but the officer only grew more irritated. 'A dancer? And a civil servant?' he bellowed, his authority evident as he wagged his stick. 'You expect me to believe such a story? You all must think I'm a fool!'

The officer's disbelief only escalated. He decided to take charge, demanding that she leave the car immediately. 'Madam, get out! I'm taking you all to the station,' he roared, convinced they were up to no good.

For a moment, the situation seemed destined for a dramatic turn, but just then, the missing musicians arrived, providing the much-needed context that finally calmed the officer down.

It was only later that Shovana learned where they had been waiting—the infamous G B Road, Delhi's red-light district. It made sense now—the officer's scepticism about their presence there. After all, who would expect a senior civil servant in such a notorious locality?

Rolling Tanks, Steady Feet

'On the day Slovenia declared its independence, I was scheduled to perform at one of the largest auditoriums in Ljubljana. However, just as I prepared for the performance, the Slovenian authorities decided to bring their Independence Day celebrations forward by a day. It was as if they were racing against time or trying to add a sense of urgency to the occasion.

'My musicians were understandably apprehensive. "*Shovana ji, mere chote chote bachche hain, kyun jana hai? Kya zarurat hai? Kuch ho gaya toh?*" (I have young kids. Why go? What's the need? What if something happens?) Even Herbert, my husband, suggested it might be safer if we stayed back. The unease was palpable—no one could reasonably predict what would happen. It was a time of uncertainty, and in moments like that, one starts to question whether dance is worth risking it all.

But, as always, I knew that art has its way of transcending everything. I couldn't let fear dictate my decision. So, I pushed ahead, determined to perform. The next day, I was supposed to perform in Grado, Italy. We finished our performance and packed up. We managed to leave just minutes before the borders were sealed.

I couldn't help but feel a sense of surreal accomplishment. Here I was, performing on a day of national significance, with rolling tanks nearby, the atmosphere thick with tension. Yet, despite everything, the auditorium was almost packed.

Despite the turmoil, the fact that people still came showed me just how powerful art can be. It was as though the people, in their way, wanted to affirm that no matter what, the show must go on. And so, it did—through uncertainty, fear, and everything. The beauty of that performance will always stay with me, reminding me of how art can stand tall even when the world seems to be on the edge.'

All things fall and are built again
And those that build them again are gay.

***Lapis Lazuli* by William Butler Yeats**

A Seeker

At the window, she sits, serene,
Bathed in sunlight's soft golden sheen.
Through the stillness, the dust comes alive,
A thousand tiny worlds begin to thrive.

Spiralling, twirling, they rise and play,
In a quiet ballet of light's tender sway.
She watches, entranced, as they shift and glide,
Each particle a story, the universe inside.

'Is this not existence?' she softly sighs,
'Our fleeting dance beneath infinite skies.
Each of us, like these motes of light,
Woven together, fragile yet bright.'

The dust whispers secrets, ancient, profound,
Of rhythms eternal, where all life is bound.
And there at the window, her heart takes its stance—
We are but fragments in the dance.

I am a seeker on an eternal journey toward enlightenment, unravelling the myriad layers of existence. With each day and breath, I delve deeper into life's mysteries, embracing the lessons that flow my way. Dance, for me, is not merely an art form; it is a profound communion with the universe, a sacred dialogue that nurtures my spirit and connects me to a higher purpose. In this dance of life, none of us is whole unto ourselves; we are fragments of a larger cosmic tapestry intricately woven into the fabric of existence. I strive to align myself with the divine plan the universe has envisioned for me.

To remain still is to deny the dynamic essence of life itself, for the cosmos is in constant motion, and I, too, must dance to its rhythm. Every being and every element around me, consciously or unconsciously, shapes my journey, and I, in turn, contribute to the grand symphony of creation.

The dance of the universe whispers its purpose into the depths of the soul.

Much like the sages of ancient times, the artist becomes a seeker, striving to touch the essence of life.

Kabir's couplets echo this yearning, reminding us of the fleeting nature of the world and the divine light within. Guru Nanak's hymns speak of oneness, of merging with the eternal through devotion and simplicity. Ashoka's transformation from conqueror to monk captures the profound realisation of life's impermanence and the pursuit of *dharma*.

This quest transcends time and geography, resonating in the songs of Meera Bai, who surrendered to divine love, and Sarojini Naidu's lyrical pleas for harmony. It continues through Swami Vivekananda's call to awaken the soul, Amrita Pritam's poignant poetry on love and loss, and Paramhansa Yogananda's spiritual revelations on the cosmic energy binding us all. Across cultures, we find Rumi dancing in ecstasy, Walt Whitman celebrating the shared soul of humanity, and Khalil Gibran seeking the divine in the ordinary.

The stream of consciousness flows further through the works of Percy Bysshe Shelley, William Wordsworth, and John Keats, who pondered the beauty and transience of nature, and Gerard Manley Hopkins, who saw God's grandeur in every leaf and cloud. Emily Dickinson's meditations on death and immortality, Virginia Woolf's reflections on time and identity, and Thomas Hardy's melancholic acceptance of life's impermanence mirror the thoughts of Rahim, who poetically captured the fragility of human connections.

These thinkers, poets, and philosophers—whether from the mystic lanes of Varanasi, the courts of Akbar, or the romantic landscapes of nineteenth century England—all share an understanding: life is transient, but in seeking its truth, one touches the eternal.

This awareness becomes both a burden and a gift for the artist, compelling them to create not only for this world but for the vast, timeless universe to which they are intrinsically connected.

Who is Ram but the embodiment of self-aware goodness, the very consciousness that guides us toward righteousness amidst the countless opposing forces of this world? Ram represents the steadfastness of dharma, the path of virtue that remains unwavering even in the face of adversity.

In contrast, Krishna, the cosmic diplomat, teaches us the art of living a meaningful life filled with values, urging us to navigate the complexities of existence with wisdom and grace. He is the divine strategist, revealing the profound balance between duty and devotion, action and detachment.

And then there is Buddha, who illuminates the path of

non-attachment, showing us how to dwell in the world without becoming entangled in its snares. His message is not to renounce life but to embrace it with equanimity, to be present yet detached, engaged yet free from the clutches of desire.

Kalki, however, is not a figure waiting to manifest in the distant future; Kalki resides within each of us. It is the *manthan*, the churning of our inner cosmos, where the forces of creation and destruction battle within. Kalki is the potential of our being—to build or to break, to uplift or to destroy.

'We are the fragments of the divine whole, and within us lies the power to be both the healer and the warrior, the creator and the annihilator.

'Turn your eyes to the mountains and behold the lives of saints who call them home. Untethered by the crutches of modern gadgets, they are bound not by technology but by the essence of life—a force connecting all beings. In their simplicity, they exist as silent observers, *sakshi,* witnessing the divine rhythm of existence, untouched by the distractions that consume us as participants, the *bhoktas.* This profound stillness reminds us of what we, caught in worldly pleasures, often fail to see,' Shovana reflects.

Leave we the common crofts, the vulgar thorpes,
Each in its tether.

To stand on a higher plane and look down upon the world is to experience a different *shanti*—an expansive and intimate peace, an *anubhuti* that transcends the ordinary. Here, you are detached yet intimately aware of the subtle, sacred flow of life, just as Robert Browning eloquently describes:

Self-gathered for an outbreak, as it ought,
Chafes in the censer.

Here, the mountains become more than a place—they symbolise a state of being where the mind, in its quietude, awaits the release of thoughts, poised between participation and pure observation.

In my dance, I have often said I am a seeker, driven by an insatiable thirst for *tripti*—that inner satisfaction which eludes mere words. This quest for the sublime led me to translate profound journeys such as *Mera Safar*, *Sujata*, and *Yashodhara* into the language of dance. Through these performances, I sought not just to express but to embody the timeless truths and to find, if only for a fleeting moment, that elusive inner fulfilment.

They told me I was digressing. In the world of Kathak, digression is frowned upon, yet such fluidity is often celebrated outside of it. I never sought the new merely for its novelty. Dance is my vessel—a journey of constant transformation. My vision flows and reshapes with each moment. Yesterday's expression carried its essence; today unfolds with another, and tomorrow will reveal yet another hue. Life, like dance, is a series of unrepeatable moments—each unique, each fleeting, and each bearing the soul of a new beginning.'

Yashodhara

Shovana says, 'In 1979, I performed as Yashodhara for the first time at Kamani Auditorium. When I announced my performance, someone in the audience corrected me, saying it should be Yashoda instead of Yashodhara. I smiled and assured them that I would be portraying Yashodhara.

'This interaction highlighted how little we know about

women's vital roles in mythology. By choosing to perform as Yashodhara, I wanted to highlight her significance and help the audience understand her story and strength. My connection with Yashodhara was profound, and I hoped to share that feeling with others.'

Sakhi, ve mujhse kehkar jaate,
Kah, to kya mujhko ve apni path-baadha hi paate?
Mujhko bahut unhone maana,
Phir bhi kya poora pehchaana?
Maine mukhya usi ko jaana,
Jo ve mann mein laate.
Sakhi, ve mujhse kehkar jaate.
Swayam susajjit karke kshan mein,
Priyatam ko, praaanon ke pan mein,
Hamein bhej deti hain ran mein -
Kshatra-dharm ke naate.
Sakhi, ve mujhse kehkar jaate.
Hua na yeh bhi bhaagya abhaagaa,
Kispar viphal garv ab jaaga?
Jisne apnaaya tha, tyaaga;
Rahe smaran hi aate!
Sakhi, ve mujhse kehkar jaate.
Nayan unhe nishthur kahte,
Par inse jo aansu behte,
Sadaya hriday ve kaise sahte?
Gaye taras hi khaate!
Sakhi, ve mujhse kehkar jaate.
Jaayein, siddhi paaven ve sukh se,
Dukhi na ho is jan ke dukh se,
Upalambh doon main kis mukh se?

Aaj adhik ve bhaate!
Sakhi, ve mujhse kehkar jaate.
Gaye, laut bhi ve aayenge,
Kuch apurv-anupam laayenge,
Rote praan unhe paayenge,
Par kya gaate-gaate?
Sakhi, ve mujhse kehkar jaate.

Shovana's dance presentation of Yashodhara, inspired by Maithili Sharan Gupt's work, explores the often-overlooked story of Yashodhara, the wife of Prince Siddhartha, who later became the Buddha. Through this performance, Shovana brings Yashodhara's voice to the forefront, portraying her not just as an abandoned wife but as a profoundly insightful seeker on her spiritual path.

The presentation reflects a deep empathy and recognition of the feminine perspective, often marginalised in historical and spiritual narratives. She highlights the inner strength, grace, and silent endurance accompanying spiritual growth by bringing Yashodhara's story to the forefront. Her dance becomes a medium to explore the complexities of sacrifice, love, and self-realisation, portraying Yashodhara's journey parallel to Siddhartha's quest for enlightenment.

Shovana's choreography likely emphasises the subtleties of emotional turmoil, the conflict between duty and personal longing, and the ultimate acceptance that comes with understanding the impermanence of worldly attachments. It explores the human condition, where every movement and gesture embody the balance between longing and liberation, the seen and the unseen. Through her portrayal, she invites the audience to reflect on the universality of Yashodhara's experience—one of resilience, wisdom, and transcendence.

Thus, this unique interpretation of Yashodhara becomes more than a dance; it is a philosophical inquiry into the untold stories that shape our understanding of spiritual quests, highlighting the silent journeys that often go unnoticed yet are equally transformative.

Yashodhara's sacrifice when Siddhartha returns to the town as a wandering ascetic is profound, layered with both emotional depth and spiritual complexity. When Siddhartha, now the Buddha, returns to Kapilavastu begging for alms, Yashodhara faces the ultimate test of her strength and detachment. Despite being left in silence years before, carrying the weight of abandonment and raising their son Rahul alone, she chooses not to respond with anger or resentment. Instead, she offers the only treasure left to her—her son—as alms to the Buddha.

This act of offering Rahul as alms is more than a gesture of surrender; it is a continuation of her selfless love and a sign of her spiritual maturity. In this moment, Yashodhara transcends personal grief and attachment, making the highest sacrifice of motherhood by relinquishing her son to the path of renunciation. It is a powerful statement of her acceptance of Siddhartha's spiritual journey and her willingness to let go of her most profound bond, recognising that true love is not possession but liberation.

Yashodhara's offering of Rahul symbolises her ultimate renunciation—she gives away not only her son but also her lingering attachment to worldly ties. It reveals her understanding that Rahul, like all beings, must find his path to enlightenment. In this poignant act, Yashodhara mirrors the Buddha's journey, showing that spiritual awakening is not confined to one gender or individual but is a universal possibility. Her sacrifice becomes a profound commentary on the nature of love, loss, and the transcendence of personal desires in the pursuit of higher truths.

Through this act, Yashodhara's character emerges not just as a passive sufferer but as a spiritual warrior in her own right, capable of great courage, compassion, and deep, unspoken wisdom. Through the emotive power of Kathak, Shovana brings to life Yashodhara's silent strength.

Narayan's subtle expressions, delicate gestures, and poignant stillness immerse the audience in Yashodhara's world, transforming them from spectators into participants on a journey of empathy, introspection, and spiritual growth.

***

Mera Safar

Phir ek din aisa aayega
Aankhon ke diye bujh jaayenge
Haathon ke kanwal kumhlaayenge
Aur barg-e-zubaan se nutk o sada
Ki har titli udd jaayegi
Ek kaale samundar ki teh mein
Kaliyon ki tarah se khilti hui
Phoolon ki tarah se hanshti hui
Saari shaklein kho jaayengi
Khoon ki gardish, dil ki dhadkan
Sab raaginiyaan so jaayengi
Aur neeli faza ki makhmal par
Hansti hui heere ki ye kani
Ye meri jannat, meri zameen
Iski subhein, iski shaamein
Be-jaane hue, be-samjhe hue
Ek musht-e-ghubaar-e-insaan par

Shabnam ki tarah ro jaayengi
Har cheez bhula di jaayegi
Yaadon ke haseen but-khane se
Har cheez utha di jaayegi
Phir koi nahi ye poochhega
'Sardar kahaan hai mehfil mein?'
Lekin main yahaan phir aaoonga
Bachhon ke dahan se bolunga
Chidiyon ki zubaan se gaaonga
Jab beej hansenge dharti mein
Aur komlein apni ungli se
Mitti ki tahon ko chedenge
Main pattee pattee, kali kali
Apni aankhein phir kholunga
Sarsabz hatheli par le kar
Shabnam ke qatrey tolunga

Main rang-e-hina, aahang-e-ghazal
Andaaz-e-sukhan ban jaoonga
Rukhsaar-e-uroos-e-nau ki tarah
Har aanchal se chan jaoonga
Jadon ki hawaayein daaman mein
Jab fasl-e-khizaan ko layengi
Reh-rau ke jawaan kadmon ke tale
Sookhe hue patton se mere
Hansne ki sadaayein aayengi

Dharti ki sunahri sab nadiyaan
Aakash ki neeli sab jheelein
Hasti se meri bhar jaayengi
Aur saara zamaana dekhega

Har qissa mera afsaana hai
Har aashiq hai Sardar yahaan
Har mashooqa Sultana hai

Main ek gurezaan lamha hoon
Ayyaam ke afsoon-khane mein
Main ek tadapta qatara hoon
Masroof-e-safar jo rehta hai
Maazi ki suraahi ke dil se
Mustaqbil ke paimane mein
Main sota hoon aur jaagta hoon
Aur jaag ke phir so jaata hoon
Sadiyon ka puraana khel hoon main
Main mar ke amar ho jaata hoon

'How do I perceive the relationship between art and life? To me, they are intricately intertwined and truly inseparable. Life is an art form, and art is my life,' Shovana adds.

She recounts the surreal experience of having the poet Ali Sardar Jafri in her drawing room, reciting verses so enchanting that she soared through the ecstatic realms of transcendentalism. In that moment of spiritual transformation, she became so lost in the profound magic of the words that she forgot to serve dinner to the poet and the other esteemed guest she had invited.

But isn't this exactly where the true essence of poetry reveals itself—when one is swept into blissful oblivion?

Shovana often reflected on this moment from years ago, tinged with admiration and regret. It was an evening etched in her memory. Even years later, the thought of her lapse lingered, a quiet reminder of her all-encompassing passion for art and the rare moments of human oversight it could bring.

When she met Jafri again after a long time, the unspoken weight of that forgotten dinner resurfaced. Shovana, however, knew that the most genuine way for an artist to convey emotions—be it regret, admiration, or affection—was through their art.

With this thought, she turned to Jafri and asked, 'Would you allow me to translate *Mera Safar* through the art form I know best? My interpretation may not align perfectly with your vision, but I promise to approach it sincerely.'

It was a profound moment of connection—one artist seeking the blessings of another to reimagine their work, to infuse it with a new dimension while preserving its soul. For Shovana, this was not merely an attempt to make amends but an act of reverence, an offering from one artistic soul to another. In that request, she exemplified how art becomes a bridge, not just for the artist to express their feelings, but to connect with those they hold close, transcending the limitations of words or time.

'At that time, I was at the peak of my career, wrapped in the illusion of invincibility that youth and success often bestow. We all interpret life through our lens, and mine was as a dancer. I believed in its continuity, its rhythm unbroken as if life itself were a seamless performance. But then, without warning, I was jolted out of that illusion. My father's accident struck me like a thunderclap, forcing me to confront the fragile, transient nature of existence. It was a harsh reminder that no matter how gracefully we may dance through life, the stage we perform on is mortal, its fabric destined to fade. Just two days after the accident, I stood on another stage at the Mathura festival, torn between the weight of grief and the demand for duty. My mother's words carried me through: "My dear, sorrow will never truly leave you, but you must continue to live your life." Her wisdom became my guiding light, reminding me that while the body may falter and the heart may break, life insists on moving forward.

'The truth of the saying, *aankhon ke diye bujh jaayenge* (The light in our eyes will one day fade), echoed in my mind. Mortality is an inevitable truth, but it does not render life meaningless. Instead, it calls upon us to create meaning in every fleeting moment—to persevere, to perform, and to honour the lives we've lost by continuing ours. For even as the dancer's steps falter, the dance itself must carry on.

Shovana Narayan with Ali Sardar Jafri

'Ali Sardar Jafri travelled from Bombay to attend every one of my performances. The piece, *Mera Safar*, was staged across the country and internationally, often in his presence. When he received the Gyan Peeth award, I had the honour of performing it again. Afterwards, his words touched me profoundly: "This now belongs to you; it is no longer mine."'

Interestingly, Shovana's initial connection was with his son, Nazim Jafri, whom she had befriended in Berlin. Later, during a visit to Bombay, she had the joy of meeting his remarkable parents, a moment that remains etched in her memory.

'Much like the Buddha, who faced the truths of old age, death, and suffering before attaining Nirvana, my journey too has been shaped by profound encounters with life's impermanence. This deep fascination with death—far from being morbid—became a powerful impetus, urging me to work with greater intensity, knowing there is still so much to create, to offer, and to complete in this fleeting existence.'

*Mera Safa*r poignantly explores life's journey, the inevitability of ageing, and the shadow of death. While reflecting on the sorrow of mortality, it also embraces life's continuity beyond the individual. This ballet brings the poet's profound musings to life, delving into the human experience of confronting impermanence.

The poet transcends the boundaries of an individual life, embracing the entirety of existence — every particle of the cosmos, every soul that has donned the robe of life, every vein in a leaf, every root entwined in the earth. It captures the unceasing flow of humanity through the epochs, from the dawn of civilisation through its settling, evolution, conquests, annexations, the cycles of learning and unlearning, decay, and resurgence. It encompasses all that was, is, and ever will be.

The performance captures the universal human fear of death—not just the act of dying but also the fear of being forgotten, of losing one's identity in the face of time. It is told from the perspective of a dancer who, aware of her ageing body and the passage of time, contemplates what will happen to her art when she is no longer there to perform it. For a dancer whose life is spent expressing herself through movement, the body becomes both a canvas and a voice. As age begins to limit that expression, there is a fear that her art might fade.

However, the dancer finds hope and a sense of continuity within this fear through her disciples. They are not just students; they are the torchbearers of her art, technique, and essence. Through them, she sees a way for her art to live on, a way for her spirit to become timeless. Her disciples represent a bridge between the finite and the infinite, ensuring that her artistic legacy continues to breathe and evolve, transcending her physical lifespan.

Mera Safar was first performed in 1991-92, with Ali Sardar Jafri reciting his evocative poem, adding a layer of emotion and authenticity to the performance. Since then, the ballet has been staged many times, each performance bringing a new interpretation and depth to its themes.

In a letter to her son, Ishan, Shovana wrote: 'The dance enactment of Ali Sardar Jafri's *Mera Safar* was beautiful. The poem beautifully reflects life's cycle, touching on our fear of death and longing for immortality. True immortality lies not in defying nature but in the legacy of our actions, traditions, and contributions. The performance captured the poem's depth and sensitivity, earning a standing ovation. I am thrilled.'

As *Mera Safar* unfolds, it reveals art's power to confront deep human fears. Reflecting the Sanskrit shloka *Ante Krishnah punararambhah* (each ending is a new beginning), it celebrates life's cyclical nature, urging audiences to ponder their lives and their legacies.

***

Shovana fondly remembers Prof Ramchandra Gandhi, a philosopher whose deep insights greatly influenced her thoughts. She called him Ramu Bhai. Though his life was cut short, he left a lasting impact on everyone who knew him, including her. More than just a philosopher, he was a visionary artist.

He once wrote a complete play for Shovana, envisioning it as a collaboration in which he would narrate, and she would bring the story to life through dance. The ballet was inspired by a childhood episode of Mohandas Karamchand Gandhi, where his maid-servant, Rambha, introduced him to the Ramayana.

Ramu Gandhi, Shovana Narayan, and Alaka Madhok formed a remarkable trio whose collaboration was magical. A series of coincidences brought them together, but once their paths crossed, they became an unstoppable creative force.

Ramu Gandhi, with his philosophical depth and unyielding pursuit of perfection, was a visionary. Shovana Narayan, an unparalleled Kathak maestro, brought his ideas to life with her grace and expressive storytelling through dance. Alaka Madhok, with her keen eye for detail and exceptional production skills, wove it all together seamlessly, ensuring each project was executed flawlessly.

Their dynamic was extraordinary—each brought something unique, complementing the others perfectly. They challenged one another, inspired one another, and supported one another through creative highs and lows. Together, they created thought-provoking, emotionally resonant, and artistically profound works.

To speak of Shovana's mesmerising performances or Ramu Gandhi's philosophical brilliance without mentioning Alaka's crucial role behind the scenes would be an incomplete narrative. Their stories and successes were intertwined and built on their shared synergy. Their partnership wasn't just about collaboration; it was about a deep, unspoken understanding that made their work timeless.

Alaka, married to an army officer, travelled across the country. She collaborated with Colonel Kapoor on the TV serial *Fauji* as a scriptwriter in Delhi. She later anchored for Jaipur Doordarshan before shifting to writing documentaries and docudramas. During this period, she met singer Suraiya Rahman, a notable singer, at a family gathering, and she created a documentary about her for Doordarshan. It was through Suraiya Rahman that Alaka met Shovana.

'Shovana and I quickly became close friends. I produced Suraiya's poetry, and Shovana beautifully interpreted it through dance. It was a powerful piece reflecting on the Ayodhya demolition and its aftermath, with music composed by Jwala Prasad ji. The performance aired on Doordarshan and was repeatedly broadcast due to public demand.'

Shovana collaborated with Ramu Gandhi, who had written five plays around the same time. They had already staged *Rambha* together, and by the time Alaka met them, they were working on *Vivekanand*.

'Shovana invited me to watch the play. Ramu ji narrated the story while she brought it to life through her Kathak performance. Shovana's performance was mesmerising, and Ramu ji's narration was exceptional.'

Alaka liked the play but was dissatisfied with the acoustics and lighting. She didn't hesitate to share her thoughts with Ramu ji. For the next performance, he asked her to take charge. Alaka brought in her team and put in significant effort to enhance Vivekanand.

When Ramu ji travelled to America, Doordarshan needed to record the play. He entrusted Alaka with the responsibility of producing and directing it in his absence. Upon his return, he was highly impressed with the results.

'The Philosophical Society of India financially backed his projects. Ramu ji was an absolute genius, his mind constantly buzzing with ideas—one emerging before the previous one was fully explored. We'd have everything set—the studio booked, technicians in place, the script finalised, the auditorium reserved, and Shovana's dates locked in. And then, suddenly, he'd announce, "Let's change the script!"

'We did our best to keep up, but it wasn't always possible with so many people already tuned to a specific plan. Yet, no matter how chaotic the process was, the final product was always spectacular. Of course, the road to perfection was paved with a fair share of bumps! We'd get frustrated, he'd get frustrated, and then we'd have to play peacemakers. Once calmed down, he'd stick to the previous version (at least for that day), and we'd finally get the shoot done, laughing off all the earlier drama.

'Getting him to commit to one idea was like catching lightning in a bottle. Locking in the plan was crucial with so many people's schedules on the line. Surprisingly, though, he was extremely cooperative when I oversaw production and directing. He'd narrate as many times as needed without a fuss. But if left to his own devices, the process could stretch endlessly—he had too many brilliant ideas. He was relentless in his pursuit of perfection. He'd spot the tiniest flaw and wouldn't rest until it was ironed out. His perfectionism was inspiring...and occasionally exhausting for the rest of us!'

Shovana, Ramu Gandhi, and Alaka were an inseparable trio. Ramu ji had his moments of fiery temper—he'd sometimes storm off the set and retreat to the lawn at the India International Centre (IIC). The two young women would chase after him, coaxing him to return. After putting on a show of annoyance, he'd eventually give in, and they'd get back to work as if nothing had happened.

There was a considerable age gap between him and the other two, yet their bond was remarkable. Despite his vast knowledge and relentless dedication, Ramu Gandhi led a simple, almost monastic life. He lived humbly in a small annexe at someone's house.

Despite the occasional clashes, the trio shared a beautiful partnership and accomplished a great deal together. Ramu ji often took Alaka to his lectures at embassies, where she would hang on to his every word.

'I was in America when I received the heartbreaking news of his passing,' Alaka shares.

Unmasking of Death based on Ramana Maharshi - written by Prof Ramchandra Gandhi

For Shovana, meaningful conversations with individuals of depth and wisdom were like a nourishing soul soup, offering sustenance for her artistic spirit and ultra-sensitive soul. Engaging with such profound thinkers allowed her to explore ideas that resonated with her inner vibrations, fuelling her creative expression. These discussions, rich with insight, deepened her understanding of the world and her art, helping her connect more profoundly with the energy that drives her performances. It was in moments like these that she found the clarity and inspiration she needed, whether in collaborating on a ballet or contemplating the complexities of peace.

Reflecting on her performance for the United Nations' World Peace Day, she had an intense conversation with Ramu Bhai about the true essence of peace. Their dialogue unveiled the inherent paradox of peace—how the very pursuit of it can sometimes lead to conflict. Peace becomes elusive when one's sense of security threatens another's vulnerability, when one's abundance highlights another's deprivation, or when success breeds envy.

Ramu Bhai and Shovana collaborated on several plays, including *Sadhu and the Sage*, *The Clown of Assissi*, *Mohan and Rambha*, *The Temptation of Vivekanand*, *The Unmasking of Death*, and *Sanmati*. Alaka participated in the filming of *The Temptation of Vivekanand*.

'Every year, without fail, Ramu Bhai would have rakhi tied by me and my sister Ranjana,' Shovana recalls solemnly.

Her formative years in Patna, particularly at St Joseph's Convent, were a period of deep learning and reflection. While her education included an introduction to the Bible and the Christian faith, equal emphasis was placed on understanding her cultural and spiritual heritage.

She observed striking parallels between different faiths: the story of Manu surviving the great deluge found resonance in Noah's ark; Krishna, the cowherd, mirrored Jesus, the shepherd. The Holy Trinity of Christianity paralleled the Hindu trinity of Brahma, Vishnu, and Mahesh. Saints protecting people in Christian traditions were akin to Hindu deities safeguarding humanity from the elements.

Shovana marvelled at the universality of spiritual symbols: the candle and the *diya,* both flames signifying purification; incense in various traditions purifying the atmosphere and warding negativity. Even the music of different faiths found commonality as Vedic and Gregorian chants used basic notes to evoke harmony and awaken the inner self.

Through these reflections, she discovered the universality of faith and its symbols—whether it was Ahilya awaiting purification by Lord Rama or Mary Magdalene finding redemption through Jesus, or the flute of Lord Krishna elevating the soul, much like Rumi's belief in its purifying power.

For Shovana, these parallels underscored a more profound truth: humanity's shared yearning for transcendence, harmony, and peace.

'My work with Ramu bhai also drew on two significant moments from Swami Vivekananda's life. These moments explored the struggles between ego and enlightenment, power and humility, and the role of inner transformation.'

The first incident occurred during Vivekananda's visit to the Ksheer Bhawani temple in Jammu and Kashmir. Seeing the damaged idol, he questioned the goddess, 'Devi, if you couldn't protect yourself, how will you protect us?' He felt her respond in a profound inner moment, 'Who are you to question me? The invaders who broke me didn't understand our culture, but you, who do, deny entry to Dalits and discriminate against your people.'

The real desecration of the sacred lies not in physical destruction but in moral failure—our inability to embrace the wholeness of humanity. It was not the goddess who was broken but society, fractured by prejudice and exclusion.

The second incident centres on a moment when Vivekananda's ego was unexpectedly humbled. During his stay at Khetri, Maharaja Ajit Singh invited him to a musical evening featuring a nautch-girl's performance. Feeling it inappropriate for a swami to attend, Vivekananda left, believing the event was beneath him. However, as the singer began her song, *'Prabhu ji mere avagun chit na dharo,'* her pure and heartfelt voice touched him deeply. In that moment, he realised the flaw wasn't in her but in his judgement. Her song, filled with devotion, dismantled his pride and reminded him that true spirituality lies in humility and openness, not in judgement or superiority.

'Ramu bhai and I often discussed how these moments reveal a universal truth—the need to look within, recognise our shared humanity, and confront our inner darkness. Life, philosophy, and spirituality are all about self-inquiry and understanding our deep connection to the universe. Growth arises from reflection, dialogue, and expression—whether through dance, music or thought.'

Ātmā vā are draṣṭavyaḥ śrotavyaḥ *mantavyaḥ nididhyāsitavyaḥ*

(The Self should be seen, heard, contemplated upon, and meditated upon.)

—Brahma Sutras

From Ballet to Ballroom

She was a dancer with dreams as vast as the sky but fears quietly nestled in her heart. Marriage, she worried, might mean surrendering what she loved the most—her career as an IAAS officer, her identity as an artist, and her unwavering bond with her homeland. But destiny, in its quiet wisdom, had plans far beyond her imagination. Into her life walked an ambassador,

Those were the days...

Dr Herbert Traxl, captivated not just by her beauty but by the soul of her dance. He fell in love with her grace, her strength, and the quiet fire within her. Their worlds couldn't have been more different—countries apart, cultures apart, even their skin bore different stories—but their hearts spoke the same language, finding each other in a way that felt like fate.

Their love became a tender journey of discovery, a weaving together of two lives that embraced both contrasts and common grounds. From the ballet stage to the ballroom, they learned to dance through life's complexities, making all little and big adjustments and treasuring fleeting moments together. With a life defined by 'quarterly marriage,' they built something enduring—something beautiful.

Now, well into their eighties, they continue to live the love story of a lifetime, filled with gratitude and without a whisper of regret.

Shovana still dances as if her heart was woven into every step, her light undimmed, her passion ageless. Herbert, as always, sits in the front row, watching her with eyes that hold the same love, admiration, and tenderness as when he first saw her. In those quiet moments, he often drifts back to that day, the first time his gaze rested on her—a luminous moon that has since lit up his world.

Dr Herbert Traxl was born on 2 December 1940, during the turmoil of World War II. His family, deeply rooted in European traditions, upheld conservative values and had never ventured beyond Europe. Both sides of the family were tied to the civil services. His father, an engineer born in 1884, had witnessed the Austro-Hungarian empire's decline and served in World War I.

Austria's struggles after the war were well captured by a French politician's remark: 'Whatever is not taken, is Austria.' The nation, reduced and divided, saw families torn between nationalism and open-mindedness. When Nazism rose and Hitler annexed Austria, life became even more perilous. Herbert's father faced interrogation by the Gestapo three times, each time narrowly escaping deportation to a concentration camp.

Though the family was once affluent, their stability crumbled due to their steadfast principles and opposition to oppression. Herbert's father, known for his friendships across diverse communities, stood against Hitler's regime, a stance that cost him his job and financial security. Despite the hardships, he lived a life of unwavering integrity, remaining true to his values until his passing in 1975.

Herbert has had a distinguished career in diplomacy and international relations. After graduating from the University of Vienna Law School with a Doctor of Jurisprudence in 1963, he pursued further studies at the John Hopkins University Bologna Centre in 1964. In 1965, he completed a traineeship at the Court of Justice before joining the Federal Chancellery's Department for Economic Coordination in 1966. His career in the foreign service began with his role at the Austrian Mission to the Organisation for Economic Cooperation and Development (OECD) in Paris in 1970, followed by his assignment in 1973 to the Federal Ministry for Foreign Affairs in the department for International Organisations. In 1975, Herbert was appointed Deputy Chief of Mission at the Austrian embassy in New Delhi.

Shovana and Herbert met when her dance career was reaching incredible heights. She dazzled audiences with her performances, but behind the glamour, she kept her heart guarded, determined not to let anything take her away from her work, dreams, or country. Herbert, an ambassador used to a diplomatic life, was unexpectedly captivated by her. Her grace, striking Indian features, and the powerful pull of her dance left him in awe.

What started as admiration for her art quickly turned into a deeper connection. Herbert was surprised by how naturally he was drawn to her strength, streak of independence, and the magic she brought to everything she did.

What was crucial to Shovana was the trust her family had in her. This trust imposed a greater responsibility on her behaviour, yet in society; such subtleties often went unnoticed.

Being single and a dancer provided ample *masala* for neighbourhood gossip. Moreover, with age advancing, life seemed ripe for such stimulating situations.

One memorable incident occurred after she returned from a performance in Himachal Pradesh. Exhausted from a night of travel by taxi to be on time for work, she fumbled with her house key when she was approached by a neighbour returning from his morning walk.

After the usual pleasantries, he noticed her suitcase and asked where she had been. When she mentioned Sunder Nagar, he looked at her with surprise and disapproval. It took her a while to realise that he had misunderstood Sunder Nagar in Himachal Pradesh for the Sunder Nagar in Delhi. She couldn't help but chuckle at the wild gossip circulating among her neighbours.

'Being gregarious, my flat saw many friends dropping in after office hours. As I was alone for long stretches, this situation, to begin with, was not taken well at all. Fragments of distasteful gossip about me would reach my ears now and then. They hurt at times; at other times I could not care less. Sometimes, I wondered how difficult the situation would have been had I not had a government flat. But amidst all the nasty comments, of which there was no dearth, there was also a silver lining. Many friendships made during those days are still there that can be counted upon, for we were young and struggling in our respective professions. Hence, there were no expectations from each other except that of a healthy friendship.'

By 1979, Shovana was well entrenched in both her professions. She was busy and happy. One day in November 1979, Monisha Khan, wife of the sitar maestro Ustad Vilayat Khan, asked her to give a lecture demonstration in Kathak for a group of friends, primarily diplomats. The event took place on 4 December 1979. Herbert was one of the invitees at this performance.

'After the performance, there was a 'meet the artist' session, but I quietly slipped out the back while the other artists mingled. The audience mostly consisted of *firangis* (foreigners), what I'd call 'the horse crowd' from the polo circuit. Monisha invited me to dinner at a guest's house the following day, a farewell for a departing diplomat. Monisha had to convince me to go. That evening, I met Herbert for the first time. From then on, Herbert often invited us to dinners or movies, with Monisha always encouraging me to join. By the end of December, Herbert began calling me directly. He invited me to join him at the polo field on 31 December. I said I'd go, but I never did,' Shovana adds spiritedly.

Herbert chuckles when recounting how love blossomed between them, weaving into the spaces between sweet nothings and meaningful moments. 'It wasn't some grand declaration,' he says, 'but the quiet exchanges that left their mark—a shared glance, a lingering smile, or the way her voice softened when we spoke.'

While Shovana speaks with vibrant energy about his persistence and charm, Herbert reflects with quiet warmth, describing how her brilliance and grace left him awestruck and utterly smitten. Together, they paint a picture of a love that grew naturally, surprising them both in the best way possible.

Their versions of how love unfolded may differ in detail but complement each other perfectly:

'On 4 December, I was invited by an old friend, Vilayat Khan's wife, Monisha. Monisha Bhabhi casually mentioned she had a good friend who was a famous dancer, and of course, it was Shovana. The introductions rolled in, and when they said she had a masters in physics, I did a double-take. A dancer? With a physics degree? I was ready to short-circuit. And as if that wasn't enough, she was also into auditing and accounting as a civil servant. I mean, who is this overachiever? Then, she performed for the gathering. We, a bunch of *firangis,* were her audience, and let's just say we were floored. But just as we thought we'd get to chat with her, poof! She disappeared like a magician's final trick.

A couple of days later, we had this big dinner planned, a long-standing event with a farewell for a colleague from the Australian embassy. I invited Monisha, hoping she'd bring the dancing prodigy along. Sure enough, she did,' Herbert quips. 'And three days after that? Well, I found myself co-starring in a Hollywood film. They needed white faces to sit on horses and pretend to play polo—the classic white team versus brown team scenario. And where do we end up? At the Taj hotel, with Shovana, of course!'

'And then?' Shovana chimes in with a smile, her curiosity piqued.

'Then, I didn't need Monisha anymore,' he says with a chuckle, referring to the once-crucial middleman who played cupid in the early days. 'The next challenge was tracking down where Shovana lived. It took me ages to find her government apartment. She even ditched me when I invited her to the polo ground!' He beams, still amused by her evasiveness. 'But eventually, we started going out together.'

Alongside the challenge of ageing, Shovana wrestled with apprehensions. Despite Herbert's resolute decision to marry her, she remained notably hesitant. The hurdles were far from ordinary. Shovana, fiercely independent and deeply rooted in her dual careers as a civil servant and a dancer, now grappled with the complexities of balancing love, work, and identity.

Most concerning was the question of her dance—a passion that was not just a career, but her very essence. Herbert's idea of consolidating her performances during her time in India seemed naive; dance, after all, was not just about scheduling but about staying connected to her art, culture, and audience.

The path ahead was uncertain, and an intense inner turmoil stirred within Shovana. Dance was not merely an art or a profession for her—it was the very essence of her being. The mere thought of relinquishing it in the name of love was unbearable.

It felt as though the mature Shovana still carried a younger self within, now awakened, pleading with unrestrained emotion, 'No, no! Do not say that! I must dance!'

Each time the idea of forsaking dance arose, her soul trembled in distress. This anguish was a relentless reminder that dance was not just an expression—it was the lifeblood that coursed through her, the core of her identity and the essence of her soul.

Their love had brought them together, but navigating these practicalities required courage, compromise, and a shared vision for a future that respected the life the two had built and the one they hoped to build together.

'Herbert, in a very matter-of-fact way, had stated that I could be with him for six months in a year while I could be in India for the other six months. Six months, I screamed aghast. He then watered it down to three months. Three months or six months, the issues were the same!'

'What happens to my official career?' I asked.

'Well, you could take up a job with an international agency.

I have seen so many other Indians do.'

'But other Indians are only single-careered. Here I am with dual careers. What happens to my dance?'

'Your agent could see that your programmes in India are bunched together during those six months,' he replied naively.

'Little did Herbert know we had no agent system in India. We still do not have one. Hence, each dancer is her own agent, travel coordinator, manager, choreographer, and publicity handler, managing every aspect of her own career. This was in stark contrast to the system prevailing in the west. Hence, to be away for so long meant that gossip would be doing the rounds that I had left dance and India forever.'

Despite the obstacles to being together, the distance couldn't keep them apart for long. They embraced each other's lifestyles, adapting and adjusting effortlessly. Whenever possible, they took assignments in places that brought them closer, always working to bridge the gap. It wasn't just love that kept them united. Their mutual willingness to compromise, understand, and cherish every moment—regardless of the distance—truly made their bond thrive.

'I arrived in Delhi in September 1975, at age thirty-five. I had never been outside Europe before. I joined the foreign service, and when the personnel department seemed eager to post me elsewhere, I chose Delhi,' he recalls with a thoughtful pause. 'Delhi in the late seventies was a completely different place, especially when it came to getting around. Everything changed with the arrival of the Maruti. Before that, it was all about Ambassador and Fiat cars. And guess what? Shovana had a Fiat.' His eyes sparkle with joy.

Shovana had a special bond with her beloved fawn-coloured Fiat car—it was her pride and joy, practically a family member!

Whether it was a simple errand or a grand outing, the Fiat was her steadfast companion. Ranjana often joked that her Didi loved that car so much she might just arrive at her wedding in it, unlike other brides who opt for grander rides, and then drive off to their honeymoon with Herbert in the same trusty vehicle! That Fiat, with its timeless charm and Shovana behind the wheel, was almost an extension of her personality—independent, practical, yet full of heart.

True to her no-frills personality, Shovana didn't believe in hiring professionals for her makeup or styling. She would do it all herself with effortless grace, perfectly complementing her understated elegance.

'On the day of my marriage, after having done my makeup, I was ready to drive myself to the marriage venue, Ashoka hotel, in my dilapidated 1962 model Fiat. My sister was aghast.

Shovana Narayan with her husband Dr Herbert Traxl and sister, Ranjana Narayan

"Didi, for once, don't be so stupid! How can you drive yourself to the marriage venue? After the wedding ceremonies, are you contemplating driving Herbert and yourself to Benno's place?"

She had a point. I called for a taxi and went to the Ashoka hotel.'

'When Herbert came to propose to Didi, he asked me and my mother for Shovana Didi's hand. My mother was very straightforward with him, saying she had no issue with him being a foreigner but made it clear that Didi would never give up three things: her dance, her job, and her country. Herbert assured her that she wouldn't have to. Over the years, Herbert and Shovana Didi have made many adjustments to keep their marriage strong. I've always seen Herbert as a father figure. He's a kind, genuine person who shares the same values as we do. My bond, even with his mother and sisters, has been very special,' says Ranjana.

Shovana's parents were unwavering in their commitment to challenging social conventions, fully prepared to face criticism for their progressive outlook. They rejected the prevailing conservative expectations of their time—by refusing to participate in dowry practices, rejecting gender discrimination, and supporting their daughters' unconventional career choices. They encouraged Shovana and Ranjana, to pursue dance and music as hobbies or full-time careers. They even broke tradition by allowing Shovana to perform the *mukhagni* (the lighting of the funeral pyre) and Ranjana to immerse their father's ashes in the Ganga—rituals traditionally reserved for sons.

These choices profoundly shaped Shovana and Ranjana's worldview, fostering a deep sense of responsibility and a desire to dismantle entrenched social myths. Their upbringing was grounded in the belief that true fulfilment comes from earning one's way.

When Shovana married, the question of dowry never surfaced. She refused to indulge in extravagant spending for a wedding trousseau. As a working woman, she saw no need for heavy brocade or *zari* saris, especially when she already had enough. She was determined to limit her wedding expenses to a quarter share of the Rs 50,000 compensation she had received after her father died in the railway accident. This decision made her feel her father was present, overseeing her wedding arrangements. She found no joy in spending hard-earned money on unnecessary luxuries. True to her self-sufficiency, Shovana, accustomed to doing her makeup for performances, didn't even visit a beauty parlour for the occasion—underscoring her commitment to simplicity and practicality.

These actions, rooted in the values imparted by her parents, reflected a lifetime of breaking away from social pressures and embracing authenticity.

Herbert's values, instilled by his parents, reflected profoundly in Shovana's character and life. The rich legacy of music he inherited not only deepened his emotional sensitivity but also honed his sense of compassion and empathy.

'I grew up in a family where music was an integral part of our lives. I played the piano, my father played it even better, and my sister was passionate about singing. Living in Vienna, we were surrounded by some of the world's finest opera houses, and European classical music became a big part of me. Shovana's passion was Indian classical music, which I appreciated over time. After courting for a long while, we faced the question: what do we do? Our relationship was a blend of Austrian and Indian cultures. Despite differences in skin colour, we shared common principles and emotions,' Herbert shares.

By 1980, he was seconded to the Federal Chancellery as

Chief of Cabinet for the Minister of State for Economic Affairs.

Herbert and Shovana tied the knot in May 1982. By that time, Herbert's father had passed away, but his mother was relieved and happy that he had finally found someone.

Herbert's friends joked about the challenges of daily life together, but the two were mature enough to understand what it took. They knew that the key was not trying to change the other person but allowing elbow room for each other.

His first ambassadorial role came in 1983 when he was appointed ambassador of Austria to Ethiopia, with concurrent accreditation to Djibouti, DVR Yemen, Madagascar, and Mauritius. He had explicitly requested assignments closer to India to minimise travel.

Amid their whirlwind life of diplomatic postings and artistic commitments, the couple found themselves at a new crossroads in 1984.

Shovana discovered she was expecting their first child.

The news brought excitement and trepidation, adding a deeply personal dimension to their already dynamic partnership.

For Shovana, this new chapter wasn't just about becoming a mother; it was about balancing her unwavering commitment to Kathak and her evolving role within the family.

Herbert, the steady pillar of support, embraced the news joyfully, eager to navigate this new journey together.

The New Rhythm

Shovana sat by the window, a cool November breeze brushing against her face as the phone conversation replayed in her mind. Dubai. A performance at an international festival. What an opportunity, she thought, her fingers unconsciously tracing her belly.

'But can I? Should I?' The questions looped endlessly. 'I've always danced with my whole being, but now… there's more than just me. Would this world of dance, so quick to celebrate youth and perfection, have room for a pregnant dancer? Would they see the art or the change in me?'

Her hand rested gently on her stomach, a connection forming between her and the child she hadn't yet met. 'You're already part of me,' she whispered in her mind, 'and somehow, I feel you'll understand. Dance is who I am, and being a Mom is already a part of me, too.'

The memory of her friend Chandni's reassuring words strengthened her, but Herbert's concern lingered. 'What if something goes wrong?' His voice echoed. Yet, deep down, Shovana felt a quiet confidence.

'This little life inside me will feel the rhythm of every beat, every movement. Together, we'll create something new—a dance that

celebrates not just the art but the journey of life itself.'

The night stretched, and as the city's lights shimmered in the distance, she resolved to embrace the challenge.

'Motherhood and dance—both are creations of love, sacrifice, and strength. And if the world isn't ready to see them together, I'll show them how it's done.'

Shovana discovered that her dear mother-in-law was much like her mother, subtly encouraging her to start a family. While maternal instincts are natural, she couldn't help but weigh the potential impact on her two demanding careers. At the same time, the realisation that she wasn't getting any younger and that time wasn't on her side began to press on her mind. After much contemplation, she ultimately decided to take the plunge into motherhood.

At the time, India was undergoing political changes. After the assassination of Indira Gandhi, her son Rajiv Gandhi became Prime Minister, and the Congress party won a historic victory in the December 1984 elections, securing 415 out of 545 seats.

Amid all this, Shovana found herself facing a personal crossroad. In late November, her friend Chandni Luthra, who worked in public relations at Ashoka hotel, called with exciting news—Shovana had been chosen to perform in Dubai at a significant food festival along with her dancers and musicians.

It was an incredible opportunity, but Shovana had a secret—she was pregnant. She hesitated to share the news, fearing that the dance world might sideline her from performing permanently. Dance had always been an inseparable part of her identity, a way to express her emotions and devotion to art. However, with her pregnancy came a profound shift. While she was excited about the journey into motherhood, she couldn't help but feel an underlying fear—how would the dance world, which had nurtured her for so long, now perceive her?

Memories of similar reactions resurfaced, reminding her of the scepticism and gossip that followed her marriage to Herbert—many had said she would leave the country and never return to dance again.

After much thought, she decided to confide in Chandni, who reassured her that the performances could be arranged to protect her role. With that support, she agreed to go ahead with the plan. Her husband, Herbert, who was stationed as an ambassador in Ethiopia, was understandably worried. But Shovana, with a mother's confidence, felt certain that her child, even before birth, would somehow understand her need to balance motherhood and her passion for dance.

Shovana's journey into motherhood was filled with love, reflection, and a deep sense of responsibility. Even before her son, Ishan, was born, she started writing letters to the child, sharing her thoughts, hopes, and uncertainties. These letters became a way for her to connect with her unborn child, even as she balanced the demands of being a dancer and a government official.

'Papa—Herbert—took me around Addis, and what a bumpy ride it was for it was our mistake that in trying to reach some place, we had lost our way and had to ride over the untarred road. I was so scared for you, but then I thought that since you had been jostled around with my dance, this jostling must be amusing you no end.'

Shovana worked until the last couple of months of her pregnancy. When she was three months pregnant, she performed in the Middle East, and afterward, she travelled to Vienna to meet Herbert. They celebrated Christmas together.

'Back then, Doordarshan was a big platform for dancers, and

we often received media coverage. I remember a funny incident: after one performance, the cameraman approached me and said, "Wow! You danced beautifully. But I must tell you something."

He leaned in and whispered, "Take care of your waist; it's expanding." My musician, Jwala Prasad ji, overheard him and replied, "She's pregnant and still dancing."' Shovana laughs.

Shovana continued performing until February 1985, with her baby expected in mid-June. Her final performance occurred on 22 February, 1985, at the Federation of Indian Chambers of Commerce and Industry (FICCI) auditorium.

'Ishan, bless his little soul, came bang on time. My maternity leave started from the day he was born, thus giving me time to devote my full three months of maternity leave to looking after the young arrival. What a bundle of joy! I could not imagine how I could have taken such a long time to decide to have him! What a joy he brought to both our families, for he was the only grandchild on both sides. Two grandmothers and three aunts doted upon him, one aunt from my side and two from Herbert's, along with an equally doting mother. My sister, who could never leave him, and he, on his part, cuddled up to her, christened him Ishan. As Herbert wanted him to have another name given by his family, what better than 'Erwin,' the name of Herbert's father, which rhymed so well with Ishan!'

Ishan was born on 18 June, and Herbert arrived from Ethiopia on 16 June.

'I arrived in India two days before Ishan's birth. Around that time, I applied for a posting in Tehran, a key embassy with a cultural institute that they managed to keep open despite the government shutting down similar institutes. It was a challenging assignment, and so was our married life,' shares Herbert.

Shovana's mother was present when Ishan was born,

and shortly after his arrival, they travelled to Vienna. Her mother-in-law eagerly awaited her first and only grandchild. Until now, whenever Shovana travelled, her hand luggage would typically be filled with her ghunghroos, a symbol of her life as a dancer. But now, that bag was packed with tiny clothes, nappies, and essentials for her baby, marking the beginning of a new chapter in her life.

Though their demanding careers often kept them apart, the two made it work. Shovana excelled in her dance career and her role as a civil servant, making her professional life even more time-consuming. Despite their full-time commitments, Shovana supported Herbert at events like National Day receptions. She attended most gala receptions, always dressed in the traditional dirndl. During Herbert's final posting in Bangkok, she had the privilege of attending the prestigious Philharmonic event, graced by the queen's presence.

Herbert chose the Bangkok posting for its proximity to Delhi, a three-hour flight. They always prioritised shorter travel distances when deciding on assignments.

Reflecting on Ishan's childhood, marked by his mother-fixation and doting affection, Shovana later writes to him in one of her letters, 'In July 1986, I was scheduled for a dance tour of England. I was there to participate in the Sanskritik Festival of the Arts of India. I first went with you to Vienna. By then, you had become very possessive of me and would cry and bang at the bathroom door if I left you even for a short period. How would I leave you for over a month when I went on this tour? That was the question. Fortunately, my flight to London was sometime in the morning, and we thought you would still be sleeping when I left. But perhaps you had an uncanny sense about my departure, for you got up much earlier than usual and started looking for me. I can still see you in your pale-yellow night suit, standing at the drawing-room door and crying your heart out. My heart cried with you, and I did not know what to do. Mamma picked you up and whisked you out of sight, but while your attention was diverted, Ilse, (nickname for Elizabeth Traxl, my elder sister-in-law) took me out quietly and drove me to the airport.

Till today, I cannot forget the sight of you crying, and my heart cries even now.'

Birendra Shankar, nephew of Pandit Ravi Shankar, who was based in London, was a remarkable organiser and one of the pioneers of large-scale professional festivals. His Sanskritik Festival of the Arts of India was widely recognised. He organised week-long festivals at the Queen Elizabeth Hall in London, featuring around fourteen to sixteen classical artists from India. Birendra was among the first to introduce the concept of collaborating on different styles for the opening and closing performances. After the London performances, the artists toured major auditoriums across England and Scotland and gave lecture demonstrations in educational institutions. These tours typically lasted a month.

Shovana's tour in England was a resounding success professionally, but personally, it tested her resilience in ways she could not have anticipated. Shortly after arriving in London, she began developing a high fever, which was soon diagnosed as malaria. Birendra Shankar and his wife even considered cancelling her performances. But Shovana refused to let her audience down. Despite the pleas of her friends, she insisted on keeping her schedule.

It was a gruelling experience—during the day, she would lie in bed, burning with fever, and just a few hours before each performance, she would take paracetamol to bring down her temperature. This would allow her to perform, drenched in cold sweat, only for the fever to return with a vengeance the moment she left the stage. Yet, night after night, she persevered, pushing her body beyond its limits.

There was a moment when it all became too much. Overwhelmed by exhaustion and illness, she found herself in a public phone booth, calling Herbert in Addis and crying in sheer despair. It was a rare moment of vulnerability for Shovana, who was accustomed to handling the pressures of her demanding double life. Herbert, too far away to help, was left anxious and helpless.

The toll of this unrelenting pace became evident when she collapsed after arriving in Vienna. Her body had reached its breaking point, and she was hospitalised for several days at the Rudolfstiftung Spital. It was a forced period of recovery, both physically and emotionally.

This experience, though painful, reaffirmed her strength as an artist and a person, revealing how the most unusual challenges in life can test one's mettle. Every step, however tricky, became part of a journey that was undeniably worth it.

'Herbert and I took a holiday with the baby, and after three months, I returned to my office and the stage. By October of that year, I was back to performing, travelling to Kolkata for a dance performance.'

Life had resumed its familiar rhythm of office work, dance, rehearsals, creating new compositions, and teaching her students. The only difference now was the presence of her newborn, Ishan, who seamlessly became a part of her routine.

In one of her letters to Ishan, Shovana wrote:

> During endless hours of music composition, you have always been sitting in my lap, playing, sleeping, but always close to me. Even when Ranju is doing her practise or teaching music, you

are THERE, sometimes in her lap, sometimes standing on your head! Even when I teach the girls, you are there, sometimes quietly watching, otherwise trying to catch my attention. And you are a little pest! Whenever I am practising dance, you love to clamber on me and hang on to me, especially when I am doing my footwork. You seem to love the movement, but for me …it is tiring. And how, of all the musical instruments it is the tabla that always catches your attention. You love to play the tabla. I would rather call it 'beat' on the tabla. But admittedly, this 'beating' on the tabla is rather rhythmic. You seem to display a good sense of timing. Kamal Sahay photographed you in such a position.

From a young age, Ishan had a faint understanding of his mother's significance, recognising her as the central figure around whom their entire household revolved. His mother was an internationally acclaimed artist whose busy schedule often meant a steady stream of visitors—admirers, collaborators, and patrons—passing through their home. Her presence was larger than life, commanding attention and admiration wherever she went, which shaped Ishan's upbringing in unique ways. This is what Ishan has to say about his childhood:

'I grew up in a household that was constantly bustling with activity, with students frequently coming and going, often accompanied by their parents. It was clear to me, even as a child, that these people weren't visiting because of me—they were there for my mother. Early on, I realised that my Mom was deeply passionate, incredibly dedicated, and exceptionally talented at *something*. At first, it was hard to grasp precisely what that was; the concept felt abstract and beyond my understanding.

'Despite her busy schedule, I always had patience and understanding for her work, even when she wasn't physically present. My Mom was often touring or performing, a stark contrast to the traditional households of my friends, where their mothers were more hands-on in daily life. Still, I never felt deprived of love. She ensured I was surrounded by care and affection, even when her career took her away.

'There were moments when I wanted to accompany her on her dance trips, and while it wasn't always possible, I knew how important her work was to her. Those challenging moments taught me to reconcile my feelings healthily.

'My childhood was spent in an environment rich with creativity and music. Our home was always alive with artists and musicians, many of whom I affectionately called *chachas*. It was a lively and unusual environment, always surrounded by ghunghroos, pakhavaj, and tabla sounds. I loved the sounds and never once, in my memory, wished for it to stop or demand my Mom's undivided attention. I was never excluded; instead, I felt deeply involved in this vibrant community. It was an open house—a big, beautiful family of art—and shaped me profoundly.

'We all worked to maintain a happy balance, and much of my good behaviour came from watching my father, who shared a loving, patient, and appreciative relationship with my mother.

'Each day, one of our domestic helps took me to a tennis club near India Gate. Once, my coach asked where my mother was, and I innocently replied, "Which one?" When he laughed and asked how many mothers I had, I sincerely said, "Five." While he looked at us puzzled, Vijay, our domestic help, chuckled and called it a bluff, but I explained: "I have my Shovana Mom, my mausi, my *badi bua*, my *choti bua*, and my nani."

'As they say, it takes a village to raise a child, and I indeed had one—spread across two continents. My father's two elder sisters doted on me, and with no first cousins, I was the sole centre of attention for all the elders in my family. It was a nurturing and profoundly loving environment.

'I was essentially "exported" to Austria for education, and life there was anything but ordinary. On a typical school day, Mom was off conquering her world, and though Dad was officially around, he wasn't always present. Enter the tribe—or as I like to call it, the village—that raised me.

'If I needed help with schoolwork or extra tutoring, my uncle was my go-to guy for everything science. He was brilliant, endlessly patient, and a great friend when we weren't stuck in study mode. We even shared birthdays, which was fun. Dad, on the other hand, took charge of history—not as a tutor but as a fellow enthusiast.

'And Mom? Well, let's just say I gave her one big headache: I was hopeless at math. She couldn't wrap her head around it, especially since she'd aced math and physics in her higher studies. My response? "Mom, people are different." Not my most endearing moment, but it worked. Summers in India meant spending time in her office, where she'd park me in the reception room with hourly math exercises that I'd struggle through like a champ—or not.

'A typical school day started early. Dad's office was near my school, so we walked together in the mornings. The school wasn't all day, so Vijay, our trusty companion who came with us to Vienna, would pick me up in the afternoons. Afterwards, it was off to the park to play. Evenings were reserved for homework sessions with my *bua*, who kept me on track. Looking back, it was a patchwork routine, but somehow, it worked—and it was mine.

'Looking back, I realise that the patchwork routine of my childhood had its charm. I was surrounded by a lively, loving tribe—*bua*, dad, Vijay, Ranjana mausi, and my uncle—all indulging me in pranks and adventures. It was a whole house, bustling with activity, though my Mom was mostly absent from this daily chaos. Yet, I never felt deprived. She had her students back in India, and I understood early on that while they flocked around her, I had an unshakable place in her heart as the star of her eyes.

'As an artist, Mom has always walked a delicate line between her public persona and private life. The balance she maintains is remarkable. Her humility and authenticity endear her to her students, who see her as a Kathak guru, mentor, and confidante. The guru-shishya parampara isn't just a tradition for her—it's a way of life, transcending the art form to encompass genuine, lasting bonds.

'And in the nineties? Oh, her pirouettes! Those spins! She has the tiniest feet, yet they command such presence and power. To me, she has always been the most beautiful dancer ever—graceful, magnetic, and utterly captivating.'

As Ishan grew, Shovana carefully guided him, teaching him important life lessons and shaping his values. From the start, she ensured that he developed an open mind, free of societal pressures, allowing small everyday experiences to influence his understanding of the world.

Shovana's bond with her son, Ishan, was rooted in profound love and nurturing, deeply influenced by his extraordinary affinity for the natural world. From a young age, Ishan had a remarkable way with animals, surprising his mother more than once with his fearless encounters and innate tenderness towards both wild and domestic creatures.

One particularly unforgettable memory involved a young leopard. During a stay in a setting reminiscent of the Flintstones—a cluster of stone huts surrounded by ancient rock formations—the family encountered a house-trained leopard, full of energy and mischief. While the other guests watched with cautious curiosity, Ishan, still a small child, became the object of the leopard's attention. After being fed, the leopard purred happily and leapt into Ishan's lap as if they were old friends. Shovana, terrified at the sight of her son playing with a one-year-old wild leopard, was in awe of Ishan's calmness. He showed no fear, only joy, as the leopard playfully jumped in and out of his lap. While Shovana's heart raced with worry, Ishan remained at ease, unfazed by the leopard's size or the mystery in its wild eyes.

Another tender moment that stayed with Shovana occurred when Ishan was only a year-and-a-half-old. A wild cat had given birth to kittens in the dance shed at the back of their house. The cat, fiercely protective of her newborns, hissed and growled at anyone approaching her kittens. Yet one day, to Shovana's shock, little Ishan waddled out of the shed with a newborn kitten in his tiny hands, milk bottle still hanging from his mouth. The cat, who had snarled at everyone else, remained silent, seemingly trusting the toddler with her baby. It was as if Ishan had a quiet understanding with animals, even at that tender age.

Ishan shares his perspective with a laugh: 'When we lived on Pandara Road, we didn't have pets, just plenty of stray dogs and cats around. I never feared them; in fact, I found them fascinating even as a kid. I was a restless child, but animals had this calming effect on me. Somehow, they always responded to me with the same calm.

'There was a 'mamma cat' who had kittens and decided to make her home in the shed at our house. She didn't let anyone near her kittens—except me. I could pick up the kittens and play with them, and she didn't mind. Everyone was worried she might hurt me, but she accepted me ultimately.

'My dad was a nature lover, and every year, he'd take me to wildlife sanctuaries. He had fantastic luck spotting tigers whenever he went alone, but we'd never see one when I was with him. Eventually, I joked that I must be kryptonite for tigers.

'Now, seeing our kids developing their relationships with animals is fun. When we visited Jaipur, Emil, who was just two-and-a-half at the time, showed zero fear of the big elephants. He ran straight toward one, thrilled, and the elephant handler even let him take a ride. Emil waved 'bye' to us like he was setting off on an adventure. Suri, our middle one, likes animals too but isn't as intense about it. Lyla, on the other hand, is very interested in animals but much more cautious than I ever was.'

'I love animals, but it's clear that animals adore Ishan,' says Perkha Ahmed, Ishan's wife. 'I've seen stray cats walk right up to him as if they've known him forever. Once, in Vienna, a cat fell head over paws for him and started bringing him dead birds as gifts. I love animals, but I don't share Ishan's effortless connection with them.'

Shovana writes in one of her letters to Ishan:

> Looking back, one remembers the lovely visit to the northeast in May 2000 and also our visit to Bobby's Resort, Karnataka. Your love for animals came to the fore. The way you handled that young leopard at Bobby's Resort and were not even scared playing with him reminded me of the time when, as a two-year-old, you could walk around, milk bottle hanging from your mouth, with the kittens of a wild cat in front of the mother cat and not being harmed by her. How did you take care of the orphan little street pups who had made the Austrian embassy their home whenever you were here on vacation? You got their inoculations, vaccinations done, and later their sterilisation! What is it in you that makes even the

wildest of animals tame in your presence? It must be your innate gentleness and goodness that must be sending the right vibrations. Darling, do not ever lose it!

As Ishan grew, his love for animals expanded. He was why Shovana and her husband, Herbert, took a rickety rickshaw to Old Delhi to buy birds for him. Later, she found herself frequenting aquariums to purchase fish. Ishan's love for pets was boundless, and when he grew tired of asking for a sibling, he made an earnest request: 'Mamma, if you can't give me a brother or sister, then give me a dog, please!' That request was much easier to fulfil, and soon Ishan had his beloved beagle, Tessa, a faithful and trusting companion.

Ishan recalls: 'As a kid, I threw all caution to the wind around animals, and thankfully, I lucked out with them. Playgrounds, though? Those were my absolute nemesis. I had countless falls, stitches, and accidents. For me, a swing was far more dangerous than any dog.'

'I had an accident in kindergarten and ended up in the hospital with stitches. The school called my Mom, assuring her not to panic, but of course, she panicked. She rushed to the hospital, only to find me just waking up after the procedure.

'When I opened my eyes, she looked at me nervously and said, "Ishan, please get out of bed." Before I could even process what was happening, she fainted and took over my hospital bed!

'So, there I was, sitting with fresh stitches, waiting for *her* to wake up. The doctors and nurses fussed over me for three hours, even giving me a Coca-Cola to keep me entertained. When my Mom finally woke up, I asked, "Mom, are you feeling better now?" She smiled weakly and said, "Yeah, I'm fine. Let's go home."' It was quite the role reversal—me with stitches, her with the drama!' Ishan has a good chuckle here.

To young Ishan, every performance of his mother's was mesmerising, and in his eyes, she was the most excellent dancer in the world. Still, he remembers that the theme of *Mukti Lekha* resonated deeply with him, especially its exploration of the mother-child relationship. As a child, he was captivated by this performance.

'For me, it wasn't just about the moments on stage—it was about the energy, the creative magic that unfolded in real life. I loved witnessing the rehearsals, the interactions between my mother and Jwala mama, the singing, dancing, and the dynamic exchange of ideas. Our home was a hub of creativity, and I had the privilege of seeing performances take shape from the beginning. Scripts, lyrics, and music were written and refined right before my eyes, with everyone contributing and correcting one another. Watching such moments felt precious, like being part of something extraordinary,' says Ishan.

'Some settings of her performances, like the ones in Khajuraho, were especially magical. I still remember the admiration her rendition of Kalidasa's *Shakuntala* received in Vienna from our friends. Unlike the audience, who encountered the finished story in the theatre, I experienced it from start to finish. Those countless hours in the living room, sipping Limca while my Mom and Ramu Gandhi debated ideas, were formative for me.

'I developed a deep appreciation for an artist's work because I had a rare insight into what happens behind the curtain—the countless hours of hard work and dedication that go unnoticed by the audience. It gave me a profound understanding of the creative process and the beauty of its unfolding.'

The adage goes, "Nothing grows under a banyan tree," emphasising how towering figures can sometimes overshadow those around them. Yet, when Ishan is asked how it felt to grow up under the shadow of his mother, the illustrious Shovana Narayan, he offers a refreshing perspective. 'I didn't grow under her shadow; I grew in her spotlight.'

Unlike a banyan tree that often monopolises the sunlight, Shovana ensured her nurturing presence didn't stifle Ishan's individuality. Instead, she acted as a canopy of care, occasionally trimming her branches of influence to let the sunlight of opportunities and self-discovery reach him.

Shovana cultivated an environment where Ishan could grow as his most authentic self by allowing space for his thoughts, choices, and personality to flourish. In her way, she redefined the metaphor—proving that with intention, even a banyan tree can foster vibrant growth beneath its shelter as long as it remembers to share the sunlight.

She cherished the purity and beauty of her son's heart, admiring his innate empathy and kindness. She took great pride in watching these qualities flourish in Ishan, nurtured by his daily experiences.

Ishan's sensitivity, especially towards orphans, the poor, and the needy, wasn't just an innate quality; Shovana had consciously nurtured this empathy through many small but meaningful incidents, ensuring he wasn't swayed by peer pressure or materialism. She was careful to instil in him a sense of being grounded, steering him away from a love for brands or superficial measures of worth. She believed in shaping her son Ishan's worldview by exposing him to experiences that nurture an open mind free from social biases.

Rather than shielding him from situations that could be misinterpreted, she embraced them as teaching moments.

One such instance came early in the year when Ishan, having

picked up a comment from their house staff, mentioned that 'cocktail parties were bad.' Shovana, alarmed and intrigued by her young son's perception, took an unconventional approach.

Instead of dismissing his curiosity or leaving it unaddressed, she called Hans Kaufmann, the Austrian trade commissioner, to ask if she could bring a rather unexpected guest to the party—her young son. Hans agreed, amused at the idea, and that evening, Ishan toddled alongside his mother to attend his first cocktail party. Upon arrival, Hans looked around for the 'guest' Shovana had mentioned, only to be met with laughter when she pointed down to where Ishan was peeking from behind her.

At the party, Ishan comfortably mingled with the guests, chatting up ladies and charming the waitstaff, who happily kept him supplied with soft drinks. It wasn't just an amusing outing; it was a thoughtful lesson in demystifying environments that often come with social stigmas.

Through these small yet meaningful experiences, Shovana instilled in Ishan the ability to think independently, free from preconceived notions. Her deliberate efforts aimed to nurture a person who would not be influenced by superficial labels or biases but would cultivate a transparent, open, and discerning mind.

***

One freezing Delhi winter in 1997-98 stands out in her memory. They were travelling, and Ishan, along with another young boy, noticed a nearly unclad ten-year-old beggar at the Safdarjung road crossroad. While his companion dismissed the boy's hardship with a casual remark about children like him being accustomed to such weather, Ishan's heart was troubled. With genuine concern, he turned to his mother and asked if he could give his old cardigan to the young boy.

Shovana quietly approved, proud of the compassion her son displayed.

Ishan eagerly handed over the cardigan, feeling like he had made a slight difference.

But a few days later, they saw the boy again, still in the same threadbare condition, begging in the cold. Puzzled, Ishan wondered aloud if the cardigan was perhaps being shared with his siblings, providing warmth to others in the family. Though they never found out, it deeply affected Ishan, who continued asking his mother about the boy after returning to Vienna.

This simple yet profound moment reaffirmed Shovana's belief that she had raised a son who could see beyond privilege and feel for others—a young man whose heart remained tender, no matter the world around him.

Despite her demanding dual career as a renowned Kathak dancer and a high-ranking government official, she was deeply committed to ensuring that her son, Ishan, grew up with the correct values. With her gentle guidance, she helped Ishan navigate through life's pressures, particularly those of materialism and peer influence.

***

One such moment occurred when Ishan was about seven or eight years old, just starting to become aware of brand names, possibly from television ads or conversations with his school friends. It was a warm day in May, and he asked Shovana to buy him a pair of sports shoes. They visited several stores around Connaught Place, and Ishan fixated on well-known brands, was reluctant to try anything else. The expensive shoes didn't quite fit right, but the allure of having what his friends wore kept him drawn to the brand names.

Shovana gently tried to explain the practicality of opting for non-branded shoes, especially since his feet were still growing and the shoes wouldn't last long. But the pull of peer pressure weighed on him, and he resisted.

She suggested they take a walk and think it over to shift the focus.

As they wandered, they noticed barefoot urchins trying to sell them small trinkets.

Suddenly, Shovana had an idea. 'Ishan let's try walking barefoot like them,' she said. Intrigued, he agreed. They both removed their shoes and began walking along the hot pavement, attracting curious stares from passers-by. It was one of the hottest summers Delhi had experienced, and soon the burning concrete began to hurt their feet. While Shovana struggled, Ishan bore it surprisingly well. They quickly sprinted across the road, put their shoes back on, and resumed their window shopping.

After a while, Ishan quietly said, 'Mamma, let's buy the ordinary ones.'

Shovana, wanting to be sure, asked, 'Ishan, are you sure? Are you saying this because I've pressured you?'

'No, Mamma. The brand-name shoes didn't fit well, nor did the others. But between the two, the ordinary ones were more comfortable.' After a pause, he added, 'You were right about my feet growing. I'll outgrow them soon anyway.'

After a thoughtful silence, Ishan said, 'Mamma, since we're saving money by not buying expensive shoes, can I have ten rupees?'

Surprised, she asked, 'Sure, but why?'

'I want to give it to the young boy selling plastic toys. He had no shoes. May I?'

Overwhelmed with pride, Shovana happily agreed. In that moment, she knew Ishan had learned a valuable lesson—one far greater than anything brand names could offer. He had seen the futility of succumbing to peer pressure, and more importantly, he had recognised the value of kindness.

With a twinkle in his eye, Ishan added, 'Maybe next time, I'll find brand-name shoes that are more comfortable.' Shovana laughed, knowing that, at that moment, her son had grown in wisdom and heart.

***

Ishan chuckles, recalling his eighteenth birthday, 'It was a big day, no doubt—*huge* for my Mom. The present she gave me—letters soaked in love, was overwhelming, something I'll never forget. Mom can pull it off. It's in her nature. But my dad? Poor Dad! I could tell he had been roped into it. He even admitted that Mom had been 'haunting' him to write some for months before my birthday, pushing him into action!'

Ishan laughs heartily. 'And my Mom's memory—wow. It's like she's a walking telephone directory and address book all rolled into one. She knows not just *who* someone is but *where* they live—down to the colony, the floor, the block. We're all amazed by it. But my dad? I genuinely feel sorry for him imagining him having to dig through encyclopaedias, old newspapers, clippings, and photos. While we all have smartphones that instantly show us metadata about when and where a photo was taken, he had to rack his brain to recall all those details!' His face lights up with surprise, fun, and admiration as he continues, 'It's incredible how meticulous she is when it comes to the people she loves. I mean, she's just amazing.'

Perkha, smiling softly, adds, 'That's what inspires me. For all my kids' birthdays, I write them letters. I talk about the year they've had. I don't know how much they'll appreciate it now, but when I look back, I'll feel good knowing I've captured those moments for them.'

Ishan found fulfilment in carving his path, free from any unspoken expectation to follow in his mother's footsteps as a dancer. Shovana always reminded him that the accurate measure of success lay not in his chosen career but in the kind of human being he became.

Today, Ishan is an accomplished corporate finance advisor and a deeply sensitive and gentle soul, reflecting his parents' values and upbringing, emphasising character over convention.

'That was her *beej mantra*: always keeping my values and principles intact. She repeated it often, like drops wearing down a stone, ingraining it deeply in me. The specific path I took in life was secondary to her. I remember accompanying Mom and nani to Birju Maharaj ji's home every week, for coffee and conversations. One day, he asked me, "*Beta, tum bhi nachoge*?" I instinctively knew I wouldn't be a dancer, and I was never pressured to follow that path. Mom's career didn't dictate mine. What influenced me most was her approach to life and her work ethic.'

Ishan does, however, love music. He used to play the piano—a hobby he regrets not continuing—and wants to return to it. For him, music isn't about a specific instrument but a broader appreciation for the arts and finer sensibilities.

'Most people only see the finished product of an artist's work and assume it's easy. A friend once told me, "I want to be an artist," and I replied, "Then you'll need to work hard." She said, "No, you just need to feel and act like one." I laughed and told her she had no idea what it takes.'

Mom has the tiniest feet but the most beautiful ones in the whole world

Ishan says he has seen firsthand the dedication, long hours, setbacks, loneliness, and sacrifices that go into being an artist.

'Mom's 'invisible hours'—writing, revising, rehearsing, sitting at her computer—showed me that being an artist takes relentless persistence and an unwavering commitment to the craft.'

Shovana, says that Ishan believes in having it all and rarely takes 'no' for an answer. However, she approaches all issues with gentleness and patience rather than rudeness or force. She's incredibly focused on her goals, even if they don't always know what their goal for the day is—she always has one.

One of the most profound lessons Ishan has learned from her is that waiting for perfection often means waiting forever. The world rarely rewards those who hesitate until everything is just right—it celebrates those who start, who act, and who learn along the way.

'She has shown me that success isn't about having a flawless plan but the courage to take the first step, even when it feels messy or uncertain. That fearless determination to begin, despite the odds, is what truly sets her apart. If someone tells her something is difficult, her immediate response is, "Why? I'm going to do both."'

In Ishan's view, his mother is a remarkable blend of physical and spiritual strength. She believes that if your mind isn't strong, your body will falter, and vice versa. Both must be in harmony.

'Her example has taught me the importance of balance—never compromising on either family or work. She's shown me that it's possible to do both.'

Kaleidoscope

The morning sun filtered through the curtains, casting a warm glow over the room as Ishan and Perkha sat side by side on the couch, their fingers intertwined. Outside, the giggles of their little ones—Emil, Suri, and Lyla—mingled with the crisp air. Shovana, their spirited 74-year-old grandmother, whom they lovingly called Oma, joined the children, her laughter ringing out as she played with them.

Emil, in the middle of one of his dramatic tantrums, came and sulked on Perkha's lap, his tiny face set in defiance. 'Alright, young man,' Oma teased with a playful glint in her eye, 'if you don't cheer up, I'm going to play your piano—and not well, mind you!' Emil's eyes widened in alarm, the hint of a smile betraying his amusement. Sliding off Perkha's lap, still pouting but now intrigued, he began chasing Oma around the room, desperate to save his beloved piano from impending doom. Their laughter, shrieks, and mock protests created a symphony of familial joy, the perfect backdrop to the quiet moment Ishan and Perkha shared.

As they gazed at the lively scene unfolding before them, their conversation drifted to memories of their own love story and the inspiration they had drawn from Ishan's parents. 'They taught us so much without ever saying a word,' Ishan murmured, his voice tinged with emotion. Perkha squeezed his hand gently, her eyes glistening. 'They showed us that love isn't about erasing differences—it's about embracing them,' she echoed, her voice soft yet firm.

Ishan smiled, his mind briefly wandering to the home he grew up in, where his parents, Shovana and Herbert, had built a life rooted in respect, trust, and mutual faith. Their marriage had transcended cultural and national boundaries, creating a haven of harmony where individuality flourished. These lessons, learned not through lectures but by observing their daily lives, had become the bedrock of his relationship with Perkha.

Now, as they watched their children grow in a household that celebrated diversity and individuality, Ishan and Perkha knew they were continuing a legacy—a mosaic of love, respect, and shared dreams that would echo across generations.

'While many focus on differences, for us, it's about celebrating similarities,' shares Perkha. 'Both of us grew up in educated, loving families with multicultural influences.'

Ishan rebounds her sentiment: 'When I met Perkha, I felt an instant connection—she understood me, and I understood her. Another shared experience was that sense of being both at home everywhere and a foreigner everywhere. I've often been asked whether I'm Indian or Austrian, and Perkha has faced similar questions. That mutual understanding brought us closer.'

Shovana's family is a beautiful blend of multicultural backgrounds. Shovana, an Indian, is married to Herbert, an Austrian. Their son, Ishan, embodies a harmonious blend of both cultures and his wife, Perkha Ahmed, brings her Pashtoon heritage into the fold, creating a truly global family.

Perkha, meaning 'dewdrops,' has roots in Peshawar, though

she was born and raised in New York. Every summer, she would visit Peshawar, reconnecting with her heritage. Her family is a traditional Pashtun one, and she grew up surrounded by a large extended family, most of whom also lived in New York.

She studied political science in New York and worked extensively in narcotics, including a few years in Islamabad. Afterwards, she returned to Johns Hopkins, where she met Ishan.

Their relationship blossomed in a diverse setting. 'We met at Johns Hopkins University in Washington, where we studied international relations—an inherently international environment. Our paths crossed at the India-China conference, where we began talking, and soon, we found ourselves part of a tight-knit group of mutual friends. It was a small university with a vibrant, multicultural community, which made everything feel natural,' recalls Perkha.

Ishan adds, 'What made our bond even more special was that we never had to choose between each other and our friends. We shared common friendships and cherished those connections. It was an organic and beautiful mix, much like our relationship itself.'

Following their marriage, Ishan secured a job in Vienna while she landed a remote position based in America. This flexibility allowed her to move to Vienna and work remotely.

Their first child, Lyla, was born in 2016, and their second, Suri, arrived in 2019. After Suri's birth, she took a one-year break from work due to the lack of maternity leave in the US, marking a challenging phase as it was her first time not working. During this period, she focused on consulting and research. In 2021, their youngest, Emil, was born.

By 2022, she had joined the UN Office on Drugs and Crime (UNODC) in Vienna, returning to her work in narcotics, explicitly addressing the global challenge of synthetic drugs. Her role involves significant international travel. Summers are often spent visiting family in America, a connection Ishan values deeply. His efforts to keep in touch with their immediate and extended families reflect the influence of his parents, Shovana and Herbert.

How did Perkha react upon learning that her future mother-in-law was a renowned Kathak dancer?

Initially, she didn't fully comprehend the magnitude of Shovana Narayan's stature.

'When I first heard Ishan's Mom was a classical dancer, I thought it was a casual hobby—something similar to what many of my Indian American friends practised growing up,' she admitted. It wasn't until a mutual friend, Neha, excitedly exclaimed, "You're dating the son of a celebrity who's always in magazines!" that the reality sank in. Shovana Mom wasn't just a dancer; she was a living legend in the world of classical art. Interestingly, this realisation came not from Ishan, who remained modest about his mother's fame, but from the enthusiastic reactions of those around him.

'My first real taste of her world was at our Indian wedding. It was my first time in India—our first wedding had been in New York—and I was already in awe of her dancing, YouTube videos, and overall presence. I even told her I'd love to try dancing myself one day! I bonded instantly with Shruti Didi, her oldest student, who had flown to New York to attend our first wedding. Meeting Shovana mamma's students in India was like stepping into this big, warm family.

'Even when she isn't dancing, her energy and stamina are awe-inspiring. Attending four or five events daily is no small feat, but her passion drives her. She exemplifies that there's no age limit to pursuing what you love. Whether writing a book, picking up a new hobby, or exploring a fresh passion, she shows that it's never too late to start something new.'

Perkha shares that she has always been open and transparent about herself and never pretended to be an artist. She never felt pressured to conform because Shovana has never fit the stereotype of an overbearing mother-in-law. Instead, Shovana is an exceptionally creative, intelligent, and sensitive individual who respects everyone's freedom to explore and nurture their talents and interests. Her boundless creativity keeps her so engrossed that she has neither the time nor the inclination to micromanage the lives of those around her.

Shovana has consistently appreciated and valued Perkha's unique strengths. Coming from a large family, Perkha is well-versed in navigating the mix of personalities, interests, and the inevitable ups and downs accompanying such dynamics. In contrast, Ishan's family is smaller, allowing her to adapt and address challenges gracefully.

'Mamma's natural curiosity drives her to understand the essence of things deeply. She recognises that no one exists in isolation and delves into the roots of ideas, traditions, and practices. This thoughtful approach is evident in her writing. She is an excellent communicator. She seamlessly explains complex traditions and mythology to children in simple, modern terms that resonate with their context. This ability to simplify and connect comes from her extensive experience as a performer. Having danced for a wide range of audiences, she understands that not every performance—or message—is meant for everyone. She adapts her communication style effortlessly, whether engaging with a villager or a senior Austrian diplomat.'

For Herbert, the foundation of a strong relationship lies in trust and respect, not constant togetherness. Physical distance is manageable when trust is solid, as seen in many couples balancing careers in different locations. The key question, he believes, is whether you genuinely trust and respect each other. If the answer is yes, everything else aligns naturally. A successful partnership, he emphasises, isn't about trying to change your partner but accepting them as they are.

'Herbert could only make it for three days when I served as the Assistant Returning Officer for the Presidential election. I was constantly busy during those days and could only spare a few hours. Despite that, he understood the demands of my role without complaint,' Shovana shares.

On a closer look, her achievements reflect her incredible time management and discipline. She essentially balanced two careers seamlessly. Her family never burdened her with guilt, which allowed her to flourish. It's a reminder that we're all part of a constellation—our relationships with colleagues, family, and children contribute to our career success.

'What I've learned from Mamma's life and career is that while everyone sees her as a singular celebrity, much of her success is rooted in her supportive community—her mother, sister, son, and above all, her husband who stood by her. Her talent is undeniable, but it thrived because of a strong support system, like a garden nurtured by those who wanted to see her bloom,' Perkha maintains.

Shovana and Herbert lived on different continents, yet they bridged the distance with unwavering commitment. With no direct calls available, communication was challenging, but they ensured they met every quarter. Shovana would travel to join Herbert for Christmas, while Herbert spent his vacations in India, cherishing their time together despite the geographical divide.

'My parents are my ultimate role models for romance,'

Ishan shares with heartfelt admiration. 'How do you sustain a long-distance marriage for so many years? They made it look so effortless and endearing. My dad was in Ethiopia, and my Mom was in Delhi. Back then, long-distance calls between India and Ethiopia were nearly impossible—neither country was significantly developed in communication. But they found the sweetest solution. They used audio tapes to stay connected. I remember seeing how it worked when Dad and I were in Vienna. He would sit in the living room, entirely focused, listening to a tape my Mom had sent. Then, he'd carefully load a blank tape, record his reply, and send it back to her. It was their way of bridging the miles with love and effort. What truly stood out, though, and something I strive to emulate with Perkha, is the unwavering trust they shared. Without trust, a relationship is built on shaky ground. But my parents' bond was solid, built on faith in each other and the determination to stay connected, no matter the distance,' Ishan shares.

Herbert continued his ambassadorial journey in 1988 with a posting to Iran. In 1991, he became the head of the Department for Development Cooperation at the Federal Ministry for Foreign Affairs. Two years later, in 1993, he was appointed Chief of Personnel at the ministry, followed by his role as Deputy Director General for Administrative Affairs in 1995. From 1998 to 2002, he served as Austria's ambassador to India, with concurrent accreditation to Bangladesh, Bhutan, the Maldives, Nepal, and Sri Lanka. He was appointed ambassador to Thailand from 2002 to 2005, where he was also co-accredited to Cambodia, Laos, and Myanmar.

Living continents apart, Shovana and Herbert maintained their bond through a steady rhythm of quarterly visits, relying on limited communication. Letters, long-distance phone calls, cassette tapes, and occasional telegrams were their lifelines, but the physical separation was sometimes profoundly felt. There were moments when the distance became almost unbearable. Shovana, known for her unyielding resilience, would sometimes crumble like a sack of dust in the face of fatigue, once even on stage—her leg going stiff, yet her poise never betraying the pain she was in. Herbert, always radiating love, stood steadfast as her rock, supporting her from afar. But even he, ever the source of strength, faced his battles with illness, each day weighed down by her absence. Despite the challenges, neither entertained the thought of the other sacrificing their pursuits.

In 2023, she dealt with personal and family health issues, including Herbert's prolonged illness, her eye problems, and skin treatment. The year 2023 was one of the most challenging times in Shovana's life. On 25 April, while rehearsing for a performance scheduled for the next day, she received a devastating call from her son: 'Papa is in a coma.' Shocked and unprepared, she faced a packed schedule with performances on 26, 27, and 29 April, 2 and 4 May, including one in Bhopal before the Chief Minister. She was also set to fly to Vienna on 11 May. Overwhelmed, she rushed home, booked a flight, and left for the airport at midnight, frantically cancelling everything on the way.

'We witnessed their love in its purest form when Dad was unwell,' Perkha shares emotionally. 'There was this raw, unfiltered longing in his eyes for her. She had to return to India while he was in the hospital, his health failing, and all he wanted—more than anything—was to be with her. I'll never forget when he woke up and saw her by his side. The look in his eyes said everything words could never convey. He was so frail, unable to speak, yet their communication was profound—an unspoken conversation through their eyes. It was louder than any words could ever be.'

Much of that year was spent postponing commitments as Shovana's priority shifted entirely to Herbert's recovery. In Vienna, Ishan and Perkha cared for him until she arrived.

Ishan recalls, 'When Dad first slipped into a coma, Mom wasn't with us in Vienna. His decline was shockingly fast, as if overnight. What started with what we thought was a simple infection spiralled into sepsis in just two days—a word I didn't even know then.

'We had a bed arranged at the hospital through a doctor friend of ours. I remember the check-in process vividly—we had tea and talked, and he read his newspaper in the hospital room. It felt routine. But within hours, everything changed. He fell into a coma.

'I had gone home briefly when my friend called to tell me things were worsening. I didn't fully grasp what was happening, but I knew it was serious. I called Mom, and she initially didn't even entirely understand its gravity. I could hear the rhythm of the tabla in the background, the familiar sound of *ta ta thai*. I did a video call and turned the camera to show her the scene—the tubes, the machines, the hospital bed.

'Ironically, the chaos seemed almost theatrical. The moment Mom saw the situation on our video call, she dropped everything—left her bags at the dance school, got into a car, and booked the next flight en route to the airport. By the very next flight, she was in Vienna.

'When I went to visit Dad in the hospital, I briefly stepped out to talk to a doctor. When I returned, I couldn't find Mom in the room. Panic set in as I rushed to the other side of the bed—there she was, fainted on the floor.

'So, there I was, in the Intensive Care Unit (ICU), with Dad in a coma on one side and my unconscious mother on the other. For a moment, I stood there, taken aback at how everyone seemed to be dropping like flies.

'As it turned out, she hadn't mentioned that she was supposed to have dental surgery in Delhi. Her pain and exhaustion had caught up with her. Once she regained consciousness, I carried her to the car and took her to another hospital. It was tough juggling one crisis after another, feeling like the universe had an ironic sense of humour in how it tested us.

'It all happened so quickly, so unpredictably. It wasn't just an existential threat to his life—it was a threat to the life we knew as a family. We grappled with this together, struggling to hold on to one another as everything shifted.'

Herbert remained hospitalised for nearly five months, until the end of September, during which he briefly emerged from a coma. However, he faced a prolonged battle with severe septicaemia, which significantly affected his blood pressure, hearing, and mobility. The recovery process was gruelling—he had to relearn how to sit, stand, and walk. Snowy months made life in a wheelchair even more difficult, but with time and determination, he progressed to using a walker.

'As a couple, Mom and Dad inspire me in countless ways. They have had incredibly successful lives, often coexisting on different continents, yet their relationship remains strong and unique. Last year, when Papa fell ill, Mamma made the remarkable decision to halt her life as she knew it and ultimately relocate to Vienna to be by his side,' Ishan adds.

Perkha praises Shovana for her dedication to Herbert's well-being despite her busy schedule, and for how she has repeatedly gone out of her way to provide care whenever any medical condition has arisen.

'Life in Vienna vastly differed from what she was accustomed to, but she adapted without complaint. While we were nearby, our work commitments kept us busy. Mamma took on the household responsibilities, from cooking meals to managing daily tasks. She started learning everything from scratch and approached it with love and grace. She even experimented with cooking, which came from a deep place of care.

'Most of my exposure to her, though, has been during her visits to Vienna, where she's not 'the legend.' Here, she's a writer, a mother, a wife, and a doting grandmother. She's written most of her books while staying with us! While I've only seen a handful of her performances—each stunning—most of what I know about her illustrious career comes from stories others tell.

I genuinely believe Papa is with us today because of her unwavering dedication. Typically, her visits would last no more than a month, but she stayed for half a year this time. She had to turn down many significant events and opportunities during that period, but she did so willingly and with a smile. It was truly admirable.'

'There were two moments when Ishan and I nearly lost hope. I was on a visa that had to be continuously extended, and I ended up staying in Vienna for eight months. We returned to India just before Christmas. Life has no hard-and-fast rules or manuals.

There's no set formula to follow. It's the sensitivity, care, and love that sustain a relationship. Love is a vast world, encompassing everything within it,' Shovana shares.

It's a marriage founded on trust, weathering life's ups and downs with resilience. Positivity and a shared sense of humour have been the anchors, helping them navigate external challenges and ironic situations.

Perkha has a wonderfully playful way of describing Shovana as a grandmother. When asked about it, she says, 'Seeing your parents become grandparents is like watching them turn into children again—it's so beautiful.'

As a mother and mother-in-law, Shovana is the perfect mix of gentleness, patience, and unconditional love. But when the kids are around, there's a surprising twist: she makes the most noise! The usually composed and graceful Shovana turns into the life of the party, matching the kids' energy, beat for beat.

'In Vienna,' Perkha laughs, 'we live in flats, and the neighbours downstairs have had their fair share of surprises.

They'd come knocking on our door, complaining about the racket, assuming it was the kids. Little did they know, it wasn't just our children—their grandmother was leading the charge!'

The image of the legendary Shovana, known for her poise and artistry, letting loose and having a ball with her grandkids, is a delightful contrast.

'Last year, Mamma was overseeing the installation of a lift in the house for Papa—a project that turned out to be anything but smooth. The workers kept making mistakes in measurements and dragged the process along for months. After three long months of delays, spiralling costs, and endless excuses, Mamma finally hit her limit. She yelled at them in a rare burst of frustration, making it crystal clear she wouldn't tolerate being taken for a ride any longer. "This is for my husband," she said, the pressure visibly weighing on her.

'When Ishan told me about it later, I could hardly believe it—Mamma losing her cool? Impossible! Even the kids were floored. Overhearing the conversation between Ishan in Vienna and Mamma back in India, they exclaimed in disbelief, "Oma? Oma got angry! She never gets angry at anyone!"

'When we shared the kids' reaction with her later, she had a good chuckle about it. It was as if this one rare moment of fiery rage had turned into a legendary family story. For someone whose patience is practically saintly, this might just be the *one* time she truly lost it—and even then, for all the right reasons.'

With her characteristic wit, Shovana recounts another amusing yet awkward incident at the Mauritius airport that led to a notable change in her passport. When she and Herbert arrived, the protocol officer, there to receive Herbert as the accredited Austrian ambassador to Mauritius, mistook Shovana for a local passenger. Assuming she was straying from the deplaning route, he gestured for her to join the other passengers. Herbert, striding ahead, quickly clarified, 'My wife.' The officer's reaction was incredulous—he looked Shovana up and down and asked Herbert, 'Are you sure?' Though Shovana found the situation humorous, Herbert was less amused.

The officer's doubts only grew when he saw Shovana's blue Indian passport instead of an Austrian diplomatic one, and to complicate matters further, her passport didn't prominently display Herbert's name.

Later, Herbert suggested making his name more visible in her documents. Upon returning, Shovana had 'Traxl' inserted between her names, ensuring no such confusion would arise again.

'People have been asking as to where we would be settling down. Where would we like to go? It will be both Delhi and Vienna for me, and I think it will be the same for Herbert. Vienna is a city that I have always loved. In my growing up years, I was fascinated by its history and particularly its role as the cultural capital of Europe. Vienna has always fascinated me with its rich cultural history, natural beauty, inviting *heurigens*, museums, churches, and palaces, and the atmosphere full of music, operas, and concerts. I always joke with Herbert that I married him because of the music and waltz.'

Anjan Banerjee reflects on Shovana's decision to remain in Delhi: 'Ours was a transferable profession, but Shovana never left Delhi, which caused some resentment among many. Dance was her passion, and she knew she couldn't leave it behind. Despite her commitment to both careers, she balanced them effortlessly, excelling in both. Highly qualified and deeply sincere in her work, Shovana stood apart from those eager to transfer abroad. She was clear from the beginning that Delhi was where she was meant to be.'

While many have speculated on her reasons, Shovana has always been fascinated with Delhi's rich history. Having lived in Delhi since 1962, she sees the city differently from those who find it chaotic. To her, it's a place filled with stories of courage, romance, and grandeur. Beneath its busy streets lies a rich history and countless memories, preserved in its ancient stones and ever-changing spirit.

Kaun Jaaye Zauq is one of Shovana Narayan's celebrated dance productions that draws upon the poetry of Sheikh Ibrahim Zauq's, *Kaun jaaye Zauq par Dilli ki galiyan chhod kar,* reflects her deep attachment to Delhi. This city symbolises the essence of culture, intellectualism, and creativity.

At eighty-four plus, Herbert is a gentleman whose eyes are the most striking thing about him—brilliant blue, like the sky on a crisp spring morning, sparkling with the same mischievous light you'd expect in the eyes of a child. His demeanour is gentle, with a kindness that seems to radiate from within, matched perfectly by his quick wit and infectious good humour. When he speaks of the love of his life, there's a magical transformation: his entire face lights up, as if under a spell that's as powerful now as the day they met. Together, he and Shovana have weathered forty-three years of life's ups and downs, but their charm as a couple remains untarnished. They pull each other's leg, gently correct one another, and complete each other's sentences, all with a playful ease that speaks of deep affection and mutual admiration.

Across Time and Space

Art has a way of dissolving boundaries, entwining hearts across nations in universal threads of love and fraternity. For true artists, the world becomes one vast stage where cultures converge and souls connect through the silent language of beauty and emotion. Shovana Narayan's dedication to Kathak has elevated her craft and drawn her into the orbit of some of the most luminous spirits in the world of art. These bonds, built on shared passion and mutual respect, have nurtured her compassion and deepened her spiritual essence.

The fluidity of an artist allows them to merge seamlessly into others' lives, finding kinship and synergy that transcends minor differences. Shovana's enduring relationship with stalwarts like Padma Bhushan recipients Pandit Rajan and Pandit Sajan Mishra exemplifies this harmonious exchange. Nurtured by her mother Lalita's warmth and hospitality, her home became a sanctuary for artists—a space where creativity blossomed and souls resonated. In this seamless merging of lives and art forms, Shovana has risen above boundaries.

Padma Bhushan awardees Pandit Rajan and Pandit Sajan

Mishra, the illustrious brothers of the Banaras Gharana, are torchbearers of a 350-year-old musical legacy, with the *sarangi* also passed down as part of their family legacy. For decades, they have graced global stages, enchanting audiences with their soulful artistry and earning admiration worldwide. Their enduring bond with Shovana spans over four decades.

Shovana frequently visited Pandit Birju Maharaj, who is Pandit Sajan's father-in-law, and in turn, Pandit Birju Maharaj often visited her home as well. With Shovana's mother, Lalita, being from Bihar, a strong connection was formed, naturally. Lalita, a sociable and welcoming figure, often hosted gatherings of artists at her home, fostering a warm environment for creative exchange.

'We often crossed paths at various performances, and Shovana ji always greeted us with warmth and affection. I vividly remember our time together in Russia in 1988. Her group and ours comprised eight artists each, making us a team of sixteen representing Hindustan. Our *jugalbandi* was received with immense appreciation by the audience. While we sang at sixteen concerts, she mesmerised everyone with her dance.

'Cars were arranged for the three leading artists—my brother Pandit Rajan Mishra, Shovana ji, and myself—to travel between venues. Often, we shared the same car when heading to the same place. At other times, we all travelled by bus, sharing light-hearted moments and laughter. We spent a month there as a team.

Food, however, was a challenge. The local bread was so tough that we'd eat only the soft middle and leave the hard crusts behind. Some of us, including Birju Maharaj ji, were strict vegetarians. He had wisely suggested we bring along Indian snacks and sweets, which turned out to be a blessing. Eventually, our manager noticed our difficulties and kindly arranged groceries to make things easier for us,' fondly recalls Pandit Sajan Mishra.

'Shakeel Ahmed and others prepared their non-vegetarian meals while we vegetarians longed for simple *ghar ka daal-chawal* or *khichdi*. Unfortunately, there were no proper vessels available to cook khichdi. We managed to find a wide yet shallow *laddoo* tray. Using some bricks to build a fire, we cooked khichdi in it. Since the tray was not deep enough, we couldn't add all the water in one go. The water kept evaporating, so we added a little more every two minutes, along with a pinch of salt. Despite the unconventional cooking method, the khichdi was so delicious that even the non-vegetarians joined us in the feast. Truly, *sahaj pake so khichdi hoye*—what cooks slowly becomes perfect.

'We had an interpreter with us, but Shovana ji once joked that she'd had her fill of all things Russian. Among our troupe was Shamim Ahmed, a talented tabla player. During one performance, we recreated an early morning scene at Jama Masjid radio station, where a tea seller called out, "*chai lo, chai lo*," as a radio played in the background. The interpreter attempted to translate the scene for the audience, but a hilarious moment ensued when the tea seller, caught up in the ambience, unconsciously began singing along to the radio tune of *Mohe Bhool Gaye Sanwariya*. Lost in the melody, he momentarily forgot he was supposed to be selling tea, leaving the audience in fits of laughter.'

Pandit Rajan and Pandit Sajan Mishra performed alongside Shovana Narayan on numerous occasions. Ranjana Narayan accompanied them for some programmes, even contributing her vocal talents during the performances.

'Our trip to Russia in 1988, as part of the Festival of India organised by the Indian Council for Cultural Relations (ICCR), was magical. We travelled from Delhi to Moscow, accompanied by the legendary Rajan and Sajan Mishra ji. I was the female vocalist in our group, while a male singer handled the male repertoire. Each performance showcased something different, keeping things exciting and dynamic,' Ranjana recounts.

Between the stage lights and the rehearsals behind the scenes, what truly stands out is the effortless way artists forge connections with the world around them. For an artist, every new place feels like a familiar rhythm, every face a potential friend, and every experience an extension of their creative journey. It's as if their art tunes their hearts to a universal frequency, allowing them to embrace the world with openness and warmth.

'In Russia, this spirit was palpable—not just in the audience's applause but in the smiles of locals, the kindness of strangers, and the shared laughter within the group. Through music, dance, or shared meals under the open sky, we found a way to make the universe our home, turning fleeting moments into lasting bonds.

'The mornings, however, were pure adventure. With three lively interpreters in tow, we'd pile into a bus and head out for daily picnics. We had a charming ritual of tying bottles with strings and submerging them in streams to chill them. Potatoes—or anything we could scavenge—became impromptu barbecue delights.

These little escapes left us refreshed and full of camaraderie. Our group of about twenty was unusually harmonious, devoid of the typical frictions that often arise on such trips. Rajan Bhaiya's razor-sharp humour kept us all in stitches, his laughter echoing through our travels. We were also fascinated by the *chai khana*, where people gathered on wooden cots in the evenings to enjoy tea. Our performances drew warm, enthusiastic audiences who made us feel incredibly welcome. Upon landing in each city, a particularly touching tradition greeted us—beautifully dressed women approached us with bread and salt, a timeless symbol of friendship and hospitality. It wasn't just a cultural exchange; it was a journey of connection, discovery, and laughter. Those days in Russia, with its scenic streams, hearty picnics, and receptive audiences, remain etched in my heart as a profoundly fulfilling and joyful experience,' Ranjana reminisces fondly.

'Our performances in the USSR went off very well. We toured and performed in several places, such as Moscow, Ashkhabad, Tashkent, Bukhara, Frunze, Alma-Ata, among others. During this tour, Ranju and I picked up a fair amount of Russian, and I started compering bits of my performances in Russian, for which I was applauded greatly. In one of my programmes, we received a standing ovation, so much so that we had to come back and perform again, not once, but many times! Such a response gladdened our hearts, I must say. Towards the end, I did abhinaya (expressional piece) to a beautiful and emotional Russian song called *Katyusha* that Ranju sang beautifully for me. We picked up a few Russian songs during this tour. Would you believe it? The audience was so deeply moved that many were brought to tears. When we finished, there was a brief, poignant silence, followed by a thunderous applause that filled the air,' Shovana shares with great joy.

The tour was a riot of laughter and adventure. Every day brought a feast of roast chicken and vegetables; afternoons often meant picnics by serene lakes, while nights turned into lively disco sessions. In Tashkent, the hilarity peaked when locals mistook Shovana for Shabana Azmi (courtesy her name) and a tall member of Rajan-Sajan's group for Amitabh Bachchan. Instead of correcting them, the mischievous troupe decided to play along, spinning tales so outlandish that even the most gullible would have second-guessed—but not in Tashkent! Watching the innocent crowd fall for the elaborate charade made everyone laugh, making the memories even sweeter.

Pandit Sajan holds Shovana in the highest regard, describing her as *karmath* (dedicated), particularly in light of the challenging decisions she has faced—whether it was navigating the loss of her father in a train accident or balancing the demands of managing her household while excelling in two professions. He also highlights her unwavering helpfulness, noting how she consistently supports her musicians and their families. According to Pandit Sajan, few artists embody such deep commitment to their craft while actively engaging in social causes, and Shovana stands out as one of them.

He attributes Shovana's refined artistic sensibilities and unique approach to the deep influence of her guru, Pandit Birju Maharaj. He acknowledges that her ability to blend tradition with innovation seamlessly stems from the guidance she received under Maharaj ji's mentorship. Observing his intricate choreography shaped her as a performer and instilled in her a profound understanding of art's emotional and spiritual dimensions. This invaluable tutelage gave her the tools to carve her niche while staying rooted in the classical essence of Kathak.

'Shovana has made significant contributions in her niche, likely influenced by her guru, Pandit Birju Maharaj ji, who considered her one of his favourite disciples. She observed his thought process, worldview, and artistic approach, learning to channel that into her performances. Maharaj ji composed numerous pieces that she enjoyed performing, and she was among the few fortunate disciples to receive personal instruction at home. From a young age, their lessons would often continue late into the evening after he finished his other classes. Her talent flourished under his guidance, both as an artist and a human being, nurtured in the *satsang* of her guru. She absorbed his teachings like a beej mantra, a seed that blossomed in the rich cultural and literary environment she grew up in. Now, as a guru herself, Shovana has sent countless disciples to the stage, and at seventy-four, she remains as passionate and dedicated to Kathak as when she first began.'

Travelling across the globe to perform exposes an artist to diverse cultures, perspectives, and artistic expressions, enriching their understanding of the universal language of art. It broadens their vision, fostering a deeper appreciation for the interconnectedness of humanity through creativity. This journey transforms the artist, allowing their craft to resonate with a more profound and inclusive essence.

Playing jugalbandi (duets) is one such tool. Jugalbandi is more than a duet—it is a celebration of harmony, a blending of forms, and a journey towards the divine. It transcends boundaries of discipline, weaving music and dance into a unified expression of art. In the spirit of collaboration, artists come together to explore their craft, inspiring and elevating each other. This union aims to lose oneself in the *kala* (art), connecting with the eternal. In every note sung and step danced, the artist seeks to complement and elevate their partner, creating moments of pure transcendence. True jugalbandi reflects that while the forms may differ, the goal remains—to touch the divine through the interplay of rhythm, melody, and expression.

The audience eagerly awaits the tender magic of jugalbandi or *sawal-jawab*. It unfolds like a playful conversation, beginning softly, almost like a whisper, only to swell with bursts of intensity, leaving everyone enchanted by its rhythm and charm.

'Jugalbandi represents a spirit of healthy competition, though we prefer to call it *sah-gaan*, where artists listen to one another, appreciating their craft and responding with their expression. Shovana ji shares this approach. We performed six jugalbandis with Pandit Birju Maharaj ji and Pandit Kishan Maharaj ji—five in India and the sixth in London. A memorable highlight was when Birju Maharaj ji danced to our composition, which felt like a great achievement for us. Jugalbandi is a collaboration. For example, if I am singing a *bandish* like *e ri e, mein kaise ghar jaun*, the dancer, or *nayika*, presents it through her bhav (expressions), and as we reach the climax, we perform the *sargam* while the nayika responds with her tatkar (footwork). All of this happens spontaneously, without prior rehearsals. Birju Maharaj ji often playfully complained, saying we never told him beforehand what we would sing, which was unfair.

'Though rehearsals are essential, and even Birju Maharaj ji was meticulous about rehearsing specific pieces, spontaneity was key in *jugalbandi*. Pandit Kishan Maharaj ji would instinctively catch the *chhand* of the dance without memorising the dance *bol.* Similarly, Birju Maharaj ji would absorb the song's fragrance after hearing just a few lines and start dancing to it.

'Our audience loved the *laykaari* and rhythmic interplay. We would also engage in *padhant,* and out of admiration, Birju Maharaj ji would often remark, "*tum gavaiyaa hokar bhi itna achcha padhte ho*!" (For a singer, you recite so well!)' Pandit Sajan remembers fondly.

Exploring the balance between *riyaz* and spontaneity, as well as the coordination between dance and music, he explains—

'Riyaz is essential, but what truly matters is the level of dedication and awareness you bring to it. *Tak tak tak tak—mein pyar paida karne ki koshish karni hai. Vo aisa ho jaye ki jaise aap phool ke upar tak tak tak tak kar rahe hain.* (You should aim to create love and delicacy in that sound as if tapping gently on a flower). Most stages today are wooden and equipped with mics to amplify the sound of your footwork. However, it's through this nuanced exploration and subtle research that you discover what we artists refer to as the *khushboo*—the fragrance in your *sangeet* (music).'

Pandit Sajan Mishra once asked Pandit Birju Maharaj ji's renowned disciples—Ram Mohan Maharaj, Kishan Mohan Maharaj, and Jai Kishan ji—how Maharaj ji 'tuned' himself before a performance, much like singers tune their *tanpura* or *swarmandal*. One disciple shared that it happened when Maharaj ji held his *ghoonghroo*, offered a *pranam*, kissed them, and put them on. Another said it was when Maharaj ji stretched his *anga* (limbs), aligning his body for the performance.

Listening to the conversation with keen interest, Pandit Birju Maharaj ji then turned to Pandit Sajan Mishra and asked when he thought this 'tuning' truly occurred.

Pandit Sajan responded that it wasn't during physical activities like *ang kholna* (stretching), *aradhya ko yaad karna* (remembering the divine), or *ghoonghroo choomna* (kissing the ankle bells). Instead, it was when Maharaj ji first stepped onto the stage and checked the foot mic, carefully sensing the spot where his feet would produce the most measured sound. His *ghoonghroo* never gave a *karkash dhwani* (harsh or jarring sound) but always had *madhurata* (sweetness), just like his *padhant*.

Pandit Birju Maharaj ji was pleasantly surprised by how closely this singer had observed this subtle tuning process before each performance.

Every moment holds a lesson for an artist. Pandit Rajan Mishra, for instance, found inspiration in Pandit Birju Maharaj ji, albeit indirectly. He once revealed that he often visualised Birju Maharaj performing bhav abhinaya while he sang. As he imagined his guru dancing to his music, his hands would float naturally, embodying the rhythm. Though some may have laughed at this, Pandit Rajan remained unfazed, saying, '*Main apne bheetar mein nach raha hoon jab main ga raha hoon.'* (I am dancing within while I am singing).

This seamless interplay of music and movement reflects the essence of a *sampurn kalakar* (complete artist), where a dancer sings within their dance, and a singer dances within their song.

A dancer need not literally sing, and a singer need not physically dance; it is about envisioning it. When you truly engage in this vision, the *jeevatma* enters your art. *Ahankar* (ego) blocks your ability to absorb music or any subtle artistic discourse fully. Without the right expression, *taav thunga* or *takit thunga* become hollow. Many may dance to *dhittam dhittam tak tak thun tat thun,* but the audience was filled with rapture when Birju Maharaj performed these steps. His body posture would transform, filled with *mulayamiyat* (softness). Only when a singer truly understands and responds to the essence of dance does divinity bless their music with *rasa*. Achieving this state of rasa is the path to the divine.

As a dance artist, if you are portraying *udveg* (intense emotion), it must be present but in a way that does not jolt the audience's sensibilities. For example, if you enact *Mahishasur Mardini,* your dance must reflect *veer rasa* (heroic emotion). Similarly, when singing a *bandish* in veer rasa, such as *badar ki dhamak suni*, the singer must be able to visualise the dhamak (rumble) of the cloud. To truly grasp this dhamak, the singer must live it in their mind, becoming the cloud. This principle applies to all art forms: artists must fully immerse themselves in their subject and become one with it.

'Seekhna shuru karte hi aapko tairna nahin aata. Aap pehle gote khate ho, paani moonh mein jata hai, phir tairna seekhte ho.'

(When you begin learning, you don't know how to swim.
At first, you struggle, swallowing water, and then you
learn to swim).

Being a sound artist and a good human is a blessing.

In art, an artist strives for love and truthfulness and carries a benevolent aura, constantly innovating and executing everything precisely.

Ananta Nrityam
The Eternal Dance

The sun dipped low over the ghats of Varanasi, painting the Ganga in hues of molten gold. The temple bells began their rhythmic tolling, mingling with the chants of priests preparing for the evening aarti. The river's bosom cradled countless earthen lamps, their flickering flames mirroring the stars just beginning to peek out. It was as if the universe had paused to revel in the magic of this eternal city.

Amidst this symphony of devotion, seated on the steps of the ghat, Bismillah Khan cradled his shehnai. The sound of its soulful notes had often become one with the evening breeze, a hymn to the Ganga. As passersby paused in awe, a curious American approached him, enraptured by the scene. Dressed in the casual confidence of a man who thought he understood the world; the visitor was visibly drunk on the intoxicating beauty of the place.

'Khan sahab,' the man said, his eyes wide with reverence, 'Your music, this place...it's heaven on earth. You must come to America and play your shehnai. We'll make it grander than anything here!'

Bismillah Khan, his fingers idly tracing the ridges of his instrument, looked up with a serene smile. The bells clanged, echoes still danced over the waters, and the air grew thick with incense.

'Hum nahin ja sakat hain, (I cannot go)' he replied, his voice steady and deeply rooted, 'kyunki yeh hamaar mamu ka ghar hai aur yeh hi hamaar ustad ki jagah hai. (Because this is my uncle's place, and this is my Guru's place.)'

Confused but undeterred, the American leaned forward, his eagerness almost childlike. 'We'll bring your house to America,' he offered with the confidence of a man used to bending the world to his will.

Bismillah Khan chuckled softly, his laughter as fluid and natural as the Ganga's current.'Aur Ganga? Oka ka? Ghanta baji hai vahan? Ganga ki lahar rahegi kaa tumhare America mein? Ganga ki arti ka ghanta aur lehar le jao, fir hum avat hain.' (And what about the Ganga? What about her? Do such sacred bells toll there? Will the Ganga's waves be there in your America? Take the Ganga's prayer bells and her waves; I will follow).

The American fell silent, perhaps for the first time, as the depth of those words sank in. Around them, the aarti had reached its crescendo. Flames swirled in perfect arcs, chants rose like waves, and the eternal and unyielding river carried the lamps' light forward, far beyond the horizon.

Bismillah Khan's music wasn't just the sound of shehnai; it was soul—a soul inseparable from its source, the sacred soil of Varanasi, the temple bells, and the Ganga's eternal embrace.

When an artist reaches this soulful connection with the arts, the experience transcends the material world. The music, dance, or art becomes a path to mysticism and inner awakening. Like a true *fakir* (ascetic), the artist detaches from worldly attachments and embraces a more profound, spiritual existence. This detachment from the *sthool* (the gross or material) and affinity with the *sookshm* (the subtle or spiritual) allows the artist to perceive the world in a way ordinary people cannot. Their art, in its purest form, reflects this higher consciousness, untouched by the fleeting concerns of everyday life.

The beauty of Indian classical music lies in its ability to evoke different emotions through *ragas*, each crafted for a specific time of day or season. With their unique sounds, these ragas carry a deep emotional essence (*khushboo*) that an artist must understand and feel from the heart. It is not just about playing the notes; it is about connecting with the raga's mood—whether it's the peacefulness of *Raga Yaman*, the joy of *Raga Malhar*, or the longing in *Raga Bageshree*. An artist lives between these emotions, understanding each raga's subtle nuances and bringing them to life in performance. Through this, the *raga* becomes a powerful medium for expression, allowing the artist to share their deepest feelings and connect with their audience on a soulful level.

'Dance offers an escape from the routine and mundane, lifting the soul to a higher plane. At its core, each soul carries a sense of melancholy—a deep yearning to connect and become one with something greater, something nameless yet profoundly felt. As the verse goes, *Birha birha aakhiye, birha tu sultan; jis tan birha na upje, vo tan jaan masaan*, the one who does not feel the pangs of separation is not truly alive,' says Rita Ganguly, a distinguished exponent of Indian classical arts. An accomplished dancer, musician, and vocalist, she was awarded the Sangeet Natak Akademi award in 2000 and the Padma Shri in 2003. She also earned a gold medal at the World Dance Festival.

Birha—separation from whom?

Rita explains that it is the longing to explore the unknown, an intrinsic desire to bridge the gap between what is and what could be. This yearning is universal, and people turn to various forms of expression—art, music, literature, or dance—to give voice to this unnameable ache for the unattainable. Even when worldly ambitions are fulfilled, this separation lingers in the soul, creating an emotional void. It is here that performing arts play a crucial role. Dance and music offer solace, transforming this longing into a creative and fulfilling journey, allowing individuals to momentarily transcend their inner emptiness and connect with something greater than themselves.

Throughout her journey, Rita has explored various artistic avenues, travelling the world with her show, *Begum Akhtar*. Yet, as the saying goes, artists are seekers, and none of these pursuits fully satisfied her. Rita always sought to express something deeper, something beyond, which continues to fuel her artistic journey. This journey is a *sadhna*.

'Agar sadhna nahin hai, to kuch nahin hai aapki zindagi mein. Yahi badi baat hai Shovana mein' (There is nothing worthwhile in your life without dedication—that's the remarkable trait in Shovana), says Rita. The sentiment perfectly encapsulates the essence of Shovana Narayan. The most noteworthy thing about

her is her unwavering dedication to Kathak. Once she embraced this classical dance form, she committed herself to it fully, allowing no distractions to deviate her focus. She consistently sought to push the boundaries of her art, ever striving to express more through ever-innovative means.

Her journey has been one of constant evolution—a search for new ways to tell ancient stories and bring fresh perspectives to the classical form. Her creations are not just performances; they are masterpieces—a seamless fusion of mythological richness and contemporary insight. Through her work, Shovana brings the timeless wisdom of classical narratives into the context of modernity, weaving together something sacred. Through her, Kathak becomes a living, breathing expression of the eternal truths infused with the pulse of the present moment.

'*Kalakar fakir hote hein agar vo sochen ki vo fakir hein aur vo badshah hote hein agar vo sochen ki vo badshah hein. Kala bhi fakkad fakir hai jiski koi Lakshman rekha nahin hoti.*'

(An artist is a fakir (ascetic) when they see themselves as one—simple, detached, and free from the chains of ego. At the same time, they become Badshah (kings) when they embrace the power of their inner confidence and expression. The essence of art lies not in what you own or claim but in how you perceive yourself. Like the fakir, art is boundless—it knows no rules, borders, or limits. It is a wandering soul, free to explore, transform, and touch the deepest corners of the heart.) As Kabir said:

Mast fakira jagat ka, sabse baith alagai.
Na uska koi rog hai, na uska koi sanai.

(The carefree fakir sits apart from the world. He has no
disease, no worldly ties.)

Dance, being a visual art form, brings emotions to life. Seasoned artists like Shovana unveil the hidden *bhavas* of the subconscious. Watching her emote can move you to shed tears of joy. It's akin to standing bare before the divine, feeling exposed, and recognising your insignificance in the presence of the supreme. Music—and any form of art—offers catharsis, touching the soul deeply. Artists, through their *sadhna* (dedication), come closer to God.

'Music touches the heart, and for a dancer, the person you are is reflected on stage. Your *bhava* (emotion) mirrors your inner self. An artist must strike the right chord in the audience's heart, leading to the *jagaran* (awakening) of the *atma* (soul). There's no definitive explanation for how one reaches the emotional melting point during a powerful performance. Music awakens the buried sensibilities of the soul. A single stroke of a *raga* (melodic framework) can transport you to an entirely different mood,' observes Subhalakshmi.

Subhalakshmi, a Bharatnatyam dancer and close friend of Shovana, has an innate affinity for all forms of dance. Married to the renowned music maestro Ustad Amjad Ali Khan, she passionately reflects on art and music. 'I am a *gulaam* (slave) to my ear,' she says. 'I consider myself a humble *sevak* (servant) of *kala* (art) and a devoted *rasik* (connoisseur). Fine arts refine life. Stepping onto the stage, applying makeup, or playing an instrument while harbouring impurities in your soul is far from ideal. Everything you do should be infused with art. It takes immense effort to transform the roughness of a diamond into brilliance. Art, likewise, demands patience, devotion, and relentless work.'

'Shovana Narayan has a remarkable ability to connect with her audience, both on secular and spiritual levels. Her performances resonate deeply with people as she brings out themes that transcend cultural and religious boundaries. The philosophy behind her dance has a deep spiritual essence,' says Guru Vijay Shanker. 'We, the artists, connect with the Almighty. For some, it's *Khuda*, for others, it's Krishna, Rama, or Shiva. But when seen through the lens of spirituality, these different names and beliefs merge into one universal truth where all words, religions, and art forms unite.'

Shovana draws from sacred texts and Sufi stories, exploring spiritual realms that resonate with people from diverse backgrounds. Her collaborations with various art forms show her belief in growing through universal connections. Her approach emphasises the universal nature of spirituality over religious distinctions.

An example is Salabega, a seventeenth century Muslim devotee of Lord Jagannath who composed Jagannath bhajans (devotional songs). Despite being a Muslim, his deep reverence for the deity earned him a revered place among Jagannath's devotees.

Shovana's dance philosophy embraces this universal spirituality, where art and devotion merge, regardless of the religious background.

For Shovana, being a good artist and a good human are closely related. She performs *Satvik* abhinaya, a pure and spiritual expression. All art forms, rooted in the Natyashastra, enable an artist to connect with the divine through different expressions—Satvik, *Aharya, Vachik, and Angik* abhinaya. Her dedication to these principles allows her to use dance to promote spiritual harmony.

As a chairperson and long-standing member of the Society for the Promotion of Indian Classical Music and Culture Amongst Youth (SPIC MACAY) since 1984, Maya Shankar, art connoisseur, former chairperson SPIC MACAY, Patna chapter, and retired professor of history, Patna University, has been deeply involved in fostering the richness of Indian classical art forms. Her journey with SPIC MACAY allowed her to interact with many legendary artists. She expresses profound gratitude to life for this opportunity, as art and artists have deeply shaped her personal and spiritual evolution.

Maya recalls her first encounter with Shovana Narayan through SPIC MACAY, describing an immediate connection. Both hailed from Bihar, a shared heritage that filled Maya with immense pride. Shovana's stature as one of the rare classical dance artists from Bihar who achieved global recognition made her an extraordinary figure in Maya's eyes. She fondly remembers the inauguration of the new auditorium at Patna Women's college, where Shovana was the first classical dancer to perform, setting a remarkable precedent for all future events.

'Beyond her artistic brilliance, what struck me about her was her humility and grounded nature. Shovana ji carries herself with such grace—there are no airs, pretensions, and ego, traits that often accompany artistic excellence. While some artists require delicate handling due to their sensitivities, Shovana ji is adaptable, warm, and at ease in any company. She has the rare ability to connect with everyone, whether it's connoisseurs of art or newcomers.'

Their shared roots have paved the way for a warm friendship. Whenever Shovana visits Patna, they make it a point to meet. 'Shovana,' says Maya, 'remains closely connected to schools in Patna that teach classical dance, ensuring that art continues to inspire younger generations.' Maya admires her commitment to cultural cross-pollination and how she nurtures the classical arts in Bihar and beyond.

Maya often hosts grand lunches and dinners for artists at her home in Patna, celebrating the magic of shared creativity and camaraderie. She, however, regrets that Shovana has not yet been able to join any of these gatherings due to her ever-demanding schedule.

Maya says Patna has long been a hub of classical art and culture. She fondly recalls the annual *Dussehra* classical programme, a spectacular event beginning at 8 pm and continuing until 8 am, immersing audiences in the transcendental beauty of Indian classical music and dance.

'Another cherished memory is the grand cultural event we organised, *Jai Bharati*, held in a vast open hall in Patna. Artists from across the country representing various classical dance forms were invited to perform under the overarching theme of how Lord Krishna united the entire nation. The setting was ethereal, decorated with fresh banana leaves and fragrant *bela* flowers; the air was filled with their divine aroma.

After the programme, the evening had a lighter, more playful side. The artists wanted to unwind and explore. Shovana ji, with her lively and fun-loving spirit, took the lead. We all went to watch the movie *Badmaash Company*, and it turned out to be an evening filled with fun and frolic. Shovana ji is a remarkable artist and a joy to be around—a perfect blend of creativity, humility, and warmth.'

At the heart of creating and appreciating art lies the essence of being a *rasik*, a connoisseur who intensely experiences and cherishes art's subtle joy. For an artist like Shovana, it means embodying the spiritual depth of her performances; for someone like Manjari Sinha, it means finding and sharing those treasures through words.

Whether on stage or in writing, the role of a rasik transcends boundaries—it's about nurturing a sensitive soul attuned to the beauty, harmony, and profound truths that art reveals.

Manjari Sinha describes herself as a *sangeet* rasik who deeply enjoys music and shares that joy through her art columns in renowned newspapers. Though she has completed Sangeet Prabhakar in tabla, sitar, vocal, and Kathak, she doesn't perform professionally like Shovana Narayan. Instead, she channels her passion into writing. Manjari is a true connoisseur of the arts with a strong foundation in both Sanskrit and music.

Much like Shovana, Manjari comes from a culturally rich family. Hailing from Hajipur, Uttar Pradesh, she considers herself fortunate to have grown up in a time where she could experience the legendary performances of maestros like Bade Ghulam Ali Khan, Siddheshwari Devi, Birju Maharaj, Shambhu Maharaj, and Vilayat Ali Khan. This shared artistic heritage forms a deep connection between her and Shovana.

Manjari uses the metaphor of the sitar to explain their bond—just as placing your hand at the right spot on the sitar strings creates a beautiful resonance, their shared love for the arts brings them into perfect harmony. Through this shared wavelength, the two women are deeply connected, united by their passion for preserving and celebrating Indian art and culture.

'I first met Shovana at a cultural conference in Lucknow in the early 1970s. Later, in 1986, I saw her perform on stage in Delhi. Over time, I heard her speak at various events and noticed how, while Kathak remained her main passion, she was always open to new collaborations. She could perform Beethoven's *Moonlight Sonata* just as easily as she could portray one of Vidyapati's *nayika*s.

To do these kinds of experiments requires reaching a certain level, which only comes from deep dedication, or *sadhana*. It's not just about how many hours you practise but about an ongoing, inward journey. Whatever theme she took on, there was always a deep thought behind it. No matter how late she went to bed, she would wake up at 4 am and practice with the tabla master for two hours before starting her day at the office. Her versatility was impressive. This love for reading, writing, dance, and music came from her mother, a knowledgeable woman who had the arts flowing through her like a lifeline. I realised that Shovana wasn't just passing on what she had learned but was adding her artistic insight and sensitivity to it. There was depth to her words, and spirituality was a core part of her personality,' Manjari observes.

Subhalakshmi deeply appreciates refinement in every aspect of life and sees Shovana as its very embodiment. Whether it is in how she interacts with people, acknowledges their contributions, fulfils her responsibilities with sincerity, or performs on stage, Shovana exudes grace and finesse. Regarding her bond with Shovana, Subhalakshmi describes themselves as birds of a feather that flock together. Shovana affectionately calls her Raju Didi, a simple yet heartfelt gesture that endears Shovana to her repeatedly.

'I have known Shovana so intimately that putting my thoughts about her into words feels like a challenge. Many years ago, she was the quintessential girl next door—simple, charming, and yet intriguingly enigmatic, especially with her radiant smile and infectious laughter,' says Salma Sultan, her warmth evident as she speaks about someone so dear to her.

A renowned Indian television journalist and director, Salma Sultan served as a news anchor for Doordarshan from 1967 to 1997 before transitioning to directing television shows.

'Immersed in our creative pursuits, we were aware of each other's presence, yet much about one another remained unexplored. However, fate has its unique way of bringing people together and fostering lasting bonds. Shovana's early morning *riyaz*, accompanied by the rhythmic chime of her ghunghroos, was unknowingly paving the way for something deeper. Eventually, I introduced my four-year-old daughter, Sana, to Shovana, entrusting her to her guidance. This nurtured Sana's artistic journey and allowed me to visit Shovana more frequently, strengthening our connection.'

Salma fondly recalls the humble home, alive with the sounds of music, a kind and gracious mother, and light-hearted conversations shared over a cup of hot coffee and freshly made fritters—all of which left an enduring impression on her.

'Shovana's growth as an artist is phenomenal. Her passion and perseverance are awe-inspiring, and her humility is worth emulating. She's touched countless lives, nurturing untapped talent and inspiring many to carry forward Kathak's timeless and precious legacy. Her concerts possess a rare aura as if infused with celestial energy that captivates and holds you spellbound. Her performances are cathartic—they elevate your spirit and transport you to an entirely different realm. Alongside her immense talent, she carries the blessings and abundant love of the divine. If I may say so, Shovana embodies *daiviya shakti*—a sacred force that radiates from her very being, illuminating every life around her.'

When artists become deeply immersed in their art, they move beyond the external world, becoming a living expression of their craft. Praise and criticism no longer affect them; they are simply the essence of their art, untouched by the material. One memorable moment Subhalakshmi recalls was when Shovana appeared in her dance costume for dinner at theirs, saying, 'Raju Didi had called, so I had to be here.' This simple act shows the genuine love and warmth she radiates and receives from everyone who knows her.

'I married Amjad Ali Khan sahab in 1976, and I met many of his associates over time. Among them was Shovana, though I hadn't seen her dance back then. I had, of course, heard much about her art and the admiration it commanded in Delhi. She was also an IAAS officer, which amazed me—her remarkable mastery and meticulousness in such diverse fields. At the time, we were living in Panchsheel Enclave. I distinctly remember the day she came to meet Amjad sahab. Her addressing him as bhaiya immediately revealed the long-standing bond they shared. The first time I saw her perform was a memorable occasion. It was a trio performance with Shovana, Sonal Mansingh, and Yamini Krishnamurthy in the presence of the President of Angola. The performance was breathtaking—Shovana danced with such joyful abundance that it left a lasting impression on me.'

The true artistry lies in the seamless blending of technical mastery and spiritual surrender. Be it music or dance, the highest expression of art seems to transcend the artist and take on a life of its own. Dance, like music, is not just a medium of expression but a profound journey—a dialogue between the performer and something infinite. The rhythm of the ghunghroos or the strings of a sarod becomes more than sound; it becomes an invocation, a gateway to timelessness. This interplay of control and surrender, discipline, and freedom, elevates the performing arts into the divine realm. It is here that the artist becomes a vessel and the art, a force that flows through them.

Ali Akbar Khan, an Indian Hindustani classical musician of the *Maihar* Gharana, known for his virtuosity in playing the sarod, once said, '*Shuru mein main sarod bajata hun; baad mein sarod mujhe bajata hai.*' (In the beginning, I play the sarod; later, the sarod plays me.)

This profound statement captures the essence of Indian classical music. It speaks to the idea that true mastery transcends the performer, where the music takes over and guides the artist.

Great artists like Kelucharan Mohapatra and Birju Maharaj embodied this transformative power of art in their performances. Kelucharan ji, for instance, would portray Radha, performing bare-chested, and his long hair flowing, yet his expression was so powerful that, for a moment, one would forget he was a man. In that moment, he was Radha, fully immersed in the character's emotion.

This is not simply the 'willing suspension of disbelief' coined by the English poet and literary critic Samuel Taylor Coleridge (the idea that readers or audience can temporarily set aside their disbelief in a story's implausible elements); this is the sheer triumph of art. It is an ecstatic transcendence where the artist and the audience are lifted beyond the physical realm into a space where the body no longer matters.

This is the magic that great artists like Shovana bring to life—through her mastery of rhythm and expression, her bhava (emotion) is so powerful that it transports the audience into a state of rapture. Whether she is portraying Duryodhana, full of arrogance and greed, throwing the dice in the fateful game of chance; or Shakuni, embodying the art of manipulation and deceit with malice in his heart; or Dushasana, consumed by lust, beckoning Draupadi to sit on his lap; and once more, in the infamous *cheer haran* (disrobing) scene, pulling at Draupadi's sari in an act of shameful humiliation; or Draupadi, pleading with the Pandavas and Kauravas to spare her dignity, or invoking Krishna to come and save her dignity—these performances are not merely acts—they are profound representations of the characters' internal struggles and flaws.

Each of these iconic scenes from the Mahabharata is brought to life with such depth and intensity by Shovana Narayan that the boundaries between the performer and the character blur, elevating the experience beyond the physical. It is a beautiful example of how, in the hands of a true maestro, art transcends the material and enters the realm of the spiritual, leaving an unforgettable imprint on the hearts of those who witness it.

For Shovana, however, as for many artists, a quiet torment lingers—a question that refuses to fade.

Will their *tapasya*, their lifelong sadhna, vanish into the whispers of the wind once they are gone?

This fear of impermanence is a universal truth, yet it carries a unique poignancy for an artist.

Every performance, every creation, becomes a deliberate attempt to defy time, to leave an imprint that will outlast the fleeting moments of applause.

It is not the immortality of the body they seek but of the spirit—etched into the collective memory, carried forward in the hearts and souls of those they touch.

As the hands of time continue to weave their inevitable pattern, one truth remains—no matter how grand or fleeting our existence may seem, it is but a thread in the vast, cosmic fabric of life.

Human life, with its joys, sorrows, triumphs, and losses, is finite. Our physical presence is fragile, bound to one inevitable end. But in this transience, there lies an unspoken truth: it is through the arts that we transcend the limits of birth and death.

Shovana Narayan, like many before her, has danced through life, carving out her rhythm against the backdrop of time's relentless march. Yet, in each step, in each gesture, there exists an echo that reverberates through eternity—an unbroken thread of human expression, of divine dance that outlasts the fleeting moments of life. The rhythm of Kathak, the language of movement, has been passed down from one generation to the next, surviving the passage of time, surviving the very concept of mortality.

When the body crumbles and the mind falters, the dance remains.

The artist's essence lives on in the movements of the feet and the undying rhythm.

We, like the fleeting notes of a melody, may fade into the silence of time. But the music, the dance, and the art continue reverberating long after we are gone. And so, in the inevitable fade of life, when the last breath is drawn and the final dance step taken, the answer is clear:

Only those who seek eternity through art shall return to it.

In Her Shadow

Yasyānke śiśavaḥ krīḍanti, yatra ca snehamandalam/
Sadā tiṣṭhati sā mātā, sarvatīrthamayī smṛtā/

(In whose lap children play, where love flows abundantly—she is the mother, revered as the embodiment of all holy places.)

Shovana's mother Lalita Narayan

13 January 1990, marked a turning point in the lives of Shovana and her sister Ranjana. The day started like any other, bustling with activity and purpose under the steady guidance of their mother. A visit to the family farm, routine political meetings, and a trip to Kamani Auditorium filled the hours. Lalita moved through her day with her characteristic vitality, teaching, analysing, and planning. Yet, as the night fell, the seemingly ordinary day transformed into a night of heartbreak. A sudden heart attack took her away within minutes, leaving the daughters stunned and unmoored.

The loss was swift and devastating, a blow that reverberated through their lives, reshaping their world in unimaginable ways.

In one of her letters to her son, Shovana vividly recalled the events of that fateful day:

> How distinctly I remember all we did on the fateful day of 13 January. In the morning, Ma, you, and I, along with Vijay, drove to the farm, where Ma did a quick round of the newly built house. She then sat under the tree near the main entrance and paid the labourers. By the time we got back, it was nearing lunchtime.

After lunch, Lalita requested to be driven to her political meetings, and they returned around 6 pm. She wanted to visit two *dargahs* (mosques) before heading to Kamani Auditorium for a classical dance performance. These visits were significant to her, as she had made a *mannat* (wish) regarding Ishan's delayed speech, hoping for his early progress and well-being. With her wish fulfilled, she wished to offer her thanksgiving through the traditional gesture of placing a *chadar* (sheet) on the shrine. They visited the two dargahs, one on Cornwallis Road near Bapa Nagar and the other at Nizamuddin Aulia, where they offered the chadar.

Afterward, they went to Kamani for a brief time before heading home. During the drive back, Lalita discussed the performance, critically analysed Shovana's past performances, and shared her thoughts on the future course of action for her dance career.

By the time the clock struck 10 pm, the household had retired to bed. Ma and Shovana shared a room, with Ishan sleeping between them, a comforting ritual that had become second nature. Shovana, still needing to finish some office work, remained in bed, reviewing her files. But before long, exhaustion overtook her, and she drifted off to sleep. Then, Ma called out to Vijay, her voice tinged with unease. She wasn't feeling well and asked him to massage her back. But moments later, a sudden urgency punctuated her words: 'Putul, wake up! I think I am having a heart attack. Fetch the doctor.'

Shovana was startled awake, a sharp panic creeping in as she and Vijay hurried to her side. Ranju quickly emerged from her room, her face ashen with concern. The first call went to Dr Narendra Bihari, their cousin and the chief of Safdarjung hospital, who lived nearby. However, he declined for personal reasons. The second call went to Dr Roy, the father of one of Shovana's students, Mishtee. Dr Roy rushed over, but Lalita's condition had worsened by then. She requested to go to the bathroom, and Shovana accompanied her, noticing the escalating pain her Ma was in.

Dr Roy's arrival brought urgency, and after assessing her condition, he insisted that she needed immediate hospitalisation. Ma, ever considerate, told Ranju to stay home with Ishan, who was peacefully asleep, and told Shovana to drive her to the hospital. Without hesitation, Shovana drove Ma, Dr Roy, and Vijay to Ram Manohar Lohia hospital, known then as Willingdon hospital.

The scene in the hospital is etched in Shovana's memory.

As Ma was given oxygen, she took her final breath. The heart monitor flatlined, and in that agonising moment, Shovana watched helplessly as her Ma slipped away. Despite the frantic efforts of the doctors, it was clear—nothing could be done. In a matter of minutes, Lalita, the woman who had guided her through life's most turbulent moments, was gone.

Shovana stood there, numb, as the seconds stretched into time without end. The life that had been so vivid moments before faded into stillness. The realisation struck—hardly twenty minutes had passed since Lalita had woken her up with those fateful words. In the blink of an eye, everything had changed.

'I called Ranju to give her the sad news, and it took me back to 23 November, 1977, when I had called home from Rewari to inform Ma and Ranju that I was bringing Papa's body home. We brought Ma's body back and laid her on a white sheet in the middle of the drawing-room floor. By then, it was around 12.40 am. She had passed away around 11.30 pm. Her very good friend, Shanta Srivastava, her son and daughter-in-law, Gopal Tandon, and a few other relatives and friends arrived immediately. Herbert was informed in Tehran, and Mamma, Ilse, and Moni-Manfred—our nickname for Erika Monika Morvay, my younger sister-in-law in Vienna. I kept touching Ma, almost hoping we were mistaken, and wondering if she wasn't truly gone—fearful that she might catch a cold lying on the floor. She looked so peaceful, so suddenly young.

By the time dawn had broken, preparations for the cremation had begun. While I managed everything at home, Ranju went to the Lodi Road cremation ground to arrange the time for the cremation, the *pandit* (priest), and the wood logs. The cremation was set for around noon. We called a hospital to arrange for a van to transport her body to the cremation ground at the appointed hour. By then, our house was teeming with friends, colleagues, Ma's political friends, and distant relatives, all coming to pay their condolences.'

To lose a parent is to lose a piece of oneself, and for Shovana and Ranju, it felt as though the very bedrock of their lives had crumbled.

Lalita had been more than a caretaker; she had been their mentor, guide, and unwavering source of strength. She instilled in them the values that would define their lives—the importance of virtue over material gains and the wisdom of the Bhagavad Gita. Her teachings were a way of life, subtly woven into their childhood through scripture and daily conversations. She showed them that success was fleeting if not rooted in integrity and that life's challenges could be overcome through resilience and faith.

The days following her passing were a blur of rituals and responsibilities. Friends, colleagues, and relatives gathered to offer condolences, but the void was irreplaceable.

The sisters leaned on each other, finding solace in shared memories and their mother's enduring influence. They now faced the sobering reality of being truly on their own.

'There is nothing more traumatic than losing your parents, those upon whom you depend so deeply. I can still recall how, for a long time, I would call home from the office and absent-mindedly ask the servant to pass the phone to Ma. The sudden silence on the other end would jolt me back to reality.'

Despite the profound loss, they knew that their mother's wisdom would always light their path, reminding them to persevere and honour her legacy in the way they lived their own lives.

'After her passing, life became difficult. My sister Ranjana and I contacted the Young Women's Christian Association (YWCA) and arranged for a governess to assist with Ishan for a few hours each day until I returned home in the evenings.'

'Shovana may have brought Ishan into this world, but to me, he's always been my son. He fondly called me mamma mausi—a name that still echoes with warmth and has become a nickname in Austria within the family. Until he was six and living in India, I was the one who took care of him the most. When he was six, Herbert took a home posting to be closer to him. Even now, I tell Ishan that no matter how old he gets—he's a father to three adorable kids—I can still scold him as his mother. Ishan is my heart. He was the most adorable baby, and I still swear he smiled at me the moment he was born,' Ranjana laughs.

Ranjana embraced motherhood in a way that blurred the lines between aunt and mother. She became a second mother to Ishan, nurturing him with the same love and care their mother had shown them. From infancy in India to his formative years in Vienna, Ranjana was his constant caretaker.

Their sisterly bond has been one for the books—solid, unshakable, and full of love. As kids, Shovana's routine was something to behold—picking up her little sister from nap class like she was guarding a priceless treasure. Her fierce protectiveness was so legendary that even the teachers probably felt like they were in the presence of a bodyguard!

And when their mother passed, Shovana didn't just step in to fill the gap; she took on the role with grace and humour that only she could, ensuring their family's love continued to flow, albeit with a bit more laughter and much heart.

They've weathered it all with a blend of love, strength, and a potential dose of fun. Life may have thrown its challenges their way, but they've kept their heads high, laughing through the ups and downs and always finding joy in the little things—like the memories of childhood routines that still make them smile.

Breath of the Universe

Shovana's artistry as a dancer and her profound intellect made her more than a teacher—she became an inspiration. Her performances were not just displays of skill but expressions of deep emotion and storytelling, capable of captivating even the most hesitant observers. For many of her disciples, including Shruti Chandra Gupta, she was not merely a mentor but a role model whose grace, discipline, and erudition they aspired to emulate.

'My grandfather, Jainendra Kumar, was a renowned Hindi writer, and my mother had a deep love for the arts. She wanted my sister and I to experience a whole gamut of artistic disciplines, encouraging us to explore and discover our natural interests. When we were young, she enrolled us in painting and folk-dance classes in Kolkata. Later, when we moved to Delhi, my grandfather, who knew Birju Maharaj ji well, expressed his wish for us to learn dance under his guidance. We were soon enrolled in Sangeet Bharati under Mr Lal's tutelage. I wasn't always enthusiastic about dance—in fact, when Mr Lal came to our house for lessons, I used to hide behind the sofa to avoid him.'

Shruti's aunt, who lived next door to Shovana Narayan in Jangpura Extension, often spoke to Shruti's mother about Shovana Narayan. 'I still remember the first time I saw Didi dance,' says Shruti, her voice softening with the memory. 'I was completely captivated. There was something in the way she moved, something so mesmerising and full of grace that it left me spellbound. At that moment, I knew—without a doubt—that I had to learn from her. And that's how my journey with dance began, with Shovana Didi as my guide.'

As a young girl, Shruti had been reluctant to attend dance classes. At first, she found excuses, hiding behind the sofa and watching Mr Lal from a distance, not yet ready to commit to what seemed like a faraway dream. But as she watched Shovana, the magic of it all started to work on her. The once simple fascination deepened into a burning desire to learn, to be like the woman who danced with such effortless elegance. 'I couldn't look away,' she continues, her voice tinged with the warmth of nostalgia. 'From those shy moments behind the sofa to when I stood there, mesmerised, wanting nothing more than to be able to dance like her, I knew my heart had found its true calling, and there was no turning back.'

Shruti's dance journey began in 1972-73 when she was just twelve and Shovana was in her early twenties. It was a time of blossoming dreams, learning, and growing. Over the years, their bond deepened into something far beyond a teacher-student relationship—a lifelong connection of shared passion, love for dance, and mutual love. 'Our bond has lasted for more than fifty years,' she smiles, her eyes reflecting a lifetime of gratitude. 'And it's still as strong today as when I first watched Didi dance.'

'We lived on Pandara Road, across from Shovana Di in B block, by the Mother Dairy. Walking to the Mother Dairy was our daily excursion. My elder sister began learning Kathak at Asavari, the school Shovana Di founded, while I, at eight, was enrolled in Shakeel bhai's tabla classes. The atmosphere was warm and vibrant. It was a large home, with dance classes held in the backyard—no wooden floors or air conditioning, just a pure love for art. Ranjana Di would often sing, Shakeel bhai would play the tabla, and our classes, relaxed and easy-going, often extended beyond the set time, with us sneaking biscuits from the kitchen,' Rahul Kumar shares.

Rahul, at seventeen, expressed his desire to become an artist. The prevailing belief was that proper financial stability came only through conventional education. 'Artists starve,' his father remarked, encouraging Rahul to pursue a mainstream profession before fully committing to the arts. Rahul reluctantly heeded the advice, embarking on a journey through chartered accountancy, an MBA, and a series of corporate roles, leading to a successful but unfulfilling career.

Rahul had a passion for the visual arts, especially pottery. Drawn to clay, he initially learned from a traditional potter in Paharganj, refined his craft, and evolved from hand-made pots to glazed studio pottery. This pursuit culminated in his first solo exhibition in Bombay. Determined to leave a mark, Rahul applied for a prestigious US government art scholarship, securing a grant to pursue a Master of Fine Arts (MFA).

After completing his degree, he returned to his corporate job but, in 2015, decided to leave the business world for good. In search of creative fulfilment, Rahul joined New Delhi Television Ltd's (NDTV's) art e-commerce venture. He later transitioned into writing and editing for various art publications. Today, with ten solo ceramic exhibitions to his credit, Rahul is a prominent curator and mentor, guiding emerging and mid-career artists to realise their potential.

Rahul credits his childhood days at Asavari Music School and the profound influence of Shovana Narayan as an artist for shaping his inner world in ways that words can hardly capture. Those early experiences, surrounded by musical rhythms and the grace of artistry, nurtured a sensitivity beyond learning musical instruments. While he had enrolled for formal lessons, the atmosphere at Asavari shaped him on a deeper, subconscious level, planting the seeds of an artistic sensibility and a quest for something intangible—a search for beauty, meaning, and connection.

Rahul sees how those days shaped him into what every true artist is meant to be: a seeker, a devotee, and a restless soul yearning for something beyond the visible measures of success. His love for pottery, like music and dance in his youth, became a way to explore the essence of human existence—the *tatva*. This tatva, the core of being, fuels his art and journey.

Shovana's devotion to her craft and constant exploration of deeper truths through art left an indelible mark on her students. Her influence taught them that the actual value of an artist lies not in external recognition but in the depth of their inner journey and the sincerity of their search.

'Though I was there for tabla, I was immersed in so much more that hung at the peripheries—dance rhythms, the discipline of song, and an unspoken reverence for the arts. Shovana Di, always affectionate and encouraging, would say, '*Ab toh tumahri ungliyon ki avaz sunai dene lagi hai. Bahut achcha kar rahe ho.*' And then she would address Shakeel Bhai, '*Rahul ko mujhe sangati dene ke liye taiyar kijiye.*' (I can hear your fingers now—you're doing well. Shakeel Bhai, please prepare Rahul to accompany me for a stage performance). Her presence commanded respect. The moment she entered, we'd stop fooling around. Over time, my interests shifted—from tabla to guitar, then violin, and finally, piano. While some people master a craft and become something, my journey was different. I was relatively young and initially coerced into learning, but the environment was a unique and tangential way to get to where I am, today.'

Despite valuing her time and packing her days with rich experiences, Shovana never hesitates to go the extra mile for what truly moves her. Immersed in profound moments, she loses track of time, staying absorbed far longer than expected. Even after a programme ends late, she quickly grabs a bite and dives into music composition, leaving those around her marvelling at how she fits so much into a single day. Her energy and vitality seem boundless, no matter her age. Whether collaborating with musicians or pushing creative boundaries, her passion consistently elevates the work beyond expectations.

People often wonder about the elusive secret to work-life balance and find themselves faltering, no matter their field. The same question has been asked countless times about Shovana: How does she pack so much into her day? The dual careers, the constant performances, award ceremonies, and gala events that take her across the globe, her role as an ambassador's wife, the responsibilities of family and friends, managing the household, her riyaz, and teaching students—all of it so seamlessly intertwined.

The question comes from all corners, and interestingly, the answer echoes back from everywhere.

Shovana's secret lies not in some mystical formula but in a mix of grit, discipline, and a unique sense of purpose. She has always believed in giving her best, no matter the circumstances. Even in the face of the biggest personal tragedies—her father's sudden and tragic passing, Herbert's critical health crises, and her ailments—she has carried on with quiet strength. No matter how overwhelming, challenges have never diminished her commitment to her work or loved ones. Instead, they seem to fuel her resolve to move forward with grace.

'Shovana Didi's work ethic is unwavering dedication—work continues no matter what. Regardless of what challenges you're facing in your personal life, once you're on stage, at the easel, or setting up an exhibition, there are no excuses. Life goes on. She maintained a clear boundary between family time and work time, and I witnessed firsthand the incredible effort she put into her craft. I would arrive at her place at 5.30 in the morning, and she had already completed her *riyaz* (practice). I would train with her until 9 am when she left for work, and I headed to my studio. At that time, I was her only disciple. In the evenings, I would return for more practice. If Didi had other commitments, I would rehearse in her mother's presence. Her work ethic left a profound impression on me and shaped my approach to life. She believed, "*Jo hona hai, vo hokar rahega. Aap bas apna kaam karte jao*" (Whatever is meant to happen will happen—you just need to keep working), Shruti adds.

Shovana takes on the role of a nurturing mother in her students' lives, teaching, training, and guiding them while imparting valuable life lessons. She encourages their creativity, inspires curiosity, and uses practical situations as teaching moments. Always receptive and open to suggestions, this quality is mirrored in her diverse group of students, representing various faiths, religions, and perspectives. This universality is what defines her as a true artist.

'Initially, we would gather at her home on Pandara Road. Eventually, we moved to a government school building where we could rehearse. We were assigned a room on the ground floor, which had an uneven floor. To accommodate this, we spread linoleum and danced there. It was only later that the authorities renovated the floor, allowing us to move our classes to the first floor,' Shruti recalls.

Guru Shovana transformed the classroom into a vibrant haven for her students. Under her guidance, every lesson became an immersive experience, fostering a deep appreciation for the art form. The atmosphere she created was educational and nurturing, making students feel valued and inspired.

Shruti represents the true spirit of devotion to dance, which showed in the most unexpected ways. When she was dating her future husband, her idea of a romantic outing was quite different from the norm. Instead of opting for typical date spots like hotels or movies, she would enthusiastically take her fiancé to events like the Kathak Mahotsav. For her, spending time surrounded by Kathak's rhythms, movements, and expressions was the ultimate way to connect, share experiences, and celebrate her passion for dance. The classroom, filled with creativity, joy, and a sense of belonging, became not just a place of learning but a second home for them.

What makes Shovana's approach remarkable is her ability to compartmentalise without detachment. When she's at work, whether on stage or mentoring a student, she is entirely present, pouring her energy into every detail. She is equally attentive with family or friends, creating an atmosphere of warmth and care. It's not about doing it all but about doing it all with intent and heart.

'You can be an inch wide and a mile deep,' says Rahul. 'You can focus on something narrow and explore it deeply, delving further without ever reaching the end. Human life is too short to fully grasp anything—whether it's science, art, or literature. Take, for example, the Japanese pottery tradition—an artist may spend twenty-five years perfecting a single form. It's not just about the physical act of creating a pot; it's the metaphorical process of birthing something with meaning beyond its physical form.'

What does clay symbolise? And what does the pot symbolise? The understanding could take years to develop. The transience of the physical world and the mortality of the human body, often symbolised as 'clay,' is a theme explored by many philosophers and poets. Kabir expresses this idea beautifully in his verse: '*Mati kahe kumhar se, tu kya raunde mohe, ek din aisa aayega, main raundoongi tohe.*' In this, the clay speaks to the potter, questioning why it is being wedged, only to remind him that one day, the potter too will be wedged back to his origin. The inevitability of death and the cyclical nature of life, where all things—no matter how magnificent—eventually return to their origins.

The process isn't just about shaping a lump of clay into a pot—it's about creating an entity that holds space, embodying the five elements: earth, water, air, fire, and space itself. This idea parallels dance, particularly abhinaya and sadhana. Nothing becomes perfect until you 'become' it.

Art has a unique way of awakening your sensitivity to the finer details of life. It sharpens your ability to notice and appreciate the subtle nuances that often go unnoticed in your daily routine. Whether it's the delicate brushstrokes of a painting, the rhythm in a piece of music, or the emotions conveyed through dance, art encourages you to look beyond the obvious and embrace the richness of what lies beneath the surface.

'My understanding of these subtleties wasn't drawn from visual arts but Shovana Di's Kathak performances. Similarly, the subtleties of shaping a pot played an equal role. A pot doesn't become happy or sad just because I adjust its curve, but I deeply appreciate the nuances.'

Rahul often draws parallels between pottery and dance. Before starting to make a pot, you wedge the clay. Wedging serves a technical purpose—to make the clay homogenous and remove air pockets, which could otherwise cause problems on the wheel or cracks during firing. His students sometimes ask why they can't wedge the clay the day before. But he insists they do it right before they begin, even if they did it the previous day.

Once, while attending a live concert of Ustad Amjad Ali Khan and his sons, Rahul asked his mother why they tuned their instruments in front of the audience instead of beforehand. The performance was scheduled for seven and started precisely on time with the tuning. His mother explained, 'They're not just tuning the instruments; they're tuning the audience, helping them prepare to receive the performance. They need those twenty minutes to detach from everything else and be present.'

Rahul later shared this idea with his students: 'Do you think you're just wedging the clay? It's about disconnecting from the world to engage with it truly.' For Rahul, all these experiences are interconnected, and they flow into his work with clay and everything he does.

'I've been influenced by everything I've learned from my mother and Shovana Di. They helped me draw such connections. At first, I didn't understand what it meant to 'become' what you learn. I thought, "I did well; my *teen taal* was fine." But I was far from truly 'becoming.' Over time, I realised what it actually meant.' Rahul admits candidly.

To be so immersed in something that you 'become it' is to transcend the boundaries of self and object. It's not merely about mastering a skill but about dissolving into the essence of what you're creating.

When you dance, you are no longer just a body moving to rhythm—you become the rhythm, the space, the silence between the beats. In music, it's not your fingers playing the notes but the sound that moves through you, as if the melody existed before you touched the instrument, and you're merely a vessel for its expression. The same is true for painting or any form of art; your brush strokes aren't just marks on canvas but a manifestation of an inner world spilling out. In this state, time vanishes, and so do the distinctions between creator and creation. You are not interpreting the world—you are who the world is expressing itself through. This is the highest form of sadhana, where the art or craft ceases to be an external task and becomes an extension of your being. You are not performing or producing; you are 'becoming'.

When an artist becomes one with the art they pursue, they transcend the need for external validation. At this point, they have developed an intrinsic understanding of their craft. The artist is driven by an innate desire to refine their art. In this state of self-assurance, the artist's relationship with their work becomes intense, personal, and immune to external approval or disapproval fluctuations.

For every true artist, the journey of creation is more important than the final product. What fuels them is the passion for the process itself: the act of creating, expressing, and honing their craft. The joy lies in the experience of immersion. While they may appreciate the result, it's the hours spent creating, practising, or exploring that truly matter. In that sense, the process becomes an artist's meditation, a form of self-expression that nurtures their inner world. The process becomes dharma.

'I took a twenty-year break from performing on stage—a long hiatus. However, Shovana Didi and I stayed in touch throughout. I had to stop dancing in February 1992 due to complications during my pregnancy. Then, in 2012, just before Didi was leaving for Vienna, she visited me at home and invited me to return to the stage. She told me about an upcoming programme at Kamani, where we would perform solos and a duet together,' Shruti shares.

Shovana has a unique way of gently pulling her students out of the inertia they often fall into, whether due to personal challenges or distractions. She reminds them that dance is not just an art form but their dharma—a calling they must fulfil. She emphasises that returning to their practice is not only about perfecting a skill but also about the therapeutic power it holds.

'There's a balance between being fluid and staying true to the path. Shovana Di exemplifies this—she can be graceful and flexible, yet she never compromises on how things should be done. I remember one of her live performances where something went slightly wrong, whether it was her error or the musicians. No one likely noticed, but she paused and said, "Let's step back and start again." Through her, I've learned about creative discipline—not just in dance but in music, instruments, and the visual arts. She's opened a vast creative world for me,' Rahul shares with deep gratitude.

How do you balance strictness and the pursuit of perfection yet be fluid, tender, affectionate, inclusive, and forgiving?

Kishori Amonkar, the renowned Indian classical vocalist, once beautifully demonstrated this on stage when, as she began to sing, she addressed a woman in the front row wearing a yellow sari: 'You are slouching. Please sit up if you want to listen to me sing.' Amonkar explained that after dedicating herself so fully—travelling and rehearsing to perfect her craft—she expected the same level of commitment from her audience so that it becomes a shared experience.

Shovana, too, a staunch believer in punctuality and decorum, holds deep respect for art and artists alike.

'One such moment that left an indelible mark on me was when the late Dr Manmohan Singh, former Prime Minister of India, along with his wife, Mrs Gursharan Kaur arrived late for one of my performances and finding the auditorium full, stood humbly in the back rows. When I caught sight of them as the stage lights briefly illuminated the audience, I immediately requested the ushers to escort them to the appropriate seating. However, in their characteristic humility, they insisted on standing, acknowledging that they had arrived late. This incident reinforced my belief that respect for time and art go hand in hand.'

Another occasion that further cemented this value in her life was when she and Herbert arrived punctually for a special event in the biting cold of December, only to find that the hosts had not yet even left their residence. After waiting for an hour, she politely called to leave her best wishes and the gift, quietly wondering why people disregarded punctuality.

Shovana also believes that the audience should never be inconvenienced due to habitual delays by guests of honour. She finds it unfair that those who have taken the effort to arrive on time should have to endure discomfort simply because a dignitary has fallen behind schedule. Her commitment to respecting the audience's time ensures that she starts her performances without excessive delays, ensuring that the focus remains on the art rather than on social hierarchies.

In numerous instances, therefore, she has chosen to commence her performances after waiting no more than ten minutes for the chief guests, prioritising the sanctity of the art over social conventions.

Shakeel Bhai, one of her accompanists, often playfully grumbles at her, shaking his head with a mix of exasperation and admiration. He can't fathom why she insists on carrying her own bag and makeup box instead of letting her *shagird*s do it for her. Or why she's always the first to arrive at an event, a solid ten minutes early, while others stroll in at their own leisure. And don't even get him started on how she sticks to the time limit given by organisers for her performances—while everyone else happily stretches theirs! But Shovana just laughs it off, staying true to her values, much to Shakeel Bhai's amused frustration.

But she doesn't just stop here. She is the first face you come across when you arrive as an audience member for her programme, standing in all humility at the entrance, hands folded, personally welcoming each guest. She poses for pictures, shares warm hugs, and makes sure every person feels seen and appreciated. It's this rare, personal touch that sets her apart—she isn't just a performer on stage, but a gracious host who makes everyone feel like they belong. It's no wonder she is called a trendsetter—not for nothing, but for all the right reasons!

She is the perfect mix of flexibility and discipline. She sometimes demands long, challenging rehearsals, pushing you to perfect every movement. But then, she can also be your friend, laughing and having fun as if there's no tomorrow. She keeps you both challenged and at ease.

'It was December 1984, and we were in Dubai after a jam-packed day of performances. As soon as the show wrapped up, still in our Kathak costumes and riding the high of the performance, the whole crew—including the musicians—headed straight to the discotheque. It was an absolute blast!

'Back in Patna, we had just wrapped up a show at Gandhi Maidan during Dussehra, with crowds so big you could barely see the end of them. They were supposed to head to a nearby village for another performance, but the event ran late. So, there we were, getting ready by lantern light in the *Sarpanch*'s house and then hitting the stage—if you could call it a stage—a tiny bamboo platform. Two villages showed up, and we danced on, full of energy, until 3 am. The stage wobbled with every tabla beat, but nothing could shake our determination. It was chaos, but the best kind of chaos! These trips are full of fun, laughter, and genuine bonding. Backstage rehearsals are always a mix of teasing, jokes, exhaustion, and the shared challenge of making it all work,' Shruti shares with exuberance.

'Shovana Di is a woman of remarkable accessibility and humility, as much at ease with individuals as with the art she reveres. Recently, as I walked her through a conversation on art, someone interrupted. She kindly asked me to wait, exchanged warm pleasantries with the person, and then resumed our discussion, effortlessly balancing respect for the individual and the art.'

Rahul emphasises the need for an academy that promotes a cross-disciplinary approach, one that cultivates respect for every form of artistic expression. This initiative transcends individual artistry and taps into the essence of what it means to be human. It would not only train individuals to become skilled dancers or musicians but also open pathways to more fulfilling lives—whether by leading a company, running a business, or engaging with the world in a more thoughtful and perceptive way.

'Much like the experiences I witnessed as a child at Asavari, this academy would offer a full-time, immersive programme that nurtures a holistic understanding of the arts and life. If she were to spearhead this, it would leave behind a legacy that profoundly contributes to our nation's cultural and human fabric, shaping future generations into more empathetic, creative, and compassionate individuals,' Rahul observes.

Shovana Narayan, as a guru, embodies the brilliance of a comet, illuminating the artistic skies with her talent. Like a comet blazing through the cosmos, she not only dazzles with her light but leaves an enduring trail of brilliance in the form of her students. Each student feels nourished under her masterful guidance, sculpted with an artist's precision.

It's an act of giving—both enduring and transformative. With unwavering commitment and an astute aesthetic sense. Shovana refines her protégés, pouring into them the blood, sweat, and tears that make their growth a reflection of her art and a legacy of her spirit.

Pavan Varma holds deep admiration for this aspect of Shovana's persona as a classical dancer:

'It's worth highlighting that Shovana has dedicated significant energy to training her students. She trains them diligently, involves them in her productions, encourages them to deliver strong solo performances, and supports their participation in independent events. Her commitment to her students' growth and success has established her as an exceptional guru.'

Bhavabhinaya

Nuances in Motion
A Palette of Narratives

The purpose of art has been debated for centuries. Horace believed art should 'delight and instruct,' while Aristotle saw drama as a form of catharsis. Thinkers like Shakespeare, who explored human nature, and Dryden, who valued art for shaping morals, also wrestled with the tension between art as entertainment and as a tool for social change.

This debate is particularly relevant in the work of modern artists like Shovana, who has pioneered dance productions that do more than entertain—they stir the soul and provoke thought. Shovana's approach aligns with the idea expressed by Cesar A Cruz: 'Art should comfort the disturbed and disturb the comfortable.' Her performances don't simply provide an escape from reality; they challenge and unsettle, pushing the audience toward introspection and growth. As Pablo Picasso said, 'Art is the lie that enables us to realise the truth'.

Shovana's work invites the audience to face uncomfortable truths, nudging them toward positive change without being overtly didactic. Her dance productions navigate the delicate balance between art as catharsis and as a powerful agent for transformation, inspiring individuals to rethink, realign, and reshape their world.

Her emotions, like the sadness of Krishna's departure, feel real and deeply moving. Her performance lingers in your mind long after it ends. A simple shift in her expression can transform sadness into *harsh-ullas* (joy) without even changing the background or costume. Sometimes, the focus is solely on her face, with no movement, just light highlighting her expressions. These subtle details are what truly connects her with the audience.

Shovana has a unique talent for emotionally connecting with her audience. In Vrindavan, she once engaged the crowd by asking if they wanted to see the *Makhan Leela* or the *Raas Leela*. When they eagerly responded, 'both,' she happily fulfilled their request.

Unlike the refined audience at Kamani, the crowd in Vrindavan was raw and brimming with unfiltered excitement, expressing their emotions through gasps, cheers, and exclamations. When Radha showed her anger at Krishna, the audience's reactions revealed their deep engagement with the story. Such interactions highlight Shovana's adaptability as a performer, tailoring her art to suit an energetic crowd. Her ability to read and respond to their energy creates a powerful connection, making the experience unforgettable.

You might find yourself smiling with her as she radiates joy, only to feel your eyes well up moments later as she embodies the sorrow of Radha yearning for Krishna, Yashodhara parting with her son Rahul for Buddha's higher purpose, or Draupadi's anguish as she faces the cruelty of being gambled away. Her expressions are so vivid, so deeply rooted in truth, that they draw you in entirely. And as you feel these emotions, something profound stirs within you. Without realising it, your perspective shifts. Layers of prejudice dissolve, and you begin to see the world with greater empathy as if a veil has been lifted. It's not just a performance—it's a transformation, leaving you forever changed.

Art has a unique, gentle way of influencing people. It speaks to the subconscious, subtly weaving lessons into its narrative without force or direct instruction. You don't feel like you're being taught; instead, the message quietly reshapes your thoughts and later reflects in your actions and mindset.

Shovana has elevated Kathak to new heights, broadening its scope beyond the traditional Radha-Krishna stories. She has infused the form with modern themes and powerful social commentary. For instance, as early as 1982-83, she presented *Dishantar*, a remarkable production centred on environmental issues. At a time when such topics were rarely discussed, her work was both groundbreaking and ahead of its time, showcasing her vision and adaptability as an artist.

Ishan shares, 'My mother is a true trailblazer, celebrated for her innovative and unconventional approach to Kathak. While I'm not an expert in dance, it's evident that her work has always pushed beyond traditional boundaries. She's endlessly curious, diving deep into research to question established norms and introduce fresh perspectives to her art. Although she occasionally repeats performances at the audience's request, her true passion lies in constantly exploring and creating something new.'

Perkha emphasises Shovana's relentless passion for exploration and her ability to redefine established norms: 'Kathak is a deeply classical art form, and she has fully embraced its traditions. Yet, it's equally true that she has reimagined them, inspired by her rich, multicultural experiences. Her impact on the field isn't about breaking the rules but reinterpreting them in ways that resonate with contemporary contexts. This approach reflects her diverse life journey and boundless curiosity.'

Through her dance, Shovana addressed essential issues like pollution and the caste system long before they were widely discussed. In her performance, *Kalia Daman*, where Krishna tames the serpent Kalia in the Yamuna river, she used the story as a metaphor. Krishna cleansing the river of poison symbolises the need to purify our environment and protect our natural resources from pollution.

'We created *Mukti Lekha* inspired by L N Singhvi's poem, addressing various societal issues. We tackled themes like apartheid in South Africa, the Satyagraha movement, trafficking of women in the Middle East, infanticide, and incest. These were disturbing issues, *and* Shovana Didi meant to disturb,' Shruti remarks.

Shovana's dance aims to provoke thought and raise awareness of society's hidden issues. Her performances go beyond beauty, conveying a subtext that reaches your subconscious. It's not necessarily about taking drastic action but raising awareness that these issues exist, and that change is possible.

In *Stri Spandan*, first premiered in 2009 in Chennai and later again on 14 October 2024, at the Stein Auditorium in Delhi, the production explores the inner worlds of three iconic women from the Mahabharata—Kunti, Draupadi, and Gandhari. Through dance and storytelling, this powerful abhinaya-based performance reimagines their reflective journeys, offering fresh perspectives on their choices, paths, and the consequences they faced. From their unique viewpoints, each woman asks, 'If I had a second chance, would I have acted differently?'

This exploration recalls a question raised by the renowned journalist and editor of the *Hindustan Times*, H K Dua, who was deeply moved by an earlier performance of Shovana's. In this performance, Draupadi, in a moment of intense fury, confronts her husband, Yudhishthir, over the humiliating gambling incident. Dua recalls, 'One performance that left a lasting impact on me was Shovana's portrayal of Draupadi at the Maurya hotel in Delhi. Sunit Tandon from All India Radio played Yudhishthir, and Shovana powerfully depicted Draupadi's anguish when Yudhishthir gambled her away, as told in the Mahabharata. Her portrayal of Draupadi's anger and betrayal was so moving that it gave me goosebumps.'

H K Dua praises Shovana's ability to breathe new life into these ancient stories, infusing them with raw emotion and deep passion.

'The act, however, ended with Draupadi reconciling, which left me with lingering questions. Years later, in 2024, I saw *Stri Spandan*. While it didn't provide all the answers, the performance offered insights into the reasons behind the decisions made at that time. It opened an intense dialogue, offering not just a performance but a contemplation of women's roles and choices throughout history.'

He nostalgically recalls his first meeting with Shovana Narayan at a diplomatic reception, where Mr Atal Bihari Vajpayee made the introduction. During the conversation, reminiscing, Mr Vajpayee told Shovana that Dua had once given him a ride on his Lambretta scooter while working as a special correspondent for the *Indian Express*.

Padma Bhushan H K Dua, a former Member of Parliament, editor, media advisor to the Prime Minister, and ambassador, overcame considerable challenges on his path to becoming a distinguished journalist. Throughout his career, he held editorial positions at leading newspapers such as the *Hindustan Times, Indian Express, Times of India*, and the *Tribune* in Chandigarh.

He deeply values his connection with Shovana and admires her commitment to dance and her willingness to explore themes beyond conventional thinking. Her ability to evoke the emotions of mythological women, with whom she shares neither time nor space, is truly remarkable.

'Although the act concluded with reconciliation, the intensity of Draupadi's accusations stayed with me,' he recalls.

Sunit emphasises that real life is complex and filled with contradictions, and great art reflects this richness. It never offers simple black-and-white portrayals. Art elevates by capturing the nuances of human nature, allowing for multiple interpretations. As actors, it's their job to embody the writer's vision, fully immersing themselves in their character's perspective, regardless of their personal views. This depth brings characters to life and makes art meaningful, leaving a lasting impact on the audience.

Kunti, the matriarch of the Pandavas, revisits the complex decisions she made as a mother, particularly her role in the birth and abandonment of Karna and the moral dilemmas that arose from her protective instincts. Her maternal sacrifices, while often seen as virtuous, carry a heavy emotional toll that leads her to question whether her choices indeed served her family or deepened their suffering.

Draupadi, the fiery queen who played a pivotal role in the events of the Mahabharata, reflects on how her actions shaped not only her destiny but the course of history itself. Was her unrelenting call for justice justified, or did it fuel the flames of conflict? Could a different response to her humiliation have altered the fate of her loved ones, or was the path she chose the only one available?

Gandhari, the blindfolded queen of Hastinapur, contemplates the burden of her loyalty and the ultimate consequences of her silent suffering. Her choice to blindfold herself in solidarity with her husband, Dhritarashtra, became a symbol of devotion and a metaphor for the blindness of her son's unchecked ambitions. Did her sacrifices hold meaning, or did they contribute to the tragic downfall of her family?

Through this retelling, *Stri Spandan* breathes new life into these revered figures, inviting audiences to connect with their deeply human experiences of love, loss, and regret. It raises profound questions: If Kunti, Draupadi, and Gandhari had chosen differently, what would have been the tenor of the Mahabharata? In today's context, are they seen as victors or victims? Would their choices stand up to the scrutiny of modern sensibilities? Did the weight of fate inevitably shape them?

The production offers no definitive answers but encourages reflection, leaving room for differing perspectives on these timeless characters and their eternal struggles.

In a way, *Stri Spandan* mirrors the timeless nature of the Mahabharata itself—an epic that evolves with each retelling, with the same characters inhabiting new dimensions, shaped by the reflections and reinterpretations of each generation. Through this lens, the women of the Mahabharata emerge not merely as historical figures, but as deeply relatable individuals whose stories resonate with contemporary audiences.

The traditional portrayal of Kunti often romanticises the birth of Karna and his abandonment to protect her family's honour, as well as the birth of her three sons—Yudhisthir, Arjun, and Bheema. Her offhand remark, 'share what you have brought,' when her sons returned with Draupadi, has often been overlooked. However, this statement becomes the central theme of *Kunti ki Vinati*.

Kunti, the mother of the Pandavas, was a woman who lived by her principles. With the lineage of mighty emperors in her blood, she demonstrated unyielding determination and purpose throughout her life. She asserted her independence through her encounters with Durvasa, the Sun God, and later by summoning different deities to father her sons. She even chose Pandu in a *swayamvara*. But how could such a strong-willed woman accept Draupadi being shared by her sons? Could she not recognise the injustice in her impulsive words, 'All of you share what has been obtained,' spoken without knowing Draupadi was the object of discussion? Where was her independence and clarity of thought?

Kunti ki Vinati explores the hidden turmoil in Kunti's mind, probing her inner conflict and anguish. Her sons, who were once bound by the chain of maternal love, now faced a dilemma—would their shared wife strengthen their bond or drive them apart? Could Kunti's rash statement be turned into an opportunity? Could Draupadi become the thread that would bind the brothers even tighter, especially in the shadow of the impending war?

Paanch moti hain anmol mere,
Maatri prem dhaage mein hain bandhe.
Par chinta kachotati mere baad,
Kaise rahenge ye saath-saath?

Swabhaav sabhi putra vadhuon ke,
Bhrata bhaav na baandh sakenge.
Bikhaarenge moti ekaaki sansaar,
Roti main isi vichaar ke aagaar.

Rahti hai kaanon mein goonjati,
Vikal vedna Draupadi ki,
'Baanton na mujhe, bacha lo ma Kunti,
Vastu nahi, hoon bhaav bhaari naari.'

Draupadi, tum kya jaano duvidha meri,
Jatil ghadi mein ghire hum sabhi,
Kaun mitr, kaun shatru, pahachanati nahi,
Putra-vadhhu kab bikhre, main janati nahi.

Vinati meri hai tumse Draupadi,
Aanchal pasare ma bheekh maangati,
Ban lo dhaaga, piro lo moti,
Goonj raha garjan Mahabharat ghari.

Kunti's decisions were driven by securing the Pandavas' claim to the throne. While she understood Draupadi's pain, she ignored her pleas, believing the survival of the Pandava dynasty was paramount. Her final words urged her sons to fight—not for a kingdom, but for an honourable life. In her view, her actions were justified by the belief that all is fair in love and war.

This piece offers a profound insight into the intricate workings of a human mind caught between duty, honour, and personal conflict.

Draupadi, born from the sacrificial fire and embodying Agni's essence, was won by Arjun in an open swayamvara. Her anguish at being asked to be shared among the five brothers has often been highlighted. She reflects on how no one sought her consent or respected her feelings. Despite her pleas, Kunti insisted she comply with the command to her sons 'share what you have brought' while the sons remained silent, offering no protest.

Draupadi's laughter at Duryodhana, calling him the 'blind son of blind parents,' ignited his thirst for revenge. Later, Yudhishthir, the *Dharma-putra*, gambled her away without her consent and lost. Her humiliation deepened when Dushasana dragged her into court and attempted to disrobe her. Outraged, she vowed not to tie her hair until she washed it with Dushasana's blood.

In the end, Draupadi lost everyone, even her children. Reflecting on her life, she questioned whether she was a victor or a victim. Turning to Krishna, her saviour during the *cheer haran,* she asked, 'O Krishna, my friend and guide, was this war the result of my vow? Was it my victory or my defeat?' Her introspection reveals her deep sense of injustice and the emotional turmoil she faced amid betrayal, humiliation, and loss.

The third character, Gandhari, queen to the blind Dhritarashtra, chose to blindfold herself for the entirety of her married life. Was this an act of devotion as a *pati-vrata stri* or an escape from reality? According to traditional texts, her sacrifice of sight and her austere life endowed her with great spiritual power.

The Mahabharata mourns the destruction caused by the Kaurava-Pandava war. Gandhari's anguish was profound as she discovered Duryodhana's death and Ashwatthama's curse of eternal suffering for killing the Pandavas' heir in Uttara's womb. Her grief led her to curse Krishna, ultimately dooming the Yadavas and marking the transition to *Kali Yuga*, a time of declining values.

Could Gandhari have changed fate? By blindfolding herself to her sons' faults, did she miss the chance to alter events?

Stri Spandan delves into such timeless questions, reflecting the enduring struggles and emotions of women across eras.

Sharon Lowen, who portrayed Gandhari in *Stri Spandan*, reflects on their collaboration, highlighting how their unique qualities complemented each other seamlessly. In art, they were equals, supporting one another's strengths and respecting each other's journeys.

An American Odissi dancer, Sharon has been trained by Guru Kelucharan Mohapatra since 1975. She has performed extensively, choreographed for film and television, and presented hundreds of concerts across India, North America, Asia, Africa, the UK, and the Middle East. Interestingly, Sharon arrived in India in 1973—the same year Shovana began her teaching career.

'Shovana, shaped by her civil service background, remains focused, avoids gossip, and never undermines others. Her energy and dedication fill auditoriums as she genuinely cares for everyone involved. I admire how she brings people together with creativity and clear direction. Once, we performed together at the Suraj Kund mela, organised by our friend and collaborator, artist Naresh Kapuria. She performed Kathak while I performed Odissi. It was fascinating to see the audience split—some preferred her Kathak, others my Odissi, but both were deeply appreciated. This diversity, like a garden of varied flowers, enriches our performances.

'Another unforgettable project was a large-scale film shot in Khajuraho, where Shovana brought together dancers from diverse styles and a cinematographer from Chennai. We performed in the temples to the recitation of Sanskrit shlokas, creating a stunning visual and cultural experience. On another occasion, Naresh designed a giant birdcage for a performance, and Shovana danced, ah, so gracefully inside it.

'Her ideas come to life with elegance and precision. She envisions concepts and executes them effortlessly, blending creativity with efficiency. Collaborations with thinkers like Ramu Gandhi have resulted in extraordinary performances inspired by philosophy, poetry, and scripture. A quick thinker and highly organised, Shovana consistently expands her artistic horizons with every project,' Sharon explains.

Ishan proudly highlights his mother's collaborative spirit as an artiste: 'Mom was a pioneer in blending Kathak with other dance forms, expanding its horizons in ways shaped by her upbringing, global exposure, and marriage to an Austrian diplomat. Her travels and broad perspective made the traditional confines of Kathak feel 'limited' and 'limiting.' Instead, she drew connections and contrasts between Kathak and other styles, using those insights to innovate. Unlike many who define themselves by a specific *Gharana*, she deliberately avoided such labels. She believes no single Gharana negates the value of another and focusing on just one can limit artistic possibilities. This inclusivity and expansive vision have been her greatest strengths.'

***

Shovana seeks to offer a fresh perspective on what has long been accepted without question. In her interpretation of *Rashmirathi* by Ramdhari Singh Dinkar, a poem about the Mahabharata, she focuses on the episode of Kunti and Karna. She brings out a seldom-explored side of Karna, evoking deep sympathy for him. The moment when Karna promises Kunti that, regardless of the war's outcome, she will always have her five sons is filled with profound pathos.

Vachan diya—main, yudh bhoomi mein,
Arjun chhod, kisi ko na maarunga!
Tum Pandavon ki ma ho, maate!
Yeh sehra na tujhse kabhi chhinunga!
Karna vachan yeh deta hai,
Ab tum mujhe krutagnata se marne do...

Women in the Mahabharata and other epics are often idealised as figures like Sati, Savitri, and various demigods, representing devotion, sacrifice, and strength. Shovana challenges this conventional perspective, urging audiences to rethink these narratives and question the roles assigned to these women.

She invites her audience to delve deeper into the emotions and experiences of women, revealing the complexities of their lives beyond the myths that have shaped them.

Men often overlook the depths of women's inner worlds, seeing them only through the lens of societal roles and expectations. They may acknowledge their contribution yet fail to grasp the essence of who they are—individuals with dreams, desires, and complexities.

Shovana feels troubled by this lack of understanding, recognising how societal norms often reduce women to mere extensions of the men in their lives.

She resonates with: '*Mujhko bahut unhone maana, phir bhi kya poora pehchaana*?'—highlighting the difference between being acknowledged and truly understood.

She feels a strong affinity with creators who compose from the female perspective as they dare to explore the nuances of womanhood. These artists dive into the emotional landscapes of their characters, bringing forth many shades of experience that define women's lives. She aims to illuminate these hidden depths, encouraging society to see beyond the surface and recognise the vibrant, multifaceted individuals that women are.

Her mission is to promote a better understanding of women's experiences, challenging the simple narratives that often dominate. She hopes to bridge the gap between perception and reality by sharing their perspectives. In doing this, Shovana honours women's voices and calls for a more empathetic dialogue, celebrating and understanding the richness of the female experience.

One of her iconic productions was the hour-long ballet *Kab*

Aogey Rama, presented in 1984. This ballet explored the women waiting for Rama—Sita, Ahilya, Shabari—each highlighting different facets of devotion and longing. Through this performance, they examined Ram's journey, reflecting on how his life was intertwined with the women who waited for him, showcasing their strength, resilience, and unwavering devotion.

Kab Aogey Rama invites reflection on the complexities of relationships and the unseen sacrifices of those who wait. It urges us to recognise the voices of these women, honouring their devotion and exploring the deeper dynamics of love, duty, and human connections.

Shovana Narayan's research-driven approach re-examines traditional tales, encouraging fresh perspectives on familiar narratives. For instance, she delves into the symbolic significance of Rama's *padukas* (slippers), placed on the throne by Bharat during Ram's exile, prompting deeper questions about their role and meaning as the story unfolds.

She probes into sensitive issues often overlooked or ignored, such as why Rama chose to subject Sita to the *agni-pariksha* (trial by fire) and the mystery of her subsequent disappearance.

Instead of offering straightforward solutions, she presents alternative viewpoints, encouraging audiences to reflect on the complexities of these situations. When Lakshman attempts to bring Sita back, her refusal to return highlights her autonomy and the symbolic importance of the paduka, representing Ram's authority and honour.

Shovana emphasises that these narratives are not merely tales but avenues for critical thinking, urging us to confront the intricacies of human relationships and societal expectations embedded within them.

Manjari Sinha observes that Shovana is always open to new

ideas, people, and experiences, continually absorbing what's meaningful. She evolves constantly, infusing new elements into even familiar performances. Her commitment to growth keeps her artistry fresh and dynamic, reflecting her belief that success requires continuous effort. She reminds us that '*Udyamena hi sidhyanti kāryāṇi na manorathaiḥ. Na hi suptasya siṃhasya praviśanti mukhe mṛigāḥ*,' meaning success comes through effort, not mere desire—just as a deer never walks into the mouth of a sleeping lion.

Shovana refuses to be constrained by the boundaries of traditional art, history, or time. Rather than simply performing what has been passed down for centuries, she delves deep into the history of civilisations, exploring their dances, rituals, philosophies, and ancient texts—such as the Vedas, epics, and inscriptions—to uncover deeper meanings. She seeks the abstract, the unspoken truths that transcend generations, holding a mirror to life itself. For her, art is not merely about preserving the past but about questioning, reinterpreting, and finding relevance for the future.

Her artistry is an intellectual journey driven by constant research, discourse, and questioning. She believes the fine arts can make us more humane, connected, and empathetic, foreseeing their role in shaping a future where art is a powerful force, not just a cultural artifact, and a guide for how we live and interact.

Manjari Sinha, a writer for publications like *Hindustan, Jansatta, The Hindu*, and *Statesman*, highlights how Shovana embraces creativity in all forms. She engages with various artistic and intellectual expressions, attending diverse events like stage shows, exhibitions, and conferences while staying connected to her artistic community and remaining unbound by any specific social boundaries.

Shovana views art as a living entity that evolves with time, using it to explore and elevate humanity. She has brought to life the stories of remarkable women like Akka Mahadevi from Karnataka, Lal Ded from Kashmir, Meera Bai, and characters from Vidhyapati, all known for challenging societal norms and following their spiritual paths with courage.

Akka Mahadevi, a twelfth century poet-saint, was devoted to Lord Shiva. She left behind material life, even shedding her clothes to symbolise her rejection of worldly attachments. Shovana captures this fearless quest for spiritual freedom.

Lal Ded, or Lalleshwari, was a fourteenth century mystic poetess from Kashmir. She spoke against religious restrictions and searched for a personal connection with the divine. Through Shovana's portrayal, Lal Ded's independence and spiritual search come alive.

Meera Bai, the sixteenth century princess and poetess, is celebrated for her love and devotion to Lord Krishna. She faced opposition from her family and society but chose to dedicate her life to Krishna. Shovana beautifully expresses Meera's deep devotion and courage to follow her heart despite all obstacles.

Vidhyapati, a fourteenth century poet from Bihar, often wrote about women's emotions, especially in love and devotion. Shovana explores the feminine aspects of Vidhyapati's work, portraying women's experiences with a depth that connects with audiences personally.

Her performances transcend dance, offering deeply researched portrayals. She immerses herself in these women's history, culture, and emotions, presenting their stories from a fresh perspective. She brings out these extraordinary figures' timeless strength and spirit through her work.

She also collaborates closely with her musicians, drawing

on her understanding of music—*rasas* (emotions), *swaras* (notes), and *talas* (rhythms). This collaboration ensures a seamless blend of dance and music, enriching the emotional depth of her performances.

Shovana has consistently been ahead of her time, pushing the boundaries of dance through innovative experiments with choreography, lighting, sound, visuals, and audience engagement. A striking example of her forward-thinking approach is the 1986 performance titled *Dvani-Pratidhvani.* In this groundbreaking piece, the dancers wore black kurtas and white churidars, creating a dramatic effect where their torsos were shrouded in darkness. The audience was drawn solely to the dancers' feet, transforming the performance into a mesmerising jugalbandi where one dancer initiated a movement, seamlessly picked up by the next, and so on. This extraordinary collaboration among six dancers redefined traditional Kathak themes through a fresh lens. The dancers aimed to convey the concept of *layakari* (harmony) as an underlying current, symbolising the *nirantarta* (continuity) of the life force that connects all humans, elements, and nature. The philosophical foundation of *Dvani-Pratidhvani* resonates deeply with the poem *Mera Safar*, highlighting the legacy passed down from one generation to another.

Through this innovative work, Shovana showcased her mastery as a dancer and her intellectual attitude, challenging audiences to engage with dance in profound and multifaceted ways.

The performance garnered acclaim, with one critic likening it to the avant-garde spirit of the Ku Klux Klan. The comparison serves as a provocative metaphor highlighting its boundary-breaking nature.

The term avant-garde refers to innovative and experimental approaches in art that challenge established norms, much like

Shovana's work that obscured the dancers' torsos and focused solely on their feet, creating a unique visual experience.

Although the Ku Klux Klan is notorious for its violent and racist ideologies, the critic likely uses this reference to emphasise the radical and transformative impact of Shovana's performance within the artistic landscape, prompting audiences to engage with and reconsider the nature of artistic expression. Ultimately, it illustrates how art can reshape societal perceptions, encouraging dialogue about innovation and rebellion.

Dance by Candlelight

Shovana was dancing at the centre of the stage, the soft hum of the packed auditorium filling the air. The evening was perfect—her ghunghroos tied snugly, the tabla in flawless sync, the crowd fully immersed in her performance. Then, without warning, the lights went out.

'A power cut?' she thought, the faint murmur of the audience breaking her concentration. 'Patna's summer heat and now this. Should I stop? Wait it out? But what if they leave? No… the show must go on.'

The silence pressed in, heavy and expectant. Her heart raced, not out of fear but from the spark of a challenge. 'Kathak is more than visuals,' she reminded herself, 'It's rhythm, sound, emotion. Even in darkness, it can breathe.'

She took a deep breath, the jingling of her ghunghroos cutting through the stillness. Her feet struck the stage, sharp and precise, carving out a symphony of rhythm. The tabla joined her, their dialogue growing more intense with each beat.

'Let them feel the dance,' she thought, her movements now painting pictures in the audience's minds. She imagined the sound

waves rippling through the darkness, drawing the audience closer.

The murmurs faded. The crowd, entranced by the rhythm, leaned in. 'This is it,' she realised, 'a moment where art transcends sight, where it becomes pure ecstasy.'

The soft glow of candles brought a new dimension to the performance. When she picked up a lantern during the thumri, using its light to accentuate the emotions of Radha's search for Krishna, the audience witnessed a transformation—what began as a challenge became an unforgettable masterpiece of innovation and grace.

Minutes stretched into eternity, and the applause was deafening when the lights finally flickered back on. Shovana smiled; the sweat glistening on her face proudly spoke of her resolve. 'Even in the absence of light,' she thought, 'dance can still shine.'

This was in 1981 when Shovana was invited to perform at the prestigious Bharatiya Nritya Kala Mandir auditorium in Patna during a hot June evening. The event was a fundraiser with an overflowing audience and high expectations. About half an hour into her performance, everything seemed to be going perfectly—until the lights suddenly went out.

After thirty minutes, the organisers brought in candles, offering light. That's when Shovana shifted to Kathak's abhinaya (expressive) aspect, performing a thumri. With limited lighting, she chose to sit and focus on the bhava-*batana*—the subtle, layered portrayal of emotions through facial expressions and gestures. Later, while emoting to a thumri where Radha searches for Krishna, Shovana picked up a lantern to highlight her eye expressions and add to the mystic charm of the scene.

The improvisation and resilience of Kathak, combined with Shovana's mastery, had turned what could have been a disaster into an unforgettable performance.

The soft glow from the lanterns illuminated the space just enough, and she rose to the occasion, quite literally. With the stage now bathed in flickering light, Shovana unleashed a flurry of rhythmical footwork, covering every inch of the stage with precision and grace. What followed was nothing short of magic.

The audience remained transfixed despite the oppressive heat and lack of air conditioning. Over two and a half hours slipped unnoticed as if time had slowed in reverence to the synergy between the dancer and spectators. Without the comforts of artificial lights or sound, not a single person left the auditorium.

The atmosphere was charged with a different kind of energy, one that transcended the usual performance highs. Shovana and her audience had been transported into a realm where the dance had become a shared experience of resilience and connection.

The next day, the front pages of newspapers featured a striking photograph of her mid-performance, accompanied by the headline: 'Candlelight Dance by Daughter of Bihar,' capturing the essence of the unforgettable evening. But beyond the public acclaim, Shovana took away a more profound lesson from that evening—navigating unforeseen challenges with grace and ingenuity. It was also a powerful reminder of Kathak's innate richness, multi-dimensionality, and capacity to thrive even in total darkness.

A journey into the origins of classical dance takes us to ritualistic performances set amidst incense and oil lamps. In such sacred contexts, when used for prayer, dance movements and expressions are minimalist, reflecting sublimation and introspection. Dim lighting aids in achieving states like *pratyahara* (withdrawal of senses), *dharana* (concentration), and *dhyana* (meditation), as bright lights distract the mind. However, storytelling and expressive dance forms, like Kathak, require more illumination to emphasise pronounced actions and expressions. Flickering oil lamps create mysterious shadows, allowing the delicate nuances of dance—such as subtle hand gestures or facial expressions—to stand out.

In forms like Kathakali, performed under the night sky with a central wick lamp, the interplay of light magnifies the slightest eye movements, enhancing the surreal, otherworldly atmosphere. The soft amber light, combined with white or pastel costumes, adds to the ethereal mood, creating an aura of finesse and romanticism in every movement.

In earlier times, while night performances were favoured for their allure of secrecy and romance, day performances presented a stark contrast. In daylight, the stage was fully exposed, stripping away the mystery. Performing under the sun or an awning required different spatial dynamics, relying on more dramatic movements, vibrant costumes, and energetic enactments to captivate the audience.

In Kathak, this meant focusing on the *tayyari ang* (technical mastery) and sequences like *gat* bhava and *kavitts*. The performer had to engage the audience entirely, overcoming distractions in a less immersive environment.

Historically, the transition from candlelight and oil lamps to gas lamps expanded the performance area, offering a bridge between day and night. Introducing electric lights created a limitless space, freeing performers to use grander, more dynamic movements. However, the arrival of dimmers brought a new dilemma—should lighting be controlled to restore the mystery and romance of earlier times? While some resisted, insisting the strength of the performance alone should create the magic, others embraced lighting's evolving role.

Lighting soon became a tool to enhance specific movements

and moods, reintroducing the mystique of the candlelight era. Intelligent lighting allowed artists to balance expansive and subtle movements, spotlighting delicate nuances. Overuse can feel gimmicky, and no amount of lighting can mask an inadequate performance.

Ultimately, judicious lighting serves as a gateway to illusion and fantasy, highlighting every delicate movement, from the flutter of fingers to the grandeur of cosmic-like explosions. Lighting enhances the magical interplay of space and motion, offering audiences a sensory escape into infinity.

When the Curtain Falls, I Rise

Spectator:

You are the star that grieves no night,
A perfect bloom in flawless light.
No tremor mars your steady flame,
No wound, no shadow speaks your name.

Artist:

Ah, but the star is born of fire,
Its light a cry, its core desire.
The bloom you see, so pure, so fair,
Has roots that twist through soil of care.

Spectator:

Yet we look to you for skies serene,
A realm where pain has never been.
Your art must rise, untouched,divine—
A mirror free of mortal line.

Artist:

But mirrors break to show their truth,
And skies are deep with storm and ruth.
What beauty lives without its scars?
What soul is shaped without its wars?

Spectator:

If cracks betray your hidden fight,
Will it not dim the sacred light?
Would not the spell, so finely spun,
Unravel, thread by thread, undone?

Artist:

No, light endures through fractured glass,
And strength is born where shadows pass.
The spell you feel, the awe it lends,
Is spun from places pain transcends.

Spectator:

Then flaw is not a curse, but grace,
The tender truth the heart must face.
Perhaps the art that stirs, enchants,
Is grown in soil of second chance.

Artist:

Yes, let no artist hide their ache,
For every fall, the spirit wakes.
Our wounds, our flaws, are songs untold—
The truest art is soft, yet bold.

Phoenix-rising from ashes

The artist's stage is a sacred space—a place where vulnerability and mastery collide and where the boundary between the self and the audience dissolves. To create art is to bare your soul; to risk exposure in its rawest form. It's a dance on a tightrope stretched between triumph and collapse, with every performance a silent question: Do I dare share this with the world?

Do you retreat, shield your humanity, or let the world see your flaws, pain, and perseverance?

Do you remain the enigmatic creator, or do you risk showing the cracks in the facade?

Art, after all, is not perfection—it is the courage to reveal oneself.

Anklet bells and painkillers

'I was basking in the glow of success. Our performances had been met with thunderous applause—standing ovations, glowing reviews, packed halls in Africa and Europe. The air was electric with validation. During one of my final performances in Prague, the mood felt celestial. The audience was alive, their energy inspiring; the gods seemed pleased. The programme began with a bang, the kind that echoes in your soul and tells you: This is magic.

But just as art can elevate, it can also betray. Amid the performance, I felt it—a sudden, horrifying stillness. My left leg refused to move. It was as though the limb had abandoned me, leaving me helpless on a stage where grace and precision were paramount. I dragged it behind me, panic creeping into every corner of my mind.

In the theatre of my mind, imaginary headlines screamed in bold: "Her feet couldn't move." Other damning voices joined the chorus, whispers of disappointment slicing through my fragile confidence: "She was not what we had heard of her."

"This won't do," I told myself, trying to mask the growing terror. In an impromptu act of storytelling, I sat down, pretending to be a heroine awaiting her beloved, massaging the lifeless limb, willing it back to life.

Nothing worked. The leg remained unyielding, time crawling in an eternal loop.

"'Can they see it?"' I thought, my heart racing. "Do they know something's wrong? What will they think?"

Inside, I was weeping, a silent, desperate plea escaping my soul: "God, help me! If I have wronged you, knowingly or unknowingly, forgive me now. Please, My Lord, don't forsake me in this moment." My frightened inner self sobbed in fear, pain, and disbelief. Why had this happened? And why so suddenly, so cruelly?

The pain that coursed through me was beyond physical—it was consuming, relentless, unbearable. Even now, as I relive those moments, I can say with certainty that the agony of that night far surpassed the time I danced on a stage littered with shards of broken glass in 1999.

This was not just a bodily affliction; it was a spiritual and emotional collapse, a kind of paralysis that threatened to strip away my identity as a dancer.

Mercifully, as is the custom in Europe, there was an interval. The moment the curtain fell, so did I. I collapsed backstage, unable to contain my anguish. Tears streamed down my face as waves of pain wracked my body.

My musicians formed a human curtain around me, shielding me from the eyes of the audience as Herbert carried me into the green room.

But the show must go on.

It always must.

I swallowed a few painkillers, forcing myself to rise again. Back on stage, I restructured my performance in the blink of an eye, adapting every movement to accommodate my condition. Miraculously, the audience remained unaware of the turmoil behind the scenes. Their applause at the end was thunderous; the reviews the next day were glowing. I could only thank the good Lord for holding me through what had felt like an impossible ordeal.

The next day brought answers I was not ready to face. At the hospital, the doctor who examined my X-rays was stunned. He couldn't fathom how I had been dancing—let alone standing—with the extent of the damage to my knees. His diagnosis was grim: permanent swelling, permanent pain, and an inability to bend. He urged me to give up all vigorous physical activity, including dance.

"Give up dance?" I asked, incredulous. The very suggestion

was unthinkable. Dance was my breath, my being, my offering to the divine. No way. I refused.

I adapted. Painkillers became my constant companions, as essential as my ghunghroos. Movements requiring deep knee bends or prolonged sitting were no longer possible. I adjusted my repertoire and even my storytelling. I often joke that earlier, my depictions of Lord Vishnu on his *Anantnaga shaiya* (serpent bed) would feature him reclining gracefully with one outstretched leg. Now, he is a 'standing reclining Vishnu'—a creative compromise born of necessity.'

The patchwork of pain

'A few years later, someone in the CGA's office where I was on deputation remarked, "Shovs, what is that dark tinge next to your eyes?"

"Dark tinge? Oh, it must be my eyeliner. I have this awful habit of rubbing my eyes, forgetting that I have *kajal* on."

'A few months later....

"Wipe your cheeks, please. There is some mark there," a colleague commented.

'I rubbed and rubbed, but the mark did not come off. Remarks like "There are dark patches near your mouth" or "You have not been sleeping well, for there are dark patches near your eyes," changed to "Gosh, how black you've become!" or "Have you burnt your skin somewhere? The texture looks burnt!" I was alarmed. In a couple of years, my smooth brown complexion had become coal black with a burnt texture! The lightest part of my face happened to be my lips!

'I am not exaggerating. The darker—rather, blacker—my skin became, the more I tried to hide it with makeup. But the more I resorted to it, the more obvious it became!

What a vicious cycle! I underwent extensive treatments across every field of medicine—homeopathy, allopathy, ayurveda—everything! In my desperation, I even turned to a beautician. Yet, there wasn't the slightest improvement. For a long time, I endured the cruel remarks without revealing how deeply they hurt me. But in April 1997, I finally broke down in the privacy of my room. Among the many harsh comments, some were intended to soothe me, but they offered no comfort. "So many verses describe dark Krishna adorned with *chandan* (sandalwood) paste. Your case is similar," they said. Do you think that brought me any solace? Not in the least! I cried and cried, overwhelmed by despair, feeling like I didn't want to live anymore. "What have I done? Why did it have to happen?" I wept aloud. "Maybe your inner strength is being tested." "But why in such a manner?"

(Extract from *Meandering Pastures of Memories)*

Shovana clung desperately to every piece of advice, hoping against hope that the toxic hyperpigmentation would fade. Each visit to the doctor's clinic became a trial, her heart sinking at the familiar faces that looked at her with shock, revulsion, or barely concealed pity. The once-confident dancer now felt reduced to a curiosity—a tragedy unfolding before their eyes.

Eventually, Dr Kalyan Sachdeva, recognising the severity of her condition, referred her to Vienna. There, Professor Dr Klaus Wolf was visibly stunned upon seeing her. Specialists from across the globe examined her and, one by one dismissed her case as hopeless. Some even urged Dr Wolf to walk away, warning that no good could come of his efforts. But he refused to give up, taking her case as a challenge.

Extensive tests followed—on cosmetics, reactions to sunlight and artificial light, and even a skin biopsy. Yet, the condition only worsened. Dark patches began to spread to areas untouched by makeup, dismantling her belief that her stage cosmetics were the culprit.

The final diagnosis was cruel: an extreme sensitivity to all forms of light, with little hope for a complete recovery.

At best, Dr Wolf could only attempt to diminish the damage.

The verdict weighed heavily, but for Shovana, the faintest glimmer of possibility was still a lifeline.

'I agreed to take the risk. Today, after four years, there has been a noticeable improvement. As promised by Dr Wolff, the path to recovery has been extremely slow.

But have the nasty barbs died down regarding my powdered face? No, not at all! How can they? The world needs food for gossip!'

***

Shovana has the gut that tells her she can still reign as the heart that captivates and the guts to unbolt the cupboard of her mind and soul, baring the skeletons the world dreads to see. Society clings to the illusion that an artist must be flawless—in craft, in appearance—but Shovana has conquered the silent war against such myths. While she has battled self-doubt in the wake of painful trials, those around her see no imperfection in her face, grace, or the charisma that binds them to her. If anything has deepened, it is not the blemishes on her being but the quiet admiration she never sought. Her dear friend, Jyotsna Suri, reflects on these deceptive beauty standards, reminding us how often we beguile ourselves, failing to honour life's true gifts.

'For me, beauty is not defined by flawless skin, perfect hair, or a sculpted form—it is something far deeper and radiates from within. A person may possess striking physical features, yet if their heart harbours cruelty, that external beauty fades, overshadowed by their inner darkness. None of us are born perfect, nor do we lead ideal lives. Perfection itself is subjective—what seems perfect to me may not be the same for you. Beauty, too, is shaped by personal perceptions. True beauty cannot be measured by appearance alone; it is reflected in one's thoughts, actions, and kindness. When I see Shovana on stage or interact with her in everyday life, I do not see merely the shimmer of the spotlight or the daylight on her skin. I see the essence of a person who exudes grace, dignity, and unwavering confidence—qualities that form the most beautiful adornment of all.'

One may wear the most exquisite brands yet remain distant and unfeeling, while another, clad in simplicity, may possess an unshakeable strength of character. True beauty lies in humanity itself. In the film and fashion world, where physical allure often takes precedence, the pressure to maintain an image can sometimes overshadow a person's genuine spirit.

'When Shovana steps onto the dance stage, everything else fades away. Her warmth, energy, emotion, and authenticity shine through, illuminating the performance and everyone privileged to witness it.'

What if Shovana had surrendered to the weight of false beauty standards, allowing them to silence her rhythm and still her dance?

What if she, like so many blessed with rare and luminous gifts, had been consumed by the relentless pursuit of perfection—of appearing flawless and achieving without falter—only to be swept away by the illusions she was meant to defy?

'Her presence is a gift to the creative world, and had she

ever chosen to step away from dance, it would have been an immeasurable loss. Likewise, had she not pursued her professional career or nurtured friendships like ours, the world would have been deprived of yet another dimension of her brilliance.'

'Shovana's courage, quick wit, and the effortless charm of her occasional one-liners make her captivating. She embraces her quirks and eccentricities with humour, and that makes her more endearing,' says Jyotsna and adds that 'Artists, like all of us, are human—flawed, vulnerable, and beautifully real. True strength is not in masking imperfections but in embracing them with grace. Shovana does so effortlessly, often weaving humour into what others might see as flaws, inspiring self-acceptance in those around her. Legends like Meena Kumari, Parveen Babi, and Marilyn Monroe bore their struggles in the public eye, never feigning invincibility, reminding us that authenticity, not perfection, is the mark of a true artist.'

***

On the morning of 29 July 2000, Shovana woke up with a jolt, startled by the realisation that she had overslept. With barely an hour left to prepare for an appointment near Gurgaon, she stumbled out of bed, her movements clumsy and rushed. Rubbing her eyes, she muttered to herself in frustration. Why couldn't she see correctly? Blaming the lingering weight of sleep, she reached for her toothbrush only to knock over the glass beside it.

'How careless,' she thought, dismissing the incident because of her haste. But the clumsiness persisted—banging into furniture, knocking over objects, and fumbling with everything she touched. A strange sense of detachment crept in as though she were floating in a suspended, unreal state.

When it became clear she wouldn't make it on time, she cancelled the appointment. Picking up the phone, she was struck by another oddity: why did she have to turn her head to see the dial pad? Confusion nagged at her, but she brushed it aside, determined to get through the morning.

At the breakfast table, the strangeness continued. Herbert, seated on her right, looked at her with concern. 'Shovana, what's wrong with you? I've been holding the toast tray for ages, and you haven't even noticed it.'

Startled, she protested, 'But I didn't see it!' Yet the unease lingered, a shadow creeping over what should have been an ordinary morning. Something was undeniably wrong.

By then, Shovana was growing increasingly alarmed. Why couldn't she see correctly? The possibilities raced through her mind—detached retina, acute glaucoma—every frightening scenario she had ever read about eye ailments.

Panic creeping in, she called the renowned eye specialist, Dr Madan Mohan, who urged her to see him immediately.

After a thorough examination, he referred her to a neurosurgeon. 'A neurosurgeon?' she thought incredulously. The gravity of the situation began to dawn on her.

Tests revealed that she had suffered a cerebral thrombosis during her sleep, affecting the right peripheral vision in both eyes.

She was hospitalised without delay.

That evening, as the shock of the day settled, she decided, 'What the hell! I can't let this cow me down!' she thought.

Gratitude tempered her fear: 'Thank the good Lord it wasn't worse. Imagine if it had paralysed my arms, legs, or even my speech!'

Determined not to let the setback define her, she told the doctor she wanted to dance again. A few days later, he gave her the green light. His reasoning was clear: with her spirit and personality, resuming her routine would aid her recovery far more than confinement to bed. Binding her to rest, he explained, would only dampen her resolve and slow her healing.

When she later saw the results of her optical field test, she was struck by its odd symmetry. It resembled a piece of abstract art, like something out of a comic book—a surreal reminder of the unexpected turns life could take.

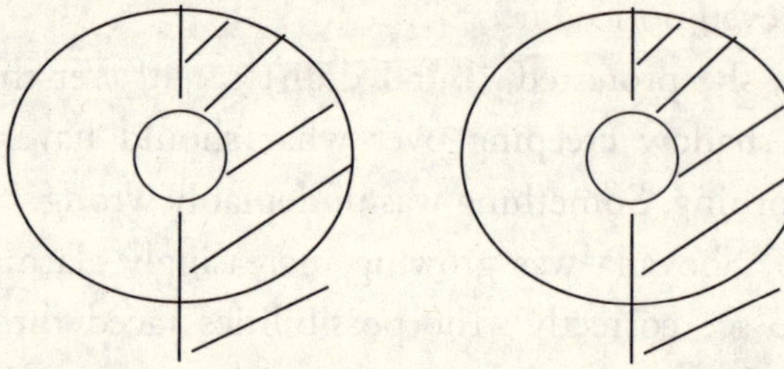

Shovana laughed when Dr Madan Mohan explained the nuances of her condition. She was fortunate, he said, that her central vision—the inner pupils—remained intact. This allowed her to see a person's full face when looking directly at them, even though her field of vision cut off abruptly at the person's left ear. The thought of seeing only half a face amused her in its absurdity, but it was also a poignant reminder of her altered reality.

She marvelled at the resilience of the human body and mind and how quickly they adapt to new circumstances. Initially, navigating her new visual limitations was a challenge. To get a complete view, she found herself tilting her head dramatically. Reading and writing were particularly confusing—should she move her book from right to left or her head from left to right? This constant adjustment persisted until her eyes as if on their own accord, adapted to the change, developing a new rhythm and speed.

On stage, the challenges were even more complex. Shovana had to mentally map out the dimensions of her performance space and the distance to her musicians, who traditionally sat to the dancer's right. With her right peripheral vision 90 per cent impaired, she had to tread cautiously to avoid stumbling into them.

Yet even her careful adjustments couldn't prevent mishaps. She recalled an incident during a concert in Delhi by an Austrian musical group, The Sound of Music. After the formal performance, the dancers and musicians invited audience members to join them on stage. Shovana was among those chosen and danced with a partner at the far-right edge of the stage. Engrossed in the moment, she failed to notice how close she was to the stage's edge and fell off.

The incident left the audience bewildered. Later, someone politely asked how she hadn't seen the edge when it had been so apparent to everyone else. She explained with a smile that her eyes had been focused on her partner, and everything to her right side was essentially a blank void unless she deliberately turned her pupils in that direction. Laughing, she often quipped, 'A person has to be on my wrong side for me to notice them!'

Moments like these often turned into amusing anecdotes for Shovana, but beneath the laughter lay a quiet interplay with her inner self—the ever-watchful observer, with the *sakshi bhav.* This *drishta* part of her stood apart, detached and calm, watching the scenes of life unfold as if they were a play. It didn't judge or react; it simply noticed, offering a perspective that brought clarity and, sometimes, humour to what could have been frustrating moments.

When she thought about the fall later, her inner commentator couldn't help but chuckle: 'There you were, elegantly dancing one moment and then making a grand exit—off the stage!' The absurdity wasn't lost on her, and the observer within wove it into the fabric of her life with a philosophical flourish. 'Isn't life exactly like this stage,' it seemed to say, 'where every step requires awareness, and every misstep is just part of the dance?'

This perspective turned what could have been embarrassing into something almost delightful. It was as though her inner self offered her a backstage pass to her life, whispering, 'Don't take it too seriously. Even the missteps have a rhythm of their own.'

Her ability to step back and see herself as both an actor and an audience member made navigating moments of chaos easier. It also brought her closer to her art, for wasn't the stage itself a reflection of life's unpredictability? With a wry smile, she often concluded, 'Well, if nothing else, it gave the audience something to remember!'

In the aftermath of the stroke, Shovana found herself in a whirlwind of experiences. The moment news of her condition spread, she was flooded with phone calls from concerned well-wishers, each eager to check on her welfare. While deeply touched by the outpouring of support, one call stood out for its unintended humour.

A particularly exasperated individual expressed frustration upon learning that she had resumed dancing, attended to her official duties, prepared for her MPhil exams, and even fulfilled her social obligations—barely two weeks post-stroke.

'You're supposed to be in bed so we can bring you flowers!' the caller complained. 'How do you think we feel seeing you up and about when we're ready to shower you with sympathy? Cheated, I say! For the sake of decency, you ought to stay bedridden. Let people grasp the gravity of your illness! Do you know what someone said? "It's all fake—a publicity stunt!" So please, Shovana, for public propriety, stay in bed for a while,' he pleaded.

Amused and touched in equal measure, Shovana continued her routine, unbothered by the whispers of doubt. 'If people want to think it's a publicity stunt,' she thought, 'they're welcome to.'

However, there were two undeniable consequences of the stroke that she deeply regretted. First, her driving days had come to an end. As someone who valued independence, relying on a chauffeur felt like a bitter pill. Second, she had lost sensitivity on her right side, leaving her unable to register the presence of anyone standing to her right. This unexpected development often led to remarks like, 'Oh, you've become so grand you can't even notice people standing right next to you!'

Explaining her condition seemed futile. Instead, Shovana decided to laugh it off and embrace her new reality with grace and humour.

Footprints

'As an artist, the impermanence of life often weighs on my mind—the inevitability of time erasing the form, the beauty, and even the artist. Kathak, for me, has been far more than a dance form; it is sadhna, a spiritual practice, a 'sadhan' for 'mukti' from the ephemeral nature of this world. Yet, the question persists: how does one preserve and pass on the essence of a lifetime's devotion?

'This contemplation deepened during my performance of 'Mera Safar', where I embodied a dancer consumed by the awareness of mortality. The 'nashwar sharir'—the transient body—bore the weight of inevitable decay, and art, too, seemed poised to fade like a lingering glance at the world one leaves behind. It was a haunting realisation that even the most beautiful creations are tied to their creators, bound by time. Thus, the impermanence of this 'sansar' often left me searching for meaning.

'What will remain of my art when I am no longer here?

'In that despair, a truth emerged: art transcends the artist through the sacred 'aavartan'—the cyclical handing over of knowledge, rhythm, and soul from one generation to the next. It is only by entrusting my students with this legacy that Kathak, the essence of

my being, will live on, defying the boundaries of mortality. Through them, I leave not just a memory but an unbroken thread connecting the finite to the infinite.

'In passing on the essence of my sadhna to my disciples through the guru-shishya parampara, I find hope that while the artist may fade, the art will continue to thrive. Though not my biological children, my disciples will be the heirs to this legacy. In their dedication, I see a reflection of my journey, a continuation of what my life has stood for—a connection to something eternal.

'These reflections drew me to the film 'Aavartan', a sensitive exploration of this dilemma, beautifully conceived and produced by Durba Sahay. The film resonated deeply with me, embodying the eternal cycle of life and art transmission across generations. It offered a profound perspective on how the essence of an artist can live on through those they nurture, even as their physical presence ceases to be. It was a theme that felt intensely personal, aligning perfectly with my understanding of what it means to leave behind a legacy.'

Durba Sahay, a filmmaker and writer, is a National Film Award winner for her film, *Patang*. She has directed several short films, including her full-length feature *Aavartan*, with Shovana Narayan in the lead role. The film, centred on the guru-shishya parampara, required an artist capable of authentically portraying the role of a guru. Durba found Shovana to be an ideal fit, and Shovana eagerly embraced the challenge. With its strong emphasis on dance, the film was elevated by Shovana's Kathak expertise, which brought unparalleled depth and authenticity to her performance.

'I scripted, directed, and produced the film. I spent hours sitting with Shovana ji, discussing the script in detail. It wasn't easy to make an artist act, still she effortlessly mastered the expressions each time, as her Kathak is deeply rooted in emotive storytelling. The film portrays the complex relationship between an artist and her disciple, with sudden emotional shifts that unfold throughout the narrative, exploring a wide range of emotions. We were also fortunate to have the veteran actress Sushma Seth ji in a significant role, and her support was invaluable. The film was selected for screening at the Goa International Film Festival and the Bengaluru International Film Festival.'

Durba, originally from Gaya, and her filmmaker husband established a cultural centre in their hometown, driven by their shared passion for promoting the arts. They built two auditoriums in Gaya, hosting regular performances by classical artists. Durba had always hoped to invite the renowned Kathak maestro Shovana Narayan to perform at their centre, believing it would elevate its cultural offerings. When Shovana finally performed at one of their auditoriums, it became a memorable milestone in their cultural journey.

'I was initially hesitant. I explained to her that our auditorium was small, with a capacity of only about a hundred people. The larger one, which could hold two hundred and fifty, was still under construction. I worried she might feel it was unworthy of her stature as a star performer. After patiently listening to my concerns several times, she finally responded, *"Durba ji, maine ek chauki pe bhi dance kiya hai."* (I have danced even on the smallest platform). After her performance, she remarked that while I had been worried about the stage being too small, it turned out to be a haven where any artist would feel privileged to perform.'

Shovana performed at Durba's auditorium many more times later. Their bond grew more robust with each interaction, sparking more collaborations. This connection eventually led to the creation of the film *Aavartan* in 2020-21.

'Shovana ji is incredibly hardworking. Talent alone is not enough; one must have a true passion for what they do, and Shovana ji's passion for her dance is unmistakable. Even her artists were so well-rehearsed that it took us no time to finish the film. She's a consummate professional—well-read, widely travelled, and deeply informed. Conversations with her are enriching. Her sharp memory stands out, as does her capacity for unconditional love and generosity. Above all, humility is her defining trait,' Durba shares.

'Acting has taught me many valuable lessons. One key difference between film and stage is the chance for re-takes in film—if something goes wrong, you can try again. But on stage, there are no second chances. My experience in *Aavartan* was particularly meaningful as it reflects the continuous cycle of life, a concept I hold close,' says Shovana.

'We travelled to Jaisalmer by train to shoot the opening scene of the film, but the journey was so uncomfortable that we quickly vowed not to take the train back. Despite the challenges, Shovana ji never showed any sign of dissatisfaction. Her adaptability was remarkable. Our team of over ten had, by mistake, booked a hotel with poor accommodation, and after a long day of work, we hoped for at least a decent dinner—but none was available. Desperate, we bribed a local to bring us food, and he arrived with *hare chane ki sabji*, which we ate gratefully, sand grains and all,' Durba giggles.

'We were staying in tent houses on the dunes, and the bathroom facilities were, as you can imagine, far from ideal. The next morning, the same man kindly prepared *puris* and *aloo ki sabji* for breakfast. While I was flustered by the uncomfortable living conditions, Shovana ji remained calm and composed. Even as we roamed about looking for better food, she handled it easily.

When we finally found a place to enjoy some authentic Rajasthani cuisine, she laughed at my complaints and said lightly, "*Ek hi din ki toh baat hai.*" (It's just for one day, after all.)'

Amid these amusing escapades, one couldn't help but marvel at how a true artist like Shovana navigates life with such grace and perspective. For her, life is a grand masquerade—a stage where every scene, whether adorned with opulence or draped in discomfort, has its own fleeting charm. The cramped train, the gritty *hare chane ki sabji*, the sand-filled tents, and the elusive perfect meal are but props and backdrops in the unfolding drama of existence. A true artist doesn't measure the stage by its size or the comfort of its trappings; instead, they revel in the impermanence of it all, finding meaning even in the seemingly mundane. The challenges become chisels, shaping their resilience and deepening their craft.

'Watching Shovana ji adapt with a light heart and a serene smile was a lesson in itself—a reminder that it is the spirit, not the setting, that elevates the performance.'

Shovana is often seen adapting to challenging situations, but she always prioritises the needs of her dancers and musicians. She ensures they have comfortable accommodations, provides unwavering support, and secures the necessary resources for them to perform at their best. Her focus remains on creating a comfortable and nurturing environment for her team.

Durba served as the secretary of the Inner Wheel Club, a global women's organisation, at the association level. The club organised a conference in Jodhpur, where Durba invited Shovana and her troupe to perform. While the club members were staying at the Taj Hotel, the troupe was given a less luxurious accommodation. Shovana gently pointed out that her dancers needed better living conditions to rest well and perform their best.

'Realising our mistake, we invited the dancers to stay at the Taj. The outcome was an unforgettable performance, one that remains vivid in our memories to this day,' shares Durba.

Shovana has always approached her journey with a deep sense of integrity, consistently striving to do justice to every endeavour without taking shortcuts. This dedication is evident in her life choices, such as participating in the Miss UN contest in 1974, where she won and celebrated a significant milestone.

'It was an instant connection, as you might say. Shovana's warmth was magnetic, drawing me in immediately. She began inviting me to her performances, and since Kamani Auditorium was just a short walk away, I made it a point to attend most of her shows. We worked together on a production called *Gora*, based on Rabindranath Tagore's acclaimed novel. Unfortunately, due to unforeseen circumstances, it couldn't be telecast, but we rehearsed tirelessly for at least two weeks. Shovana portrayed Sucharita's mother, and I played Gora. During that time, we even stayed at her grandfather's haveli, which further strengthened our bond. There was an unspoken understanding between us—a connection of thought and ideology.

'Later, we collaborated again for a stage play called *Mirdad*, where I handled the theatre aspects, and she brought the story to life through dance. Shovana truly inspires me. Despite her immense accomplishments, she remains deeply grounded. Her grace is ever-present whether in her dance class, at home, on stage, in the office, or anywhere else. She serves like a mirror in many ways, reflecting parts of myself. But more than anything, she is giving—so wonderfully, selflessly giving,' Joyoshree Arora, a close friend of Shovana Narayan, adds.

Joyoshree began her journey with Kathak at age four. However, due to her fragile health, she had to take breaks from dancing and eventually transitioned to Manipuri, a style that demanded less physical stamina. Joyoshree was always drawn to the arts, excelling in dance, drama, and television. Her television career took off in 1980 when she auditioned for the role of Bhagvanti in the iconic TV serial *Hum Log*, directed by Manohar Shyam Joshi. During this period, through a women-oriented programme, she first met Shovana Narayan, marking the start of their enduring friendship.

Joyoshree strongly believes that theatre and dance should be integral to the school curriculum, as they play a crucial role in nurturing a person's sensibilities. These art forms cultivate emotional intelligence, creativity, and a profound understanding of human emotions. At their core, both theatre and dance centre around the art of expression. They provide individuals with a medium to channel their emotions, represented by the *nava* rasas (the nine essential emotions), and bring them to life.

In Indian tradition, theatre and dance are closely linked, both being branches of the same artistic tree, yet each has distinct characteristics. Dance relies on movements, *mook* abhinaya, music, and rhythm, following a codified grammar perfected through years of sadhna, while theatre focuses on dialogue, voice, gestures, and emotional delivery, with less reliance on stylised movements. Both art forms share the need for rigorous preparation, a deep understanding of accompanying literature, and attention to music and costume.

A dancer or actor assumes multiple roles and emotions, expressing joy to sorrow and love to anger. Yet, once the performance ends, they learn the art of detachment, stepping away from those characters and returning to themselves. This process enriches them as performers and offers a valuable life lesson—how to connect deeply, express fully, and then let go gracefully. Through these forms, artists learn empathy, self-awareness, and the ability to engage with the world more profoundly.

Joyoshree reflects that learning an art form is a divine experience. It instils a sense of calm and raises awareness of the self and the world. As you immerse yourself in the nuances of an art form, you begin to understand the subtleties of your body—how your movements, gestures (mudras), and emotions (rasas) align to tell a deeper story. Your eyes become windows to your soul, revealing emotions far beyond words. On stage, when you emote, there may be moments when your lips form a smile, even while your heart holds sorrow. It's not about deceiving the audience in those moments but rather about deceiving yourself. The smile becomes a veil, a marker of composure that conceals inner turmoil.

'With Shovana, this depth of emotion is always present. Every time I meet her, it feels as if another layer of her personality, of her artistry, unfolds. Each encounter reveals something new, and each of her performances holds a fresh vitality, no matter how many times she's presented it before. Her enthusiasm is infectious, and it never wanes. Shovana continues to surpass herself with every piece she performs, elevating her art to new heights with renewed passion and dedication every time she steps onto the stage.'

Shovana has consistently embraced challenging paths, ensuring her work aligns with her values and remains deeply connected to her art. In 1995, while working on the telefilm *Akbar's Bridge,* Shovana visited the very bridge that inspired the scenes. The final shot featured this bridge, which had been meticulously reconstructed in Bhopal for the film. Dedicated to authenticity, Shovana fully immersed herself in her role as a *kumharin* (potter), even learning the craft of pottery-making firsthand from a local potter.

Humility is the mark of a true artist, the quiet surrender of ego as they become one with their art, aligning themselves with the universe. To be truly an artist is to see divinity in all things, in every being—even in rivals and disciplines other than their own. It is to recognise that pursuing art is not for personal glory but a journey of the soul that brings them closer to a universal truth.

Joyoshree reflects that while we are social beings, we guard our personal boundaries. Yet, Shovana is the one person who has gently crossed into her safe space—a 'happy intrusion' that has blossomed over forty long years.

Sahar Zaman, a journalist, author, and cultural curator, considers herself fortunate to have Shovana as a friend. To Sahar, Shovana is the very definition of a 'complete woman.'

'When I first met Shovana ji, her humility and warmth immediately stood out. Despite being an iconic Kathak guru, her presence is remarkably charming and approachable. As a journalist, I interact with people from all walks of life—politicians, lawyers, activists, artists, performers, ministers, diplomats, and more. I interviewed her first in 2010 and instinctively sensed a genuine sincerity that hinted at the possibility of a great friendship.

'She even suggested I consider learning Kathak, as she believed I possessed a natural grace. I laughed it off, never finding the time to pursue it amidst my busy schedule at the news studio. Despite the 30-year age gap between us, her youthful energy bridges that divide effortlessly.

'Nearly a decade later, in 2019, I reconnected with her while curating *Jashn-e-Talat*, a tribute concert for my grand-uncle, Talat Mahmood. Unlike the conventional approach of organising live orchestras with singers to perform his film songs and ghazals, I envisioned incorporating dance pieces set to his original soundtracks. I contacted Shovana ji to see if she would be willing to perform classical dances to film songs.

'Anticipating the need to select only those compositions with classical undertones, I was pleasantly surprised when she responded, "Sahar, choose any song you like; I have no reservations about dancing to any of Talat sahab's iconic hits. You focus on your script and selecting the songs that best complement your narration. Leave the dance to me."

'Her approach to collaborations is incredibly comforting. She poured her heart and time into ensuring that the one-hour skit on Talat Mahmood's life became a heartfelt tribute. Since then, we've collaborated on two dance shows and several talk shows exploring her dual careers as an IAAS officer and a Padma Shri danseuse.

'Her remarkable ability to excel in every role—nurturing a long-distance marriage, supporting her husband's diplomatic journey, or authoring numerous books—is truly inspiring. I felt compelled to acknowledge her selfless contributions to my tribute to *Talat Mahmood: The Definitive Biography*.'

One of Shovana's most inspiring qualities is her ability to recognise talent and nurture it with unwavering support. She promotes those whose work she genuinely believes in, becoming a catalyst in their growth—not just as professionals but also as individuals. Her encouragement helps them evolve into influential representatives of their niche fields. This nurturing spirit is beautifully reflected in her decades-long bond with Seerat Narindra, founder director and design head.

Seerat was doing her professional design courses in Milan, Italy, when Shovana connected with her family in Delhi.

'When I came from Italy, mummy would say, "*Badi soni kudi aayee si*" (a beautiful girl had come). She still is one of the prettiest women I know, not just in physical terms but a ‘pretty human being,’ so to speak. You can’t describe her sufficiently—professionally, personally. It is a delight to relate to her. I feel blessed to be in her orbit.’

Seerat was just an out-of-college person. When she returned to India, she got the opportunity to see Shovana’s dance. Seerat was doing work for India Tourism Development Corporation’s (ITDC) cultural wing. All the senior dancers were regular visitors there, performing off and on. The cultural wing of ITDC used to organise VIP programmes. Most cultural programmes held even at the Rashtrapati Bhavan were routed through this wing.

‘I was awestruck to see all these senior dancers perform, but I found Shovana Didi exceptionally warm. She created a comfort zone for me, a young artist.’

Seerat began her journey in designing costumes for ITDC in the late seventies. At that time, she was unfamiliar with the classical dances of India and couldn’t distinguish one form from another. Eager to learn, she started studying Odissi.

Her first collaboration with Shovana was in 1993 for the production *Moonlight Impressionism*.

‘One day, Didi casually asked me, “Seerat, would you like to do the costumes?” Without hesitation, I jumped at the opportunity, replying, “Yes!” *Moonlight Impressionism* was set to piano music, blending elements of ballet with both eastern and western influences. I chose a colour palette of white and sky-blue with touches of silver to complement the ethereal theme. The performance was staged at the FICCI auditorium. Excited by the creative process, I asked if I could also dance, and Didi graciously agreed.’

Seerat believes understanding dance movements is key to designing costumes that enhance the performance. For her, makeup, costumes, and lighting all contribute to a dance’s visual appeal, making aesthetics essential to her craft.

One of her career highlights was designing costumes for the classical dances at the Commonwealth Games, which she views as the premier platform for classical art.

'Shovana Didi led the opening and closing ceremonies from conceptualisation to execution. It was a massive responsibility—balancing interactions with authorities and senior officials while coordinating with artists, musicians, composers, designers, lighting technicians, and dancers. Ensuring that every detail was perfect, and the paperwork was accurate was no small feat. Didi selected the creative team purely on merit, without any favouritism. Her attention to detail and fairness made her stand out. She documented everything meticulously, shielding the artists from personal criticism.'

Seerat believes that only someone with Shovana's vision, knowledge, and experience could have successfully managed such a monumental task.

'One beautiful quality of Didi that stands out is that she will never criticise anyone, even those who backstabbed her. She will still be a smiling face to that person. She steers clear of politics, staying focused on her art, work, and students.'

Shovana has cultivated deep and meaningful connections with remarkable individuals from diverse walks of life. H K Dua reflects on his close bond with both Shovana and Herbert, highlighting what makes them a wonderful couple:

'Shovana is a delightful person to be with and her energy is boundless. Herbert is equally a pleasure to be around—a skilled diplomat who, on a personal level, is incredibly supportive of Shovana. As a dancer, she thrives on the freedom to express herself, as dance embodies the pure joy of "being," a freedom Herbert wholeheartedly ensures she has. He deeply appreciates

Indian culture and values. Shovana's joyful laughter fills any room, while Herbert's gentle, tender smiles reflect his admiration for his life partner, much beloved in their social circles. Our conversations often revolve around politics and foreign affairs, topics that I, as a newsman, always enjoy.'

H K Dua observes that Shovana never criticises fellow artists—a rare trait in fields often marked by rivalry and critique. She gracefully redirects the conversation if someone speaks negatively about another in their absence.

Pavan Varma appears to echo this sentiment when he observes: 'Shovana's greatest strength lies in her temperament. It's rare to find someone like her in the artistic community—I've never heard her speak ill of another artist. She doesn't indulge in gossip, especially the malicious kind. Instead, she is genuinely appreciative of everyone around her. Her infectious laughter, openness, warmth, hospitality, and sincere concern for others make her extraordinary.'

Distinguished figures hold Shovana in the highest regard, celebrating her multifaceted persona as a performer par excellence, a relentless seeker of truth, a mystic deeply rooted in the spiritual essence of her art, a disciplined practitioner, an inspiring guru, a steadfast friend, and a source of unending inspiration. They marvel at her extraordinary ability to seamlessly weave these diverse roles into the fabric of her life, living each with authenticity and grace.

'She is one of the most hard-working people I have ever met,' says H K Dua. 'An achiever and a guru to many, she nurtures her students like a mother, shaping their futures with love and dedication. Constantly on the move, she doesn't know how to relax, which I see as her only flaw. She gives her all—whether as a dancer, host, professional, or friend. If I had one suggestion, it would be for her to make more time for herself.'

Joyoshree compares Shovana to water, praising her fluidity and adaptability. She navigates all her roles gracefully, though Joyoshree notes that sometimes Shovana's commitments seep into her personal life.

Dr Anjan Banerjee emphasises Shovana's deep connections, both socially and professionally, shaped by her aristocratic background and success as a celebrated artist. She is well-acquainted with the 'who's who' and often hosts gala dinners with notable figures, yet she never feels the need to name-drop. Confident and secure in her identity, Shovana does not rely on others' status to affirm her own.

Pandit Sajan Mishra also attests to Shovana's integrity and dedication both on stage and in life:

'Much like the legendary figures such as Pandit Birju Maharaj, Bhimsen Joshi, Pandit Ravi Shankar, and Ustad Amjad Ali Khan, Shovana Narayan embodies true mastery. She never places herself above her art. She uplifts emerging artists, offering them the space to excel, while remaining deeply committed to her own journey. For her, the stage is a sacred space for all artists to shine. She is one of the humblest artists I have ever met.'

Jyotsna reflects on the challenges of ageing, changing appearances, and mental health, noting that denial often leads to inner turmoil. In the fleeting world of performance, those who embrace honesty and evolution find greater fulfilment.

'In every sphere of life, stepping aside to make space for others is vital, as our scriptures illustrate through the four ashrams—*Brahmacharya*, *Grihastha*, *Vanaprastha*, and *Sanyas*. Today, *sanyas* isn't about retreating but embracing *aavartan*—the cycle of life completing itself. The timing of this transition is entirely personal and should never be dictated by others. Just as one must know when to lead, one must also recognise when to become the *sarathi* (charioteer), guiding others forward. Shovana embodies this rhythm of life—seamlessly transitioning from dazzling pirouettes to refining the depth of her expressions. She enters the stage gracefully and exits with the same effortless poise, allowing the rhythm of time to move forward uninterrupted.'

For Shovana, the world is a boundless canvas, each moment an invitation to explore its infinite possibilities with the wonder of a child gazing at an endless horizon. She walks into the unknown gracefully, unafraid to let her talent dance through uncharted realms. But beyond her artistry lies a heart just as radiant—one that finds joy in uplifting others, going the extra mile to bring warmth where needed. In her, artistry and compassion entwine, crafting a life as luminous and inspiring as the performances she breathes into existence.

'I've known Shovana ji for years. Long before we became friends, I attended one of her performances and was completely captivated. Over time, we met more often, both in India and abroad, and with each encounter, I was drawn further to her exuberant, warm nature. I remember once, when she wore Art Karat jewellery for a promotion, she was as joyful as a child, admiring herself in the mirror. I felt nervous during her performance, though I had ensured the jewellery stayed in place while she danced with her usual gusto. She also performed for Art Karat at Taj Bengal, an event that garnered great press coverage. Despite being an icon in her own right, Shovana never says no. I never miss her events—because I admire her as an artist and individual. While many artists worry about imperfections, Shovana redefines beauty with pride. Being around her reminds you that true beauty goes far beyond the surface. Her confidence is her greatest accessory,' says Asha Modi.

Kamal Modi and Asha Modi, founders of Art Karat, blend their love for fine arts with their work in jewellery and fashion, creating a home that mirrors an art gallery.

Asha, a self-taught designer, began nearly four decades ago, challenging traditional gold jewellery with her innovative silver-based designs featuring semi-precious stones. Despite initial resistance, her styles gained popularity, and under Kamal's marketing expertise, Art Karat grew into a global brand, now expanding with a gold line led by the next generation.

Kamal remembers meeting Shovana through a mutual friend and being impressed by her quiet confidence and strong presence.

'Shovana focuses on her growth, avoiding petty rivalries, and stays deeply committed to her work. She's also fearless in reimagining mythological stories, bringing new perspectives to epic characters. Her ability to connect with people and her passion for her craft make her unique.'

Kamal emphasises the urgent need for greater support for both, performing arts and fine arts, through both government and private initiatives. Recognising the value of art and artists, he advocates for funding institutions like the National School of Drama to foster talent and preserve India's cultural heritage.

Sushma Seth, a trailblazer in Indian arts celebrated for her versatile contributions to theatre, television, and film over six decades, beautifully captures the essence of an artist's devotion to their craft, mainly reflecting on Shovana's unwavering commitment to her art:

'The appreciation of a piece of music, a moment in drama, a composition in a painting, or a movement in dance arises from within. It is this creative process which enriches our lives, and the joy it brings is described in the *Natya Shastra* as rasa—the essence that resonates within, evoking a euphoric connection. It is this profound feeling that artists strive to create and audiences long to experience. This connection drew me to performances of plays, music recitals, art exhibitions, and dance. Kathak enchanted me with its storytelling, abhinaya (expressive gestures), and rhythmic footwork. I had the privilege of watching masters like Pandit Birju Maharaj, Durga Lal, and Shovana Narayan. Shovana stood out for weaving stories not only from Hindu mythology and spiritual themes but also from contemporary and socially relevant issues. Her movements and abhinaya were a seamless blend of fluidity, grace, and dramatic intensity. Our friendship developed during art meets, seminars, social gatherings, Shovana's recitals, and the performances of Arpana Trust's students. We both believe that to preserve and refine any art form, it is imperative to pass it on to the talented and enthusiastic students with dedication and devotion.'

'*Ek guru ko agar ek yogya shishya mil jaye, toh apne paas kuch nahin rakhna chahiye, sab de dena chahiye.*' (If a teacher finds a worthy disciple, they should withhold nothing and pass on everything.)

The words capture the heart of the guru-shishya parampara—a relationship built on trust, selflessness, and the passing on of knowledge without holding anything back. Shovana Narayan lives by this principle as a guru. She has trained thousands of students worldwide, not just in the technicalities of Kathak but also in its deeper essence. She teaches theory, abhinaya, choreography, and the art of storytelling, nurturing her students to find their voice while staying rooted in tradition.

Her lessons are about more than dance—they teach grace, humility, and a love for the art that goes beyond performance.

On 20 November 2024, Suparna Singh and Mahima Satsangi, two of her talented students performed *Sumang*, a beautiful tribute to the guru-shishya bond. Their performance wasn't just about dance; it was about connection—how a guru's guidance shapes a student's skills and their understanding of life.

The bond with a guru is not just mentorship; it's a deep, spiritual journey. A guru's wisdom helps the disciple grow, reflect, and discover their potential. Through this relationship, they learn that the guru is not just a teacher but a guide who helps them to see the divine within themselves.

It's a journey of trust, surrender, and transformation, where art becomes a bridge between the guru and the shishya, and the legacy lives on.

Debadhara Festival, Kamani Auditorium, right to left-
Guru Shovana, Pallavi, Mahima, Suparna

Pic Credits:- Rahul Naag

Dil se...
From the Heart

Guru-shishya parampara

In the heavens, Vishwakarma, the divine architect, crafted the universe with his magical chisel. His creations were not just beautiful; they held the essence of life itself. Every stroke of his chisel shaped not only the form but the spirit within, bringing balance and meaning to the cosmos. Whether crafting the resplendent halls of Indra or the celestial weapons of the gods, Vishwakarma's creations were not just objects—they were embodiments of the divine.

Centuries later, in a small village, a boy named Aarav sat at the feet of his guru, learning to play the veena. Aarav struggled at first—his fingers clumsy and his tunes uneven. But his guru, known for his unparalleled skill, guided him with patient care. 'Place your fingers here; let the strings breathe,' he would say, his voice carrying the weight of countless years of wisdom.

Aarav admired his guru, thinking he was the unshaped stone and his teacher the sculptor.

Over time, Aarav noticed something began to shift. As his guru taught him, his own passion and questions seemed to energise the teacher. His innocent curiosity reawakened the teacher's sense of wonder, his persistence refining the guru's methods. One day, Aarav asked, 'Guruji, who is shaping whom? Are you shaping me, or am I shaping you?'

The guru smiled and pointed to a sketch on the wall—a drawing of one hand sketching another. 'This is us,' he said. 'Like Vishwakarma's chisel, our bond shapes not just your music or my teaching but our souls. We are both transformed in this journey.'

Years later, Aarav became a renowned veena player, touching hearts with his music. But he never forgot the allegory of Vishwakarma. As he began teaching his disciples, he realised the eternal truth of their shared journey: the guru and shishya shape one another, creating not just art but a deep connection that changes them both.

This chapter, *Dil se*—from the heart—delves into the lives of Shovana Narayan's students, revealing the profound and lasting influence she has had on them. To her disciples, she is far more than a Kathak guru; she is a mentor who shapes their lives with equal measures of love, discipline, and steadfast support.

With compassion at her core, Shovana gently nurtures her students while maintaining the discipline necessary for growth, ensuring they evolve not just as dancers but as well-rounded individuals. Through every challenge and success, their Shovana guru ji remains a constant source of wisdom and warmth, standing by their side.

For many, her guidance has been a pillar of strength during trying times. Their heartfelt stories, often shared with deep emotion, speak of a bond that transcends words—a connection that has profoundly transformed their lives, imparting lessons that extend far beyond the stage.

Ruchi Arya

Ruchi Arya, one of Shovana's students, recalls how, as a fourth-grade child, she began learning Kathak under Guru Shovana's watchful eye at Pandara Road. Today, while pursuing her MBA, Ruchi still cherishes those early years when the dance form and life itself intertwined through her guru's teachings.

Her journey, like so many others, is not just a tale of mastering an art form but of growing into a better person.

Dil se….

'Shovana Guruji has given me more than I could ever imagine, and I am deeply grateful for all the opportunities she has provided. I'm one of the lucky few students who never had to pay for Kathak classes, something I'll always cherish. My journey with her began in fourth grade at Nirmal Primary School, where she taught. After finishing fifth grade, I still wanted to continue learning, but my family couldn't afford it. Guruji understood my love for dance and kindly allowed me to keep learning without asking for a fee. It's not something you find often—a guru who is so giving and compassionate. I have also had the privilege of being part of her repertoire group for a year, performing with her—each moment has been a true blessing.

'One performance in Udaipur stands out in my memory. We needed plates for the act in the first scene, but the organisers only gave us two instead of three. We went on stage and performed anyway. Backstage, Guruji was upset and reminded us never to depend on others to get things done. Her words stayed with me: we must always take responsibility for ourselves and our work. From that day on, I've made it a point to be extra careful and handle things independently, just as she taught us.

'At the Lalit Arpan festival on 14 and 15 October 2024, Guruji entrusted me with an incredible responsibility—managing the backstage music. It felt like stepping into uncharted territory, but she guided me through every step, patiently sending instructions and reassuring me. At first, I was overwhelmed and nervous about handling such a critical task. But as soon as I spoke to her, the fear vanished. There's something magical about her presence—the calmness in her voice dissolves your worries. That experience wasn't just about responsibility; it was about trust and her belief in me, something I'll always carry with pride.

'There was another time when we had two back-to-back programmes to prepare for, and I hadn't fully memorised my part during rehearsals. Let's just say Guruji's strict side made a grand entrance! She scolded me firmly, and oh, it stung. It's always tough to hear, and I felt so sad knowing I'd let her down. But if there's one thing about Guruji—her discipline is like a tough-love boot camp! She pushes you because she knows your potential. Her scolding is less about punishment and more like a mother eagle nudging her chick to fly. Behind the strictness is her deep care, which makes her incredible. You can't slack off under her watchful eye, but you'll always know it's done out of love.'

***

Shuchi Chaudhry

Shuchi became a part of Asavari in 1986, and since then, she has had the privilege of witnessing her guru, Shovana ji, in countless shades and roles. Shovana ji's impact on Shuchi has extended far beyond the boundaries of the dance class—it has been transformative, shaping her not just as a dancer but as a person. Shovana ji has subtly moulded Shuchi's personality through her quiet yet powerful influence, instilling values of discipline, grace, independence, and resilience.

For Shuchi, Shovana Guruji is not just a teacher but a guiding light who has inspired her to explore her fullest potential both on and off the stage. Whenever Shuchi speaks of her Guruji, her words are steeped in gratitude, as she credits her guru for much of who she is today. Her Guruji's influence is deeply woven into the fabric of her life.

'Shovana Didi has been a trailblazer on so many fronts that it's hard to keep count! From a young age, she shattered stereotypes about women and showed, through her own life, that you can have it all: a successful long-distance marriage—she married Dr Herbert Traxl, the Austrian Ambassador—and a relentless pursuit of dance, reaching the very peak of excellence without letting work or marriage stand in her way.

'As an IAAS officer, she worked gruelling hours with the Government of India, yet nothing could deter her from her *riyaz* at 4 am every morning! After long workdays, she still teaches her students thrice a week from 6 to 8 pm and even on Sunday mornings. We, her "old-timers" from the '80s batch, often wonder, "Does Didi ever sleep?" Her dedication to her art is legendary—whether it's performing on stage or teaching her students, she doesn't just give 100 per cent, she gives 500 per cent! And, true to her disciplined nature, Shovana Didi is never late for a class, whether online or offline.

'Even in her post-retirement years, Didi's thirst for learning remains insatiable. She mastered the technicalities of online teaching, creating a global platform where her old students—now solo performers or Kathak teachers—reunite to learn from her again. Her teaching doesn't just cover the technicalities of dance; she brings to life the subtle beauty of both Lucknow and Jaipur Gharanas, blending delicate abhinaya with the electrifying energy of tayyari ang.

'Didi's intellectual pursuits are equally inspiring. Her deep study of Sanskrit and Hindi literature and her love for history, art, and spirituality find expression in her timeless productions. She's a pioneer in blending Kathak with global forms, from performing a duet with Spanish Flamenco dancers to choreographing *Moonlight Impressionism* to the strains of a piano. Her productions span epic tales like the Ramayana, Mahabharata, and Buddha to lesser-known gems like *Rashmirathi*, as well as stories of strong women protagonists—Yashodhara, Gandhari, Draupadi, and Sita.

'In class, she doesn't just teach dance but ignites curiosity. Her favourite *mantra*, "Don't take my word for it—research and explore," has inspired countless students to think deeply about the art form. And let's not forget her immense generosity—Didi didn't charge fees for her classes in the early days, and even when she started charging a token of Rs 40 per month, she often waived it for students who couldn't afford it.

'Shovana Didi has always emphasised independence, especially for her female students, encouraging them to follow their passions without being dictated by boyfriends, husbands, or in-laws. At the same time, she instilled discipline among male students and musicians, ensuring a healthy, co-educational environment—a rarity in many institutions.

'As an old student of hers, my greatest wish is to make her proud—not just as a dancer but as a person. Shovana Didi is a phenomenal artist and an extraordinary human being. I wish her the best of health and happiness and hope she continues to shower us with divine grace for years.'

***

Pallavi Lohani

Pallavi, a doctorate in Kathak and assistant professor at Tecnia Institute of Art and Design reflects on her nearly decade-long journey with Guru Shovana Narayan, which began in 2014. Hailing from Almora, Uttarakhand, Pallavi sees Guru Shovana as a life-changing presence—not just as a mentor in dance but a guiding light through life's challenges. There were moments of despair when Shovana Guruji was the only ray of hope, offering more than just professional support; she extended compassion, understanding, and her unwavering presence.

For Pallavi, Shovana Guruji's dedication goes far beyond the teacher role—she intuitively knows when her disciples need her the most and goes out of her way to offer guidance, comfort, or simply her presence. This deep, personal connection highlights the selflessness with which Shovana nurtures her students, making them feel trained and cared for, shaping their lives in ways that transcend the art form.

'I lost my mother during the COVID pandemic—a devastating loss that left me heartbroken. Having already lost my father in 2000, I felt completely shattered. After my mother's passing, I took leave of absence from my job and our dance class, Asavari. Shovana Didi reached out to me with deep compassion during this dark period. She acknowledged my grief and offered her unwavering support, but she also posed a profound question: after six months or a year, would I choose to continue dancing, or would I let it go forever?

'Her question wasn't just a casual inquiry—it was a gentle yet powerful reminder of what dance meant to me. She encouraged me to reflect on whether I could genuinely navigate my grief without this creative outlet. While she gave me the space I needed to grieve, she also urged me to think about my future. She even asked if I planned to stay in Almora permanently, prompting me to consider life beyond my immediate sorrow.

'At the time, I didn't have an answer. I felt lost, alone, and unsure of the path ahead. But as I sat with her words, a realisation took root—I could never abandon dance. It wasn't just a practice; it was my essence, my way of making sense of life's complexities. About two weeks later, I found the courage to return to my troupe. Reconnecting with dance reignited my passion and reminded me of the joy and healing it brought me.

'Through her sensitivity and wisdom, Shovana Didi guided me back to what truly mattered. She showed me that art has the profound power to heal and transform even in the darkest times.

'When the COVID era hit, Shovana Didi decided it was time to dive into the world of online classes. Typically, we'd head to the studio on Tuesdays and Thursdays, but class schedules were anyone's guess this time. Our families quickly learned that our phones may as well have been buried in the backyard when we were with Guruji.

'About a month into the pandemic, Guruji announced it was time to embrace technology—even though she openly admitted she had no idea how to use Zoom. But hey, why not figure it out together? For her, learning new things is second nature; for us, it was like stumbling through a tech jungle. What was meant to be a one-hour class somehow transformed into epic four- or five-hour marathons. Yes, we had jobs, but apparently, Guruji believed our stamina had no bounds. We'd rush home from work, grab a bite, and then dance until the moon decided it was bedtime.

'Meanwhile, our families were busy becoming gourmet chefs, experimenting with fancy new recipes, while we barely managed to cook up some *tukdas* and *parans* between spins and leaps. And just when we thought things couldn't get busier, Guruji announced online classes for the younger students. Guess who got roped in to teach them? Yep, us senior students! It was like a dance relay—perfecting our moves one minute and corralling a group of overexcited kids the next. Between tech mishaps, endless hours of practice, and her unshakable energy, Shovana Didi ensured the pandemic didn't stand a chance against her passion for Kathak—and she dragged us along for the ride!' Pallavi, and Komal, a fellow disciple of Guru Shovana, break into laughter as they exchange tender anecdotes about their Guruji, a bond that draws them closer.

'We always thought being an artist meant sticking to the classics—a sculptor, poet, writer, painter, musician, or dancer. Simple enough, right? But then Didi came along and flipped the script. She declared, *Kalakar*! Now, hold on a second because this isn't just any old term. *Kala* means art, and *kar* means… well, a motor car!

'Since Didi has been juggling dual careers for years, she spends most of her time zipping around in her car. So, with her, it's all about that 'kala' in her 'car.' Honestly, I think I've absorbed more *bandish* (musical compositions) in her car than in the actual dance class! I've created a filing system for it: 'Bandish in the Car,' 'Bandish on the Train,' and the all-time favourite, 'Bandish in the Aeroplane.'

'And let me tell you, traffic jams hit differently when you're belting out a rhythmic masterpiece. Who knew you could be stuck in traffic and still be in the flow—literally! With Didi, art finds its way into every corner of life, even a car stuck at a red light.

'The other day, while we were waiting at the airport for our flight to Udaipur, we were all gossiping and having a good time when Didi suddenly went quiet. We didn't think much of it until she suddenly erupted, "*Sawa panch ki tihai aa gayi! Aa jao!*" (The *sawa panch tihai* is here! Come on!) I mean, seriously! People around us started gawking, clearly intrigued about what kind of rehearsals we were conducting in the middle of an airport. They probably thought we were auditioning for the next big dance blockbuster!

'We always get nervous about Didi's spontaneous eruptions and wild innovations. I mean, really, who's going to remember all of it later? It's not like we carry notepads everywhere, so we must rely on our memory!

'During one of her creative moments, Didi was clapping and creating a *taal* (rhythmic cycle) when suddenly, an adorable little infant, clearly captivated by her energy, crawled over and handed her his milk bottle. And what did Didi do? She started teaching him *teen taal* by holding his tiny palms and singing, "*Dha! Dhin*!" The scene was so cute that people around us whipped out their phones to record it. We were a mix of embarrassed and amused, but hey, that's just a regular day in Didi's world!

'Now, when we travel by plane, we often find ourselves strategically sitting far away from her just to escape her unexpected bursts of creativity.

'Even when travelling alone, she has this habit of clapping and developing new *tukdas* (musical phrases) and *parans* (patterns). She's like a one-woman band who startles the other passengers with her enthusiasm, flashes them a smile, and then just settles back into her seat like nothing ever happened.

'Didi is head-over-heels in love with dance; it's her heartbeat. She practises it in her mind every single moment. Sometimes, we've had to plead with her not to perform when she's running a high temperature, but good luck getting her to listen! We feel embarrassed even mentioning we're sick and might need to sit out. She's a living example of dedication.

'During one of our choreographies, I was coughing like crazy amid the COVID wave, worried that Didi might catch something from me. So, I was masked up for safety. But Didi, with her trademark passion, grabbed the mic and insisted we all take off our masks. She said she couldn't see our *bhav*—our expressions! We tried explaining that we were concerned for her health, but she was adamant, saying she wouldn't catch anything. It's moments like these that remind us how fiercely she loves her art—and how often we must play the role of worried parents!

'During the COVID pandemic, we found no editors to help us with our projects. In true Shovana Guruji style, she learned video editing from her dance disciples, who were quite skilled at it. Now, she edits almost all her dance productions herself. What's truly special is how she always acknowledges everyone who has helped her along the way. She teaches us the importance of giving credit to those who contribute to our learning, which she practises. She is so humble that she calls the disciples who teach her anything, her Gurus. This attitude encourages us to recognise the efforts of others.

'From her, we've learned that saying no to new experiences is never an option. She motivates us to embrace every opportunity without hesitation, showing us that growth often happens outside our comfort zones.

'Guruji always ensures that we receive our payments on time, no matter what. Sometimes, we find out later that the production house or show organisers hadn't even paid her yet, but she had already ensured we were compensated. She's incredibly particular about this.

'On stage, she gives us immense credit and respect, acknowledging our contributions in front of the audience. If our parents or other gurus are present, she'll invite them on stage and honour them. She instils a strong sense of ownership in us, letting us be ourselves and giving us the freedom to grow. And when it's time to celebrate, everything feels even more joyful with her presence. Her warmth makes those moments more memorable.'

Komal Biswal

'Alright, today we're working on something different. I want to see if you can feel what drawing water from a well is like. Do you remember when we were in the countryside, and I asked you to try it?'

'Yes, Guruji, I remember! We were all struggling to pull the bucket up. It didn't feel natural.'

'Exactly! And that's because it's not just about moving your arms. It's about feeling the weight, the effort, and connecting with the earth. When you draw water, there's this pull and tension in your body that you must sense. It's not just a move—it's a moment of work, of life.'

'So, when we do it in the dance, we must show that

weight and struggle?'

'Yes, that's it! You must put effort into your movements as if pulling that heavy water up. The audience should feel it, too. It's about feeling the earth under you, the work in your body, and the rhythm of it all. Let's try again, but this time, really feel it. Imagine the water, the weight, everything.'

Komal Biswal, a senior disciple of Guru Shovana Narayan, holds a master's degree in Kathak and currently teaches at Dayanand Anglo Vedic (DAV) school. She teaches beginner Kathak batches at Asavari and is part of the performance repertoire.

Komal first approached Guru Shovana when she was in the seventh grade. At the time, Kathak classes were being held at Pandara Road under Guru Bhai Teerath Ajwani, as Guru Shovana, busy with her civil service duties, could only attend once a week. Despite her limited time, Guru Shovana often kept a keen eye on Komal's performance during annual functions. On one such occasion, she praised Komal's dancing and suggested she join the repertoire class—a dream opportunity for any young student.

Awestruck by Guru Shovana, Komal eagerly agreed. However, when she stepped into the repertoire class, she was overwhelmed by the advanced skills of the senior students. Insecurity crept in, and feeling out of place, she stopped attending and returned to her regular class.

Noticing Komal's absence, Guru Shovana contacted her, asking why she wasn't attending the repertoire sessions. She encouraged Komal to observe the senior students closely and learn from their expertise. With this guidance, Komal slowly built her confidence. Over the next six months, she grew more comfortable in the repertoire class and began to grasp the nuances that set the senior students apart. It was a turning point in her journey, showing her the value of perseverance and learning through observation.

'Guruji gave me my first big break to perform at Vrindavan, and from that moment, there was no looking back. But, oh, those early days came with some hilarious lessons! Back then, I had this terrible habit of hunching my shoulders—thanks to lugging around an absurdly heavy school bag. A straight posture? It was not even on my radar.

'One day, after we got off a train, I stood with the troupe, utterly unaware of how slouched I looked. Suddenly, *whack*! Shovana Guruji slapped me on the back! I jumped like I'd been struck by lightning, spinning around in utter confusion. For a split second, I thought, what did I do wrong this time?

'Then it hit me—literally and figuratively. She was just trying to get me to straighten my posture. And guess what? It worked like a charm. From that day on, I've never dared to slouch again. Guruji's methods might have been somewhat unconventional, but they were effective!

'Guru Shovana ji entrusted me with teaching beginner dance classes, which was both exciting and humbling. It's something I often think about, especially when I see how many people today call themselves a guru—even students fresh out of training are quick to adopt the title. To me, an acharya teaches skills, but a true guru offers something far more profound: a complete transformation of life. A guru is like a guiding parent to your soul.

'In her unique approach, Didi never directly intervenes in my classes. Instead, she observes quietly, stepping in only when necessary to offer feedback in private. She gives me the freedom to lead, and that trust boosts my confidence. When she sits back and watches the beginners, they feel seen and valued, which makes their learning experience that much more meaningful.

Her presence adds an unspoken depth to everything we do.

'Among all the performances I've participated in, one that holds a special place in my heart was portraying a young girl. She had been married off as a child, faced the stigma of widowhood, remarried, and eventually had a child. The role was based on a real-life story, and I truly cherished bringing it to life.

'Through such performances, we step into multiple lives, experiencing emotions and stories that we might never encounter in our own lives.

'More recently, I had the unique challenge of playing Rama and Ravana in the same production. The pace in such situations is intense—there's no time to breathe! We must be incredibly fast in changing costumes, shifting from one character to the next, and immediately re-entering the stage. Of course, there are fillers in between, but the transitions are demanding. Sometimes, we wear double-layered lehengas to shed one and continue dancing in the other quickly. In Guruji's world, there is no room for hesitation. We aren't taught to say no or offer excuses—there are no statements like, "Guruji, I can't do this."

'So, one day at Pandara Road, I had one of those classic klutzy moments. I slipped in the washroom and twisted my ankle. In a panic, I called Guruji to tell her I wouldn't make it to class, expecting sympathy. She listened patiently, then asked, "Can you walk slowly to your gate?" I said, "Well, yeah, I can manage that." Without missing a beat, she said, "Great! Get ready, I'm coming to pick you up!" I was stunned, but sure enough, she showed up, took my hand, and helped me into the car. I ended up attending the full three-hour class—but instead of dancing, I was sitting there doing the *padhant* (reciting rhythmic syllables).

'That day, I realised something mind-blowing: there's no room for self-doubt when you're with Guruji. She's like your personal cheerleader, seeing your potential even when you're too busy questioning yourself. And if you think you're done for, she's there to prove you wrong and get you back in action—no excuses!

'Shovana Guruji has a unique way of teaching—she makes every lesson come alive through real-life experiences, helping us grasp the most intricate aspects of dance. I remember one such lesson vividly. Guruji wanted us to understand how the weight and content of a vessel could influence our expressions and movements. We were to lift the vessel once on our waist, giving the impression that it was empty, and then again on our heads as though it were full. No matter how often we tried, she wasn't satisfied with our efforts.

'That's when she decided to show us what it felt like. She brought in a large earthen pot, filled it with water, and had us place it on our heads, one by one. She then asked us to look at ourselves in the mirror. The weight of the pot immediately changed our postures, and we could see the subtle difference in our facial expressions—the strain, the caution, the heaviness. Then, she asked us to repeat the movement with the pot on our waist. That experience made us understand the nuance of expression in each situation, a lesson no amount of verbal instruction could have conveyed.

'Didi always stressed the importance of our bends, especially our *kalai* (wrist). She used to say, "*Aap kahin bhi baithe ho, gaadi mein ho, aapki kalai hamesha chalti rehni chahiye*" (No matter where you are, even while sitting in a car, your wrist should always be moving). Didi placed equal importance on grace and strength. She often said, "*Nritta mein bhi aapko utna hi nipun hona hai jitna ki bhav mein*" (Your technical precision should be as refined as your expression).

'Didi would spend hours perfecting even the most minor details, like a glance. She would insist, "Keep practising your *nazar* (glance) until I feel it's right." She was incredibly particular about coordinating our gaze, hands, and nose, ensuring everything was perfectly aligned.

'Guruji often uses props to teach us these subtleties. A simple *dupatta*, for instance, can reveal the posture our bodies assume when we dance. She teaches metaphorical dance movements, emphasising that nothing is ever direct. If we are depicting the streets of Vrindavan, it isn't about creating a replica but hinting at it through subtle gestures: the middle partition of your hair, a distant glance, or the wave-like motion of your hands—all these gestures suggest a street without ever stating it directly.

'Similarly, when portraying complex characters like Ravana, Guruji delves into their multidimensional nature. When I was cast as Ravana, I initially found it amusing. How was I supposed to bring such a larger-than-life figure to life? But then Guruji began to explain his character, not just as a villain but as a powerful, noble and learned king—who also happened to be arrogant, angry, and flawed. Once she described his traits, both positive and negative, I began to understand the depth of the character. It became less about acting as Ravana and more about embodying all the complexities he represented. By the time I performed the role, I had fully immersed myself in his persona and received much appreciation.

'In one production, we performed a one-*shloka* Ramayana with just four of us, each playing multiple characters, each requiring its own distinct set of nuances. In another performance, I was cast as Jahanara. Initially, I didn't know much about her, but Guruji took the time to guide me through her history and character, revealing that she was the daughter of Shah Jahan and Mumtaz Mahal. This deeper understanding of her story enriched my performance and expanded my perspective on the world.

A family get-together with Guru Shovana Narayan's senior disciples-
Shruti Gupta, Kartika Singh, Mrinalini and Shuchi Rastogi, 2023

'Guru Shovana's thought process is never simple. She often chooses complex themes and characters from mythology, asking questions that make us think deeply. Instead of giving direct answers, she inspires us to explore and reflect on these ideas.

'One of the most memorable productions we did was *Shunyata,* which presented the story of King Ashoka and his profound disillusionment after witnessing the horrors of war, juxtaposed with the peaceful presence of monks. Sharing the stage with real monks was a surreal, almost spiritual experience. Even the Dalai Lama attended that performance, which felt like a moment of true transcendence.

'These performances have not only helped us grow as dancers but have also shaped our worldview. Through them, we've come to appreciate the richness of our history and the deeper meaning behind every movement, expression, and character. As Guruji's disciples, we have evolved not just as performers but as individuals with a broader understanding of life.

'Shovana Guruji is like a mother to us. When we're upset,

she feels it too—she goes out of her way to figure out what's bothering us and helps us work through it. Back when we had classes at Pandara Road, we'd rush straight from school or college, toss our bags aside, and head straight into the kitchen like it was our own home. There were no formalities—she always made us feel like we belonged. Whether eating, resting, rehearsing, or even sleeping, the door was always open to us.

'We could ring her doorbell at any hour, even after midnight, and there'd be a warm meal waiting. Even today, when we visit her farmhouse, we never need to ask which room to stay in—the whole house feels like ours. Guruji has this incredible ability to make each of us feel like we share a unique, special bond with her—that's her magic. She's always present, performing alongside us or sitting in the front row, watching with pride. No matter what, she's there, cheering us on.

'One year, during our annual day, we had to manage everything without her, as she was in Austria taking care of her husband, Mr Herbert, who was unwell. But she sent us a voice note that we played in the auditorium, and there we were, teary-eyed, taking care of everything from invitations to costumes to rehearsals. But that's her trust in us—she empowers us to handle things ourselves, knowing we can.

'Guruji's style is like a sneaky ninja—she'll appear out of nowhere, whisper a quick correction in your ear, and vanish just as fast. Performing alongside her is always a big deal for us. Recently, we had a trio performance—me, Pallavi, and Guruji. We had practised everything she asked, so we thought we were ready. But just before the show, she casually strolls up to the mic and announces an entirely different production than what we had rehearsed! We stood there with our jaws on the floor, trying not to freak out. And then she says, "If I make a wrong move, just whisper, 'Didi, go there,' and guide me!" So, during the performance, whenever we turned our backs to the audience, we whispered like secret agents, frantically correcting each other's placements. It felt like a covert operation!

'I still laugh when I think back to when I first joined Guruji. I had memorised every single detail of the performance we were supposed to do. We were performing exactly what we had rehearsed, and then, out of nowhere, Didi leaned over and whispered, "Present *raudra* rasa, Pallavi!" I was like, "What on earth is *raudra*?" I had no clue! Panicked, I quickly whispered to Komal, who thankfully filled me in on what to do. Talk about a last-minute challenge! Guruji keeps us on our toes, doesn't she?'

"Why can't you show the gagari properly?" I yelled. "It looks like an awkward dhobi bundle and not a gagari!"

"What is the difference in holding the two?" the young student shot back.

"Your hands and the curve of your arms must reflect the curve of the earthenware pot. And mind you, it is different when held on the head and at the waist!" (An extract from 'Meandering Pastures of Memories')

Pallavi and Komal speak of their Guruji with such bubbling affection that their words often tumble over each other. One begins a story, and before it can find its full shape, the other—eyes alight, voice eager—leans in to add a memory of her own. Their sentences crisscross, laughter and reverence woven together, as though the act of remembering is a shared performance. They happily interrupt, not out of haste, but out of joy, carrying the conversation like a rhythmic jugalbandi.

Praveen Parihar

Praveen Parihar of the Jaipur Gharana grew up in a family where music and dance were a cherished legacy. Initially drawn to western culture, he showed little interest in classical arts until a 2004 performance by Pandit Manish Gangani at Kamani Auditorium inspired him. Shortly after, the family moved to Janakpuri so Praveen could train under Pandit Manish Gangani. Beginning formal training at seven, he trained with Pandit Manish for eight years before completing his post-diploma at Delhi's Kathak Kendra under Pandit Rajendra Gangani.

'I was performing with both of my Gurujis at the time but sought a place to work consistently on dance productions. I reached out to Guru Shovana ji after learning about her repertoire. She warmly welcomed me and encouraged me to start learning pieces from her archives. Her humility, calm demeanour, and immense knowledge struck me as I joined the ongoing rehearsals for her past productions. Soon after, I began travelling and performing with her, and it's now been nearly twelve years of sharing the stage with Guruji.

'Many years ago, I attended the cultural event Lalit Arpan, which Guruji organises annually and features legendary dance performances. At the time, I had just joined Guruji's repertoire as a twenty-four-year-old dancer. I dreamt of performing at Lalit Arpan one day. Hesitantly, I shared this wish with Shovana Guruji, who gently explained that the dancers for that year had already been selected. I took it as a sign to focus on perfecting my craft, and from that moment, I dedicated myself to practising diligently.

'In 2023, I once again expressed my wish to perform at Lalit Arpan, only to be told, yet again, that I was too late—the dance pieces had been finalised months earlier. I accepted it with quiet resolve, unaware of what fate had in store. During a trip to Vietnam with Shovana Guruji for a performance of *Yajnaseni,* we were casually chatting when she suddenly turned to me and asked if I had received the letter. Puzzled, I looked at her blankly. That's when she smiled and announced that I would perform at Lalit Arpan. Her words sent shivers down my spine—it was the fulfilment of a dream I had nurtured for years. The following day in Vietnam, with a heart full of gratitude, I began practising earnestly.

'During our intense rehearsals, Guruji casually mentioned that even Rama Vaidyanathan would perform on the same day. I was stunned—these were living legends! I've always held Shovana Guru ji in such reverence and her presence feels so powerful that I hardly dare ask too many questions. The details don't seem as important as simply meeting her expectations.

'It wasn't until the day before Lalit Arpan that I finally gathered the courage to ask, "*Didi, mera samay kitna hoga?*" (How much time do I get to perform?) She smiled and replied, "*Praveen, jab tak audience bore nahin ho, lage rahna.*" (Praveen, continue until the audience begins to get bored.)

'That evening felt like stepping into a dream. Sharing the stage with legends was surreal, and to have senior artists shower me with their appreciation was a moment I will cherish forever.

'Shovana Guruji doesn't impose discipline—it's something you instinctively pick up by simply being around her. Her dedication speaks louder than words. No matter how far she's travelled or how exhausting her journey might have been, she always heads straight to the repertoire from the airport, as her commitment fuels her energy.

'I made it a personal goal to arrive early for class, hoping to be there before her, but every time, I'd find her already there, calm and focused, ready to begin. It was humbling and awe-inspiring as if she operated on a plane of discipline and devotion that we could only aspire to reach.

'She emphasises the importance of rehearsals for every artist, saying that if you skip even a single day, you fall behind by at least a week. *Nirantarata*—consistency—is key. Her agility and boundless positive energy come from her commitment to regular practice. For her, dance is akin to yoga and sadhana, connecting you to higher, divine energies.

'Shovana Guruji acted in *Aavartan*, where I played a character named Bhumi. Guruji was choreographing for the movie and preparing us for a stage performance at Kamani Auditorium, scheduled just three days later. Balancing film shoots and rehearsals for the show was intense, but exhilarating.

'Then, just two days before the performance, I was in a serious accident. My arm was fractured in three places, requiring a steel rod to be inserted. I was devastated. The thought of losing my role in the film and missing the performance after a month of dedicated rehearsals was heartbreaking.

'Didi visited me during this difficult time. She reassured me with her characteristic calm and compassion, saying I would heal soon and that everything would eventually return to normal. Her words were a source of immense comfort, reminding me of the strength and patience required to overcome challenges.

'A few days later, *Aavartan* was screened at the IHC auditorium. Despite knowing I was no longer part of the film, I watched it. Surprisingly, my role remained intact—precisely as it had been filmed! Guruji had thoughtfully and gracefully crafted a safe exit for my character, preserving everything we had worked on together.

'It was an overwhelming moment that left me deeply moved. Guruji's decision wasn't just about choreography or storytelling; it reflected her immense kindness and respect for her students. With her, you never feel left behind or forgotten. She has a unique way of ensuring that everyone shines in their own way.

With Guruji, you only gain—there's never anything to lose.

'Guruji imparts the most profound nuances of the performing arts, teaching us to embody any character—male or female, authentically. She showed me that the key lies in fully immersing oneself in the role and gracefully letting it go once the performance ends. There's no need to carry the feminine gait or emotions into real life. Over the years, I've played powerful and complex characters like Ravana, Duryodhana, and Krishna, each time marvelling at Guruji's instinctive ability to assign roles ideally, trusting her deep understanding of our strengths.

'When she asked me to play Ravana, I was taken aback. How could someone as delicate as me portray such a commanding and formidable figure? But her explanation changed everything. She told me that Ravana was more than physical strength—he was a concept, a force of nature. To help me understand, she demonstrated Ravana's persona, and in that moment, he came alive in her every gesture, movement, and expression.

'Watching her transform was a revelation. I realised that acting isn't about the physicality of a character—it's about capturing its essence, its soul. That lesson has stayed with me ever since, guiding every role I take.

'This philosophy extends far beyond the stage. Like stepping into roles written by a divine script, life calls us to embrace its abstract essence, not just the tangible aspect. Acting mirrors life: we take on each role fully, perform it wholeheartedly, and then release it without attachment.

'Under Guruji's wise and compassionate guidance, I've become a versatile artist capable of embodying any character. One of the most transformative experiences was my portrayal of Ravana—a role I once thought was beyond me. Yet, it revealed my growth as a dancer and a person. The appreciation

I received for that performance affirmed how deeply Guruji's teachings had shaped me.'

Praveen envisions a long career as a stage performer and aspires to become a dance guru, carrying forward a cherished legacy. He understands that while the physical agility and vigour essential to dance have their limits with age, the deeper, timeless elements of the craft endure.

'Shovana Guru ji, a living example of this wisdom, often revisits her works from the eighties, infusing them with fresh relevance and meaning. She reminds her students, "*Tezi ek samay tak hai. Bhav aur bhumika hamesha rahenge*". This profound teaching highlights that while speed and physical prowess may fade, the essence of storytelling, roles (bhumika), and expressions (bhav) remains eternal.'

Dancers who wish to sustain their artistry into later years must embrace these subtleties, for they hold the true soul of dance—transcending physical limitations. Inspired by his Guru's journey, Praveen hopes to master these timeless aspects, ensuring his connection to dance remains unbroken throughout his life.

***

Suparna Singh

Suparna is currently pursuing a PhD in Kathak at Sri Sri University, Cuttack, and holds a master's degree in Kathak from Indira Kala Vishwavidyalaya, Khairagarh. She has also completed diploma and post-diploma programmes from Shriram Bharatiya Kala Kendra, Delhi. Suparna began her discipleship under Guru Shovana Narayan in late 2017, marking the start of an ongoing journey of artistic growth and learning.

'I remember our exam papers often included multiple-choice

questions like, "Who among the following is a disciple of Birju Maharaj?" Without hesitation, I'd tick "Shovana Narayan." As I grew older, I happened to watch her interview on Doordarshan. Her screen presence and thoughtful answers completely captivated me. I turned to my father and said, "I want to learn from her." Little did I know that the moment would mark the beginning of an incredible journey—a journey that has only deepened my admiration and connection with her over the years!'

'I vividly remember my first day. I stood there, unsure and hesitant, but she gently encouraged me to dive in. She reassured me with her signature words: "*Peeche khade hokar bhi bahut kuch seekh sakte ho.*" It didn't matter if I was a beginner or more advanced—what mattered was being present and open to learning. That's the beauty of her teaching; she is incredibly generous with her knowledge, leaving it entirely up to us to decide how much we are ready to absorb.

'I've never encountered a mentor quite like her. She radiates warmth and makes us feel at home, like a foster mother. We confide in her about our lives beyond dance. Even outside of rehearsals and performances, we maintain a close bond. During the month-long holidays in June, she often calls us to say she misses us. Despite her busy schedule and numerous performances, she always finds time to contact us. She truly feels like family. We admire her immensely as a public figure, but the simple, heartfelt gesture of her calling us without any reason—just to let us know we're on her mind—makes us feel truly special.

'In 2018, I endured a severe illness that left me hospitalised for an entire month, just as I was beginning to get to know Shovana Didi. During this challenging period, I realised that she is much more than a dance guru—she is also an incredible therapist and counsellor. Her presence carries an unspoken healing power, one that soothes not just the body but also the soul.

'Since meeting her, I have built a resilience I never knew I had. My horizons have expanded, and my perspectives have shifted dramatically. It's like undergoing a rigorous training programme akin to army training, where every facet of your personality is meticulously nurtured and groomed.

'When we perform, you can truly see her influence in us. She has an extraordinary ability to bring out the best in each of her students, transforming the chaos of our lives into a cohesive and beautiful expression of art.

'It's as if she weaves her essence into our very being, crafting us into magnificent individuals ready to take on the world.

'The journey under her guidance is not just about dance; it's about becoming the best version of ourselves.'

***

Mahima Satsangi

'I began my journey with Guru Shovana Narayan ji in February 2019, and with each step, my gratitude for the opportunity to learn from her has only deepened. Initially, I was recommended for the junior class, but soon, Shruti Chandra Di and Mahaveer Bhaiya suggested I move to the senior group. That's when I started learning directly from Didi—a privilege I still find hard to believe.

'A few months later, during an event, Didi watched me perform for the first time. I was overjoyed when she allowed me to present a solo piece. It was my first solo with live music—a moment I will forever cherish. Later, she offered me another solo in her production *Noor Jahan*. With each new opportunity, my heart swelled with gratitude, knowing she believed in me.

'Didi's teachings go far beyond dance. My greatest lesson from her is patience—not just in the art of movement, but in life itself. She guides us with such gentleness and warmth that our classes feel less like lessons and more like home. Even more remarkable is how this sense of belonging extends beyond the classroom.

'Didi has an open house and an open heart for her students. I never imagined I would have the opportunity to learn from her so closely—visiting her home, sharing meals, and sometimes even staying over. These experiences have shown me the deeper connection she fosters with us. It's in these moments outside of class that the real magic happens—watching her compose music with musicians, seeing her interact respectfully with dignitaries and her staff, and journeying with her through everyday life.

'One of the most profound experiences has been travelling with her for performances. I've accompanied Didi several times, witnessing how seamlessly she adapts to any situation. She remains unshaken, whether it's adjusting to less-than-ideal accommodations, handling inexplicable delays, navigating clashes of time, or managing untoward challenges that arise. Her ability to stay calm, positive, and gracious in the face of such challenges has taught me invaluable lessons in resilience and grace.

'It's not just about learning dance—it's about observing how she lives and embodies grace, respect, and patience in every interaction. Being around her, I've realised that true artistry is about living the values you teach. Didi does this so effortlessly, making us feel part of a larger, loving family.

'My trip to the Allahabad Museum is one experience I hold very close to my heart. It was my first dance trip with Didi, where I performed alongside Suparna during Didi's lecture demonstration. Being with her on that journey, I witnessed firsthand the immense respect and admiration people have for her. As we travelled, I couldn't help but marvel at how Didi, so revered in the world of art, carries herself with such grace and humility. Despite her status as a highly respected figure, she remains grounded, making everyone around her feel seen, heard, and valued.

'In that moment, I realised how fortunate I am to have her as my guru. She teaches us the art of dance and cares for us like a second mother, offering guidance, love, and support in every aspect of our lives. I felt incredibly humbled, aware of how much she invests in our growth, both as artists and as people.

'Now, as I teach dance at a school, I carry Didi's lessons daily. Her patience and unwavering kindness have shaped me as a dancer, person, and teacher. What she has given me goes beyond words—her wisdom, humility, and love for her students are immeasurable. I am deeply grateful to be a part of her world, and I feel blessed to walk this path under her guidance.'

***

Anupama Jha Kumar

'My transformative journey with Didi, Padma Shri Guru Shovana Narayan, began in July 2020. I never anticipated that I would forge such a profound bond with her in such a brief period. I often reflect that I've experienced two significant births: my physical arrival into this world from my biological parents and the profound awakening of my soul, my atma, through Didi's guidance and wisdom. These past four years have felt like an eternity, enriched by the intensity of four weekly classes, each a step deeper into dance and spirituality. She carries the essence of a godmother, nurturing my art and the substance of who I am. This sense of belonging and connection is something I cherish deeply.

'As I reflect on the intense relationship between Paramhansa Yogananda and his revered guru, Yukteshwar Giri, a bond that elevated Yogananda to extraordinary spiritual heights, I find echoes of that sacred connection in the relationship between Ramkrishna Paramahansa and Vivekananda. Today, I proudly acknowledge my deep connection with Didi. Every moment spent in her presence feels like reaching for and plucking stars from the vast, boundless sky, a constant reminder of the beauty and magic life offers through her mentorship.

'I wholeheartedly attribute my happiness and my direction of life to her. Over these past four years, Didi has diligently shaped my spirit and artistry. Her mentorship has been nothing short of transformative, leading to my breakthrough in 2022, when I danced to live music for the first time—made possible by her unwavering encouragement and benign guidance. She also helped me bring my dance production on women's empowerment to life, titled *Yajnaseni - Born out of the Fire*. However, this journey was not without challenges; Didi's support helped me overcome them.

'Through her, I have discovered my true calling: to immerse myself in Kathak's captivating world. I feel truly privileged to have her as a part of my life. No matter what I achieve, I can never fully repay the boundless love and support she has graciously given me. This sense of fulfilment and gratitude is something that I carry with me every single day.'

***

Geetika Tewari

'I first encountered Shovana Didi when I was just three years old, sometime around 1982-83. Given how young I was, I don't remember that initial meeting. However, my earliest, most vivid childhood memories revolve around being in her class, silently observing her with awe and admiration. I was mesmerised by her presence, her dedication, and her grace. In those early years, I remember Didi correcting us with utmost patience and emphasising the nuances that make Kathak an extraordinary art form—the importance of precise bends, fluid wrist movements, *bhava* (expression), speed, and technical perfection. Her teachings left an indelible mark on my young mind.

'There is one moment, among many, for which I will forever remain deeply grateful to Didi—it was the time I lived with her.

'I was around seven or eight when my family moved from New Delhi to Old Delhi. This relocation and my father's demanding work schedule made it increasingly difficult for him to manage my pick-up and drop-off for dance classes. The long commute took a toll, and eventually, we had to discontinue my lessons with Shovana Didi.

'Months passed, and one day, my father received a call from Didi's mother, the respected Lalita aunty. She inquired about me, concerned as to why I had stopped attending. When she learned about our situation, she and Shovana Didi made an incredible decision that changed the course of my life. They arranged for me to come directly from my school at Curzon Road on Fridays and stay at their home until Sunday. For months and years, I spent my weekends at Didi's place, learning Kathak under her care.

'Not only did she ensure I continued my training, but she also treated me like her own child. I vividly remember how she ensured I slept right by her side in her room as though I were her little daughter. This act of generosity is something I will never forget. I could continue learning Kathak despite the challenges only because of her love and support.

'Life took its course, and after twenty-eight long years of living in Mumbai, building a career as a corporate marketing professional, and raising two teenagers, I felt an intense pull to return to my first love—Kathak. By a divine blessing, I found my way back to Shovana Didi. It is solely because of her that I got this second chance.

'She is my *rahnuma* (guide) in my journey. Today, as I humbly pass on her teachings, values, and legacy to my students through my dance school in Mumbai, I am reminded every single day of the incredible debt of gratitude I owe her.'

***

Bela Shah

Today, Bela Shah is forty-six and first enrolled as an online student of Shovana from the lockdown batch of 2020. She has a delightful tale to share about her journey of learning Kathak under her revered guru. When she first joined, she was admittedly terrified of Shovana Guru ji, but it didn't take long for her to discover her warm and approachable personality.

Bela's commitment to learning is as remarkable as it is meticulous. She makes it a point to write down every detail of what Shovana Didi teaches—from abhinaya explanations to choreography nuances. 'When I perform on stage, I think of Guruji's explanations, and the abhinaya flows effortlessly,' she shares. Bela's precision in documenting every movement—down to whether the right hand or left hand is to be used—has earned her the nickname, the *Hard Disk* of the class. Guruji herself often says, "*Kuch bhi ho, Bela ke notes mein sahi movements likhe honge!*"

Bela fondly recalls moments when she, with the utmost

respect, gently reminded her guru of specific details. 'Sometimes, Guruji changes a particular movement, and I politely say, "Guruji, you mentioned the right hand, and I've written it down, so I'll follow that!"' she laughs.

Bela's story doesn't stop at her devotion to her guru—it extends to her admiration for other stalwarts of Indian classical dance, like Sonal Mansingh. Once, Bela expressed her heartfelt wish to meet Sonal Mansingh, who was scheduled to be the chief guest at one of their events. However, due to health reasons, Sonal ji excused herself midway through the programme. But Shovana Guru, determined to make her student's dream come true, went above and beyond.

'In the middle of the event, Guruji called out loudly, "*Bela ko jaldi bulao*!" Everyone was looking for me, and before I could understand what was happening, Guruji told me to run towards the exit. I didn't even ask why and just ran, with Guruji running right behind me!' Bela guffaws as she recounts the chaos. 'At one point, I ran in the wrong direction, and Guruji screamed, "*Abe idhar nahi, udhar bhago*!"'

Finally, Bela reached the exit, and to her astonishment, there stood Sonal ji. Shovana Guru ji graciously introduced her star-struck student to the iconic dancer. 'I was so lucky to receive blessings from Sonal ji, and it was all because of my Guruji's kindness and effort. How many gurus would go to such lengths to fulfil a student's wish?'

***

Mrinalini

Mrinalini's journey through life is deeply intertwined with her journey in dance, and at the heart of it all is her bond with her Shovana Didi. To her, Shovana Didi is more than a mentor; she is a guiding star whose presence has shaped and illuminated her path in Kathak. Mrinalini's love for this classical dance form is as profound as her admiration and affection for Guru Shovana Narayan.

Her tryst with Kathak began as a legacy passed down by her mother, a passionate art practitioner. Rooted in the Banaras Gharana, her mother envisioned a future for Mrinalini steeped in Kathak's rhythm, grace, and tradition even before she was born. With years of experience and wisdom to draw upon, her mother charted a course for Mrinalini, believing deeply in the transformative power of the art form. It was not just a dance she was passing on; it was a way of life, a lineage, and a heritage of beauty and expression.

For Mrinalini, the journey has been one of discovery, discipline, and devotion—anchored by her mother's dreams and nurtured by the inspiration of Shovana Didi, whose artistry and guidance continue to shape her as a dancer and a person.

'When I was just three or four years old, my mother would show me dance videos of Guru Shovana Narayan ji. At that time, the thought of ever learning directly from her felt like a distant dream—she was a celebrity, someone we admired from afar. I still remember how Doordarshan used to sell tapes of classical dancers, and one of them was a recording of her performance at Purana Qila, a dance production called *Moonlight*.

'My mother spoke of her dance with such admiration that it inspired me—the ideal I hoped to follow. Watching those videos was my first introduction to Kathak and the incredible artist who would spark my love for this beautiful art form.'

As destiny would have it, Mrinalini's father was posted to Delhi, a turn of events her mother saw as a sign from the universe.

This move allowed them to connect with Asavari, the dance school run by Guru Shovana Narayan. It was the year 1999, and Mrinalini was just six years old. Thanks to her mother's guidance, she already had a strong foundation in Kathak and was ready to take her first steps in formal training.

'When I first stepped into the class at Pandara Road, Delhi, my little heart felt something profound—I knew I had arrived at a special place, the pinnacle of my dreams, and that life was about to unfold in the most beautiful of ways. It felt like this was exactly where I was meant to be.

'I started in the kids' batch, and Shovana Didi occasionally passed by. We would catch glimpses of her rushing off to a party or returning from work, her sari's edge trailing gracefully behind her. For us kids, those fleeting moments were magical. She was like a goddess to us, a vision of elegance and inspiration, always moving with the energy of a fresh, uplifting breeze.

'Different teachers taught our classes, but Shovana Didi oversaw everything. She worked with the senior students and managed the repertoire at Asavari. During water breaks, we'd sneak peeks into her private room, where she taught her most senior students. I was often caught in the act, peeking through the curtains. She would call out, "Who's there? Come inside!" And in that moment, my heart would race as I thought, 'Oh no, she saw me watching her! What do I do now?'

Since Shovana would oversee all the batches at Asavari, she noticed Mrinalini and remarked that she liked her form. She invited her to join her personal classes—a moment that, in hindsight, feels as monumental as graduation day. It was an incredible honour for young Mrinalini.

The senior class she was invited to was far beyond her level then. Overwhelmed yet eager, she would sit quietly, watch, and absorb everything she could. From that point on, there was no turning back. Mrinalini grew steadily under Shovana's guidance, performing solos and eventually achieving the milestone of her *Rangmanch Pravesh*, marking her formal entry into the world of professional Kathak.

'I was under the tutelage of someone who was not only a master performer but also deeply rooted in the science and architecture of Kathak—an intricate framework that audiences consume as beauty and art. For the audience, it's mesmerising and aesthetic, but the precision behind it—the stencil, so to speak—is incredibly complex to learn.

'From day one, Shovana Guru ji emphasised the importance of being theoretically firm and grammatically correct as dancers. "Looking good on stage isn't enough," she often reminded us. "If something about your dance is questioned, you must be able to explain it." This focus on intellectual and technical depth sets her apart as a Kathak guru.

What sets her apart as a human being and an artist, however, is her warmth. As a performer, her grace and beauty on stage reflect the genuine love she carries in her heart for the art. It's this combination of brilliance and humanity that makes her extraordinary.'

Mrinalini adds, 'Shovana Didi is at a level of excellence and achievement that most can only dream of reaching in a lifetime.' Over the last twenty years, travelling extensively with Shovana Guruji, Mrinalini has witnessed a remarkable quality in her that leaves a deep impression—her unwavering kindness.

'No matter where she is, Shovana Didi treats everyone with respect and warmth, including the staff and those helping behind the scenes. This humility and compassion are striking, especially for someone of her stature. In a world where people at her level often find it easy to overlook those at the base of the pyramid, mainly when racing against time to be on stage, her thoughtfulness stands out as both inspiring and rare.

'Didi would always pause, even if for ten seconds, to thank the driver who dropped her off or the person who carried her belongings. Sometimes, we would grow impatient, but for her, this gratitude is second nature. Over time, we've learned so much from her beyond dance, and the first lesson we can all agree on is kindness. While kindness is something we're all taught about in theory at school, I've had the privilege of seeing it in action through her. Another beautiful quality I've observed, especially during national or international dance festivals, is her simplicity and lack of demands. All she needs to know is where the stage is and when she's expected to perform.

'She nurtures us as if we were her children, and in return, we revere her as a mother figure. We often feel the urge to ensure her comfort and even debate why she asks for so little. But Didi, true to her nature, is more concerned about whether *we* are comfortable, placing our well-being above her own. Her selflessness continues to inspire us.'

Mrinalini has learned from her Guruji how to truly show up on stage, assess the audience's needs, and be attuned to the emotions in any room. This is how she crafts her performances. Under her guidance, Mrinalini has developed the ability to connect with people from all walks of life, understanding the importance of genuinely immersing herself in whatever she does.

Mrinalini has learned to dive deep into the roots of things, to understand and appreciate them fully. Many people go through the motions, but few truly grasp what they're doing and why. Shovana's diligence and attention to detail are remarkable. For example, even though she doesn't have many opportunities to cook, whenever she does, she follows the recipe with meticulous precision—whether it's something as simple as making *dal*. One of the key lessons Mrinalini has learned from her is to approach everything wholeheartedly, no matter the task.

'She wouldn't let us off easily. She was a tough taskmaster. I remember when we would be dancing, she wouldn't even allow us water breaks. We'd start, say, at 7 am, and the practice would go on until 1 pm, leaving us so exhausted that our legs could hardly carry us. This was our routine, and she was very strict about it. "Until you get it right, you're not going on stage," she would say. I'm so grateful to her for this discipline, and I feel today's young performers—and their parents—need to understand this. While it's easy to get on stage these days, the true essence of the guru-shishya tradition lies in staying grounded in the traditional values of the art form.

'Shovana Didi's brilliance is multifaceted, and it is what gives her an undeniable charisma. Not only is she a master of Kathak, but she is also bilingual and a prolific writer in both Hindi and English. Her command of multiple languages is impressive, but above all, the language in which she excels the most is the language of love.'

The bond between Shovana and her students is built on deep affection, admiration, and reverence, much like the pure relationship between a mother and her children. Her students don't just cherish her for her unparalleled expertise in Kathak; they also deeply value the warmth and care she extends to them. To them, she is more than a guru—she is a source of inspiration, a role model, someone they aspire to emulate in every aspect of their lives. For Mrinalini, this admiration goes beyond just learning the art—she even aspires to embody the grace and presence of Shovana, wishing to reflect the qualities she so profoundly reveres.

'Shovana Didi looks most beautiful in saris. Every time I step out, I wear one too. To me, she is both the dancer and the dance, the artist and the art. If I ever reach a point where I can proudly say I've achieved something or become the person I aspired to be, it will be because of her. My love for the arts and the creativity I now nurture have all flourished from the love, wisdom, and guidance she has so generously given me.'

There have been moments in Mrinalini's life when she wrestled with self-doubt, questioning whether dance was truly her passion or just a dream her mother had for her. These moments of uncertainty were pivotal, driving her to search deeply within herself for clarity.

'Throughout this journey, I've often asked myself whether this is what I truly wanted to do or if I was following a path I had been conditioned to take. It was crucial for me to reflect on these questions, and I spent a lot of time contemplating them. What if my mother hadn't encouraged me to pursue dance? What would I have chosen instead? But the moment I step onto the stage, become part of the creative process, and express myself through dance, I realise that this is what I would have done, regardless of the circumstances. I feel incredibly fortunate to have been guided in this direction by my parents. In a way, half of my journey was already set in motion. I would have eventually found my way to dance, perhaps a bit later in life. Dance, for me, is an inner calling that I could never ignore.'

A true guru is not someone who imparts knowledge or teaches technique but one who continues to learn and explore with the curiosity of a seeker. This is the essence of what makes a guru truly exceptional—the constant pursuit of growth, understanding, and wonder. A guru who keeps exploring is enriching their own life and sharing that ongoing discovery with their students, guiding them through an ever-evolving process.

In Mrinalini's journey, the path laid out by her Guruji has been more than just mastering the basics to perform on stage. It has been a continuous, immersive process of learning—rehearsing dance, delving into poetry, studying texts, and engaging with others in the art world. Guruji's discovery of the Kathak villages, her travels, her decoding of the *Natyashastra*, and her research into various dance forms influenced her understanding of the art.

Shovana's students feel particularly blessed by the realisation that their guru is, in essence, a disciple of life itself. Every day, she explores uncharted territories and uncovers new dimensions of knowledge. This lifelong learning journey is not confined to the guru alone but is shared generously with her students, who are invited to walk with her on this path of constant exploration.

'All I did was attend dance class—whether after school, on weekends, or during holidays. Dance class was my refuge, my source of healing. It was my entire world then, and it still is. Even if I haven't performed on stage in a while, I never stop being a dancer.'

Mrinalini has had the privilege of performing solo on many stages and travelling extensively, but she doesn't seek material goals in her dance journey. For her, Kathak is not something to be measured or quantified; she hopes to carry it within her for as long as she breathes. Looking ahead, she envisions herself becoming a teacher of Kathak in the coming years, continuing to perform in various parts of the world.

In addition to teaching and performing, Mrinalini plans to delve deeper into research on dance, while her *riyaz* will remain a constant part of her life. She wants to stay in tune with the art form, as it has become an integral tool for navigating life's ups and downs.

Kathak is a versatile and expressive dance form, and Mrinalini hopes to make it more accessible to audiences worldwide, sharing its beauty and depth wherever she goes.

'What I truly love is when the audience connects with the art form, even if they don't understand the language. For example, when I perform abroad in front of a culturally diverse audience, they mostly do not understand the Sanskrit *shlokas* I dance to. Still, many tell me they feel goosebumps or even cry during my performance. I experienced the power of art in a personal way during the COVID times when I created a video expressing the ennui and anxiety that we were all feeling. It went viral, even though it was a solo dance performed in my flat's gallery, with no ghunghroos on my feet.

'People connected deeply with the video, and my inbox was flooded with heartfelt messages and blessings. Many of the viewers were far from home and shared how the video gave them a sense of hope, believing that life would return to normal soon. Of course, they weren't just connecting with me as a person; they were connecting with the art itself, which allowed them to release their pent-up emotions during tough times. I want this cross-cultural connection to reach all parts of the world.

'My future goal is to attract more of these positive energies because, in the end, it's what you leave behind that truly matters.'

***

Kristina Luna Dolinina

Kristina Luna Dolinina from Lithuania was interested in Hindi while studying at university, which led her to visit Agra's Kendriya

Hindi Sansthan twice. Although she had always been passionate about theatre and somewhat interested in dance, her time in Agra deepened her fascination with dance, making her realise it was her true calling. Determined to learn Indian classical dance, she pursued a scholarship to study in India. However, she was initially unsure about which classical dance style to choose.

She was informed that she couldn't learn classical dance directly but could pursue a master's degree in Hindi in India. On her application form, she listed Delhi for Kathak, Banaras Hindu University also for Kathak, and Hyderabad for Kuchipudi as her preferred choices.

'Getting Delhi was a stroke of luck that changed my life completely. My world flipped upside down,' Kristina recalls with a spark in her eyes. Her journey took an unexpected turn when a professor who taught her about the Bhakti movement mentioned an exceptional Kathak dancer he had once seen at a conference. Intrigued, Kristina tracked down the dancer's name—Shovana Narayan.

In 2003 she arrived in Delhi, ready to embrace the city and its vibrant culture. Determined to pursue her newfound passion, Kristina made her way to Pandara Road, where Shovana Narayan lived. Nervously, she introduced herself, unsure how the legendary dancer would respond.

To her relief, Shovana listened patiently as Kristina shared her story and her commitment to staying in India for at least two years while completing her master's at Jawaharlal Nehru University (JNU). After a thoughtful pause, Shovana responded with words Kristina would never forget: 'Okay, I will make a dancer out of you in two years.'

With that promise, Kristina was accepted as a *shishya*, a disciple. It was the beginning of a transformative journey that would shape not just her dance, but her entire life.

'After that, everything I did was connected to India,' Kristina reflects. She completed her master's degree, continued her dance training, and became deeply involved with Shovana's Asavari repertoire. In 2010, she returned to Lithuania when she was pregnant, but her bond with India remained strong. She would fly back to Delhi every year, staying for three to four months to practice under Shovana's guidance.

'I was living two lives,' she explains. 'In India, I was her disciple, completely immersed in dance. Then, I'd return to Lithuania, balancing my job and caring for my baby.' It was a unique rhythm—shuffling between continents, switching roles, but always staying true to her passion.

In 2007, she performed at the Lalit Arpan annual programme organised by Shovana. By 2015, she was dancing solo on stage, a pinnacle of her artistic growth. 'The dance studio at Pandara Road was more than just a practice space—it was my second home,' Kristina smiles. 'I found a family in Didi. She wasn't just my guru; she became my anchor.'

Her connection with Shovana also helped her seamlessly integrate into the IIC society in Delhi, opening doors to a vibrant cultural community. 'None of it would have been possible without her,' Kristina admits. 'She didn't just teach me dance; she shaped my entire journey.'

People often advised Kristina to leave Delhi due to the air pollution, but the city's vibrant artistic scene kept her rooted. It was the cultural hub, buzzing with grand events, art shows, and endless opportunities for socialising. She felt privileged to witness this world and play a small, humble part in it.

'Shovana Didi truly lives a dual life, inspiring us to excel on multiple platforms at once,' Kristina says of her guru. 'She makes us believe it's possible to do it all in one lifetime.'

Whenever Kristina struggled to balance her passions—wondering if she should abandon her studies to focus solely on dance—her guru answered firmly: 'No, you don't have to quit anything. You must do it all in this life, and you must do it now.'

Kristina often marvels at her Guruji's boundless energy. 'I don't know when she rests or sleeps. She's always teaching, performing, or supporting her friends and family,' she says. Despite the odd hours of online dance classes—sometimes at midnight or even at 3 am—her guru never misses a session. 'She adjusts her schedule to ours, no matter the time zone. Honestly, who does that?'

'I get thrilled whenever she visits Lithuania—for workshops, film screenings, or performances. And every time, without fail, my partner watches her bouncing around with that spring in her step and jokes, "Are you sure she's not younger than you?" I mean, seriously, she's so fit and full of life, it's hard to keep up! She's like this unstoppable bubble of energy. During those marathon practice sessions, all of us—her girls, including me—end up completely wiped out, practically melting into the floor. But not her. Oh no! She's clapping her hands, all fired up, yelling, "*Chalo chalo, utho utho*, we're not done yet!" I don't know where she gets that energy from, but it's contagious...and a little terrifying!

'We worked on this incredible project called *Aham Prithvi*—a fantastic mix of classical dance, a Lithuanian song dedicated to Mother Earth, and a powerful message about how we're treating our planet. It was brilliantly metaphorical, using the Draupadi *cheer haran* scene to show how we're playing Dushasana, stripping away Earth's vegetation just like he tried to strip Draupadi's sari.

'And get this—the legendary Odissi dancer Sharon Lowen was part of the production! I was helping conceptualise and choreograph some of the contemporary dance sections, feeling proud of myself...until Shovana Didi pulled off the ultimate showstopper.

'Picture this: Didi was hospitalised at the time. The doctors were dead serious, saying, "You're not leaving this hospital, no matter what." But what did she do? She waltzed right out of there, with a cannula in her wrist and all! Anyone else would've played the "Sorry, I'm sick" card (and no one would've blamed them!), but not her. Nope! She showed up because she had committed and would keep it—no excuses.

'So, there she was, doing Kathak with the same grace and power as ever, Sharon Lowen ji killing it with Odissi, and the rest of us girls doing contemporary dance and storytelling about the state of the Earth. But honestly, the real story was Shovana Didi, rocking that stage like she'd just walked out of a spa day instead of a hospital bed!

'Shovana Didi has shaped our futures. She has become the embodiment of her art, sharing it selflessly. When a guru chooses to be an instrument of their art, they transcend the ordinary—they become the art itself. For her, teaching isn't a transaction. I was just another student in Delhi when she took me under her wing, not because she was selling her knowledge but because her passion for Kathak demanded to be shared. She trusted and supported me, and I hope I honoured that. She has given me the strength to navigate life's ocean with grace. She is my axis—my anchor.

'For Didi, dance is more than art—a purpose she shares with unmatched passion. You see it in her choreography, hear it in her narrations, and feel it as she weaves literature and scriptures into her performances.

'People often say that performing arts heal, cultivate dedication, and grant spiritual strength, but to truly understand this, you need a guiding hand. She is that guiding hand.

'Through her, I found the purpose of my existence—of living this life and moving toward self-actualisation. Under her guidance, I've learned to experience life with open eyes, heart, and body.

'To me, art is about bringing the past and the future into the present, letting them blossom in this very moment. It's a state beyond time, without boundaries—a complete harmony where everything coheres. In Shovana Guru ji's world, this present moment feels eternal, suspended in time.

'What she imparts to her disciples is beyond measure, beyond words. It's a gift of purpose and awakening.'

***

A Mesmerising Evening: Ruby Mathur's Kathak Performance Captivates Abu Dhabi
26 February 2025, Media House

Anandini—The Joy of Being

Abu Dhabi: The stage was set, the rhythm was alive, and the air was filled with devotion as Ruby Mathur delivered a spellbinding Kathak recital, '*Anandini*: When Movement Becomes Meditation,' in Abu Dhabi. The performance was an enchanting journey where movement met devotion and rhythm became a heartbeat, leaving the audience in awe.

The Joy of Being—this performance was more than dance; it was an intimate embrace of Ruby's Kathak journey, a celebration of the divine feminine. From the delicate nuances of abhinaya to the powerful resonance of intricate footwork, every step was a prayer, every movement an offering. The energy in the auditorium was palpable, amplified by the presence of the esteemed guests, including Mrs Vandana Sudhir, the wife of the Indian ambassador, whose unwavering support and kind words added to the magic of the evening. His Excellency Dr Etienne Berchtold, Austrian ambassador to the UAE, further graced the performance, whose admiration for Indian culture and participation made the event even more memorable. A heartfelt tribute was paid to Ruby's gurus—Dr Shovana Narayan, Mulla Afsar Khan, and Kundan Mukherjee, whose guidance has shaped her artistic journey. Performing solo on this milestone birthday was a dream come true for Ruby.

'I had long cherished the dream of performing my first solo recital—a dream that found its perfect moment on my fiftieth birthday. And yet, dreams need wings. Mine came from my Guru, Shovana ji.

'I still remember the day I called her last February. Doubt clouded my mind—could I genuinely embark on this journey? Didi not only listened; she lifted me. She infused me with the strength I needed. Her words became my mantra. As I danced that night, every movement and every expression carried the weight of her wisdom, grace, and blessings.

'What made this milestone even more special was her presence. Shovana Di travelled from India to Abu Dhabi with her musicians to be there for me in this defining moment. That is the Guru she is—one who fuels the dreams of her disciples with boundless devotion, no matter the odds. Her presence alone was a reassurance, a silent promise that I was not alone.

'For her, Kathak is not just about perfecting footwork or rhythm. It is about storytelling, about embodying emotions deeply. She taught me how it was vital to feel every emotion—to internalise a woman's longing for her beloved, the surge of joy upon seeing him, and the delicate emotions stirred by his touch. Even during the final rehearsals, she was there, adjusting my posture, perfecting my footwork, reminding me to look at the audience and to hold their gaze. Every detail mattered—a step closer to perfection.

'Didi has shaped me as a dancer and as a person. She has shown me that Kathak is not merely an art form—it is humility, devotion, and a constant journey of self-discovery.

Guru tere upkar ka kaise chukaoon mein mol, laakh keemti dhan bhala, guru hai mera anmol. (For me, she is more than a guru. She is a blessing, an eternal rhythm, a timeless grace.)'

***

Dil Se….

For all the brilliance, wisdom, and inspiration that Shovana Guruji brings into her students' lives, there's no denying that learning under her is no walk in the park. She demands excellence with an intensity that leaves little room for breathers—sometimes quite literally! Water breaks are a luxury, mistakes are met with merciless precision, and 'no' simply does not exist in her vocabulary.

'Learning under Shovana Guruji is like stepping into a tornado of perfection—she expects us to absorb years of wisdom in minutes, and heaven help us if we dare to ask for a water break!'

'She calls a spade a spade, and sometimes a whole shovel—our mistakes in dance, our posture, even our social etiquette isn't spared under her sharp eye!'

'There are no no's in her class—only "Yes, Guruji" and "I'll try harder, Guruji," even when our knees beg for mercy.'

'Her passion is so intense that her dinner goes cold during class—along with ours—but who needs food when you have Kathak to sustain you?'

'Shovana Guruji's merciless focus on precision means we don't just learn dance, we learn discipline, humility, and how to gulp down water in five seconds flat when she isn't looking!'

'Her love for dance is so all-consuming that she forgets time exists—if you ever find yourself in her class, make peace with the fact that mealtime is a distant dream.'

'We joke that Guruji doesn't just teach dance—she runs a boot camp where even a second's distraction is a crime! But in the end, we wouldn't have it any other way.'

'She corrects us not just in our dance, but in our attitude, our discipline, even our way of interacting with fellow dancers. Sometimes we wonder if she secretly runs a finishing school on the side!'

'We adore her intensity, but sometimes we wish she'd be just a little kinder—to herself. She gives us no breaks, but she gives herself even less. We wish she would take a breath, sit down, and enjoy a meal without a *tatkar* soundtrack in the background. Just once, let the world wait while she gives herself the same patience and love she showers on dance.'

'If only she'd allow herself the same grace she demands from us—less chasing, more cherishing. After all, even the fiercest of gurus deserves a moment of stillness.'

***

The relationship between a teacher and a disciple is one of profound synergy, where both evolve through the exchange of energies, wisdom, and understanding. The bond between Krishna and Arjuna epitomises this sacred connection.

When Arjuna, overwhelmed by doubt and despair, surrenders to Krishna, he says:

Sishyaste ham shadhi mam tvam prapannam
(I am Your disciple, surrendered to You. Please instruct me.)
—*Bhagavad Gita* 2.7

This marks the transformation of their relationship from friendship to one of divine mentorship.

In return, Krishna assures Arjuna with his eternal promise:

Sarva-dharman parityajya mam ekam sharanam vraja
(Surrender unto Me alone, and I shall deliver you from all sins; do not fear.)
—*Gita* 18.66

The *Taittiriya Upanishad* (1.11.2) also underscores the mutual respect and growth in the teacher-student relationship:

Acharya Devo Bhava, Shishya Devo Bhava
(Treat your teacher as a god, and treat your student as a god.)

And again:

Acharya padam adatte, padam shishya swamedhaya emphasises the collaborative nature of learning—a teacher offers a part, and the disciple refines it with their understanding. Much like the divine chisel of Vishwakarma that sculpts perfection, the energies exchanged between guru and *shishya* carve not just the art but the essence of each soul, leaving both transformed in the process.

A sculptor shapes a stone into a masterpiece, the stone, in turn, refines the sculptor's art.

Kamani Auditorium backstage, Vasantotsava Programme, 2023

Chandrotasava Festival, India Habitat Centre, right to left-
Mahima, Guru Shovana and Suparna

Pic Credits:- One Framed Story

The Asavari centre for Kathak group, a workshop led by Padma Shri Dr Shovana Narayan, Chowmukha, City Palace Museum, Udaipur.

India International Center
Dr. Shovana Narayan's disciple Dhriti Swarup's Manch Pravesh, 2017
Right to left- Shuchi, Mrinalini, Pavaki, Guru Shovana, Dhriti, Shruti, Komal, Suparna and Urvi

Kristina Dolinina, The Festival of Indian Classical Arts Sur-Sadhana 2017,
Theatre Hall, Vilnius, Lithuania.

Photo credit - Jovita Ambrazaityte

Anandini – The Joy of Being, Ruby Mathur's solo Kathak production choreographed by Guru Shovana Narayan, 15 Feb 2025, the Indian Embassy, Abu Dhabi

Right to left- sitting Mahima, Ishita and Mrinalini.
Standing right to left- Suparna, Dhriti, Sukriti, Shivani, Komal

"Didi wanted me to bend more for a certain pose. I was initially stiff until she taught me the exact angle." Pallavi
Rehearsing for Vedaaranya Heritage and Healing Festival 2022
The Moment of Love

Sadhna (Dedication), *Ananda* (Joy), and the Art of Being

The journey of a classical artist is a sacred dialogue between sadhna—the discipline of devotion—and ananda—the bliss of transcendence. For Shovana Narayan, dance is not merely an art form but the essence of her being, a river flowing ceaselessly through life's depths and heights. Honours such as the Padma Shri and Sangeet Natak Akademi award are fleeting reflections of a much larger truth: the eternal pursuit of meaning through art.

'The Sangeet Natak Akademi award was a beautiful surprise, a recognition I hadn't anticipated. It was for 1999-2000, a special award given and chosen by the artists themselves. I remember it vividly—one serene morning, I received a call from the esteemed journalist Shanta Serbjeet Singh. She told me that I'd been selected. It took a moment for the words to seep in. Knowing that it is artists honouring fellow artists adds a unique depth to this award. It's a quiet, yet profound affirmation of our collective journey in the arts.'

Shovana embraces each award and honour with genuine gratitude, seeing them not as personal achievements but as affirmations of the timeless value of classical arts. She is deeply moved by the respect they represent—not only for her work but for the cultural heritage she strives to uphold. The respect she has garnered fuels her resolve to give back to the art form and the audiences who have embraced her with such warmth and regard.

'Every honour—the Padma Shri, the Delhi Government's Parishad Samman, the Bihar Government's Rashtriya Samman, or any other—brings immense gratitude and joy. These moments feel like an acknowledgment of the sadhna, the lifelong dedication I have poured into classical dance. Yet, as cherished as these recognitions are, they are milestones in an ongoing journey. Life doesn't halt with accolades; the path of sadhna flows endlessly, like a river. Dance is the essence of my being, breath, and soul.

Recognition holds deep meaning, whether a prestigious award, a heartfelt thank you, or a warm hug. Such gestures inspire an artist, encouraging them to delve deeper, refine further, and continuously strive to give their very best.

'I hold government and state honours particularly close to my heart, as they represent the cultural value of classical arts. The memory of receiving the Padma Shri remains as vivid as yesterday. It was a calm morning, and I was giving a visitor a small tour of our farm, enjoying the serenity of the surroundings. Suddenly, I noticed my sister, Ranjana, at a distance, waving a newspaper high in the air and calling out to me with excitement. Curious and slightly puzzled, I walked toward her, and that's when she shared the news—my name was listed among the Padma Shri awardees.

'The moment was surreal. My visitor and I stood there in astonishment, taking in the gravity of the news. It was a moment of joy, disbelief, and overwhelming gratitude. I feel deeply blessed, and I can only bow my head and thank the Lord for such a precious honour. Such moments reaffirm my purpose and inspire me to give my best to the art form that has shaped my life.'

Do classical performing arts hold the power to heal?

Shovana reflects on this with profound sensitivity, emphasising that the healing power of the arts lies within the individual rather than the art form or profession itself. Everyone's response is uniquely personal. She explains, 'Think back to the COVID lockdowns—creativity emerged from the most unexpected places. Even in those isolating times, how many classical artists truly gave in to despair? The answer is telling.'

For Shovana, the resilience of classical artists comes from a focus on art, not materialism. 'We're not driven by commercial gain but by devotion to the art itself,' she says. 'Classical arts connect us globally, offering a quiet message: Do you seek quick fame or lasting fulfilment? Wealth or *ananda* (inner joy)?'

In 2021, the passing of Pandit Rajan Mishra left Pandit Sajan Mishra in profound silence, too grief-stricken to even speak, let alone sing. He remained in *maun* (silence) for a year, and it was only through the power of music and the persistent encouragement of his disciples that he eventually returned to singing.

Pandit Sajan Mishra distinguishes between a *satvik kalakar* and an artist with a specific *udeshya* or motive. One seeks to achieve the purity of art, while the other pursues money and fame. He reflects on his guiding principle and values, stating, 'Our *uddeshya and samskara* should be *sai itna dijiye ja mein kutumb samaye; mein bhi bhookha na rahun, sadhu na bookha jaye.* (Give me just enough to support my family; let neither me nor any sage go hungry.)'

Pursuing a path in classical arts is a choice that demands unwavering dedication, patience, and integrity. It is not a swift ascent but a profound journey shaped by purpose and resilience. For Shovana, this path was inspired by a quest for *ananda*—a deep, enduring joy that nourishes the soul. She affirms, 'Hard work is the only way; there are no shortcuts. Avoid them. Embrace diversity. Be true to yourself and approach everything with sincerity and devotion. Immerse yourself in your learning, and from that depth, let the inner *rassaswadana* (joy of experience) and *anandam* (bliss) flow naturally. Excellence will follow in its own time.

'Trust that success may greet you tomorrow or even later if you falter today. There is no need to fear or rush. Others may ascend quickly, but life tests us all in different ways. Resilience is essential because surrendering to adversity is akin to giving up on life. Life is a cycle of light and shadow, of day and night. Dance, in its essence, teaches us to embrace this rhythm, to discover harmony in each phase, and to find strength in both stillness and movement.'

Her reflection highlights an essential truth: classical arts, for those who embrace them wholeheartedly, offer beauty, skill, and resilience. They provide an anchor, a steady light that continues to guide and uplift, even in the darkest of times.

Shovana emphasises that worldly recognition or accolades should never define the worth of one's talent or the purpose of one's passion. She urges aspiring artists to follow their hearts, immerse themselves completely in what they love, and give their utmost without being consumed by the desire for external validation. For her, the joy of creation and the process hold far greater significance than any award or applause.

She reflects on the poignant story of Guru Dutt, the legendary Indian filmmaker and actor, and his masterpiece *Kaagaz Ke Phool,* which she holds close to her heart. During his lifetime, Guru Dutt faced harsh criticism and rejection. The film into which he poured his soul was deemed a box office failure, and he was branded a disappointment by the very world he sought to move. Yet, years after his passing, the same film was celebrated as a cinematic marvel, and Guru Dutt came to be revered as one of the greatest actors in Indian cinema.

This story exemplifies the transient nature of worldly acclaim and the importance of staying true to one's craft. 'Recognition,' she says, 'is fleeting, often arriving when we no longer seek it or sometimes when we are no longer here to witness it. But the love and honesty we bring to our art are eternal. When we create with sincerity and passion, the work becomes our legacy, regardless of how it is received in our time.'

Rama Vaidyanathan, one of the directors at Ganesha Natyalaya—one of India's leading Bharatnatyam institutes—has taught dance for over four decades, performing across India and the world. Reflecting on the book, *Indian Classical Dances: The Healing Powers* by Kanaka Sudhakar, Rama shares insights into the healing impact of dance, especially for young learners. She reflects on how dance is a powerful medium for students, especially women, to reconnect with their bodies and rebuild self-esteem. Many who come to learn dance carry the weight of body shame, domestic violence, or unhealed childhood traumas that have left them feeling alienated from their physical selves. Through dance, they discover a sanctuary where they can confront these buried wounds.

Rama likens the process to catching the bull by its horns, where pain is expressed and transformed through art, offering a therapeutic release. Even seemingly simple acts—standing tall, combing their hair, adorning a *bindi*, or stretching their arms wide before a mirror—become profound gestures of reclaiming their bodies. These moments ignite a sense of ownership and joy, a liberation that is both physical and emotional.

Dance, she emphasises, is more than movement; it is a journey of self-love and reclamation, teaching individuals to embrace and celebrate their bodies. For every dancer, this reconnection is not just empowering but essential, a profound step toward healing and wholeness.

'As dancers, you may not possess grand assets or luxurious jewellery, but you hold something far more profound—the space around you. When you lift your arms in dance, that space becomes yours to claim and embody. Embrace it with confidence and grace. I have witnessed the incredible transformative power of dance in countless lives, especially among women who come from challenging circumstances. Many arrive burdened with shame about their bodies, hesitant and unsure. Yet, as they begin to move and express themselves, a beautiful shift occurs—they start to love and accept themselves.'

This newfound sense of wholeness as dancers creates a harmonious balance between their body, mind, and soul. It is one of the most rewarding gifts a dance teacher can offer. Dance teaches them to express their emotions freely, not to suppress them in silence. In the studio, they learn to embody love, anger, and wonder—whether it's Radha's deep love for Krishna or Durga's fierce, unyielding strength against Mahishasura. These expressions transcend language, awakening a spiritual awareness and connection within them. Through dance, they don't just perform; they reclaim their identity, emotions, and inner power. It becomes a path to self-discovery, healing, and liberation.

'At the Natya Kala conference in Chennai, I invited trans individuals—auto drivers, cleaners, labourers—who learned Bharatnatyam. On stage, they felt a sense of belonging and pride. Dance allowed them to express deep, sensitive poetry, taking them into another realm and awakening a sense of inner spirituality. One dancer, who transitioned from male to female, shared that the *ardha mandala* posture was difficult for her due to the strain on the crotch area and the inner thighs. Still, she felt joy in the experience, moving in her true body.'

Even differently abled children, says Rama, find joy and connection through dance, sharing laughter and stories backstage. Their joy in movement, despite any limitations, is a reminder of the power of dance to heal and uplift.

Rama has experienced the joy of teaching dance to seniors in their eighties living with Parkinson's. Simple tasks like pouring water can be daunting, yet rhythmic, cyclical dance steps help them reconnect with their bodies and minds. Movements become a guiding rhythm—one, two, three, four—transforming into a melody that aids daily tasks, like brushing teeth or picking up objects. These small victories bring a sense of accomplishment, independence, and joy, helping them rediscover the beauty in life's simplest acts despite their challenges.

Shovana explains that Kathak is therapeutic in its essence—its grammar encompasses this healing quality entirely.

She recalls her experience as a student when her guru tied an auspicious thread around her wrist, symbolising the continuation of tradition, like the *janeu* ritual in Hindu culture. She was also given *chana* and *gur*; the former represented the *kathor sadhna* (tough training) a disciple must undergo, while *gur* symbolised sweetness, *rassaswadan*, or *rasanabhuti*. Through this sadhana, one becomes one with the art leading to profound inner joy.

Art is a form of complete yoga. *Yama* is the resolve to learn; *niyam* represents discipline, which mirrors life's own *niyam* and *jeevan chakra* (cycle of life). *Asan* is the *mehnat* (hard work), and *pranayam* involves controlling one's breath while dancing, especially during *padhant* (recitation). If breath control falters, the rhythm is lost. In just thirty or forty minutes of dance, one

Yoga with Guru Shovana Narayan: Asian Art Center, Vilnius, Lithuania, 2nd June, 2022.
The Yoga Dance performed along with Yoga Guru Gražinė Genė

experiences physical exertion equivalent to an hour of jogging; this is reflected in the artist's glowing face, creating a surreal effect.

Each dance form possesses unique qualities and beauty, making them distinct in expression and style. In Kathak, intricate footwork and rapid spins, or *chakkars*, are central to its dynamic expression. In contrast, while also rhythmically rich, Kuchipudi has a lighter technical approach, with dancers placing their feet gently and maintaining a graceful, bouncing quality throughout the performance. Bharatnatyam, recognised as the oldest classical dance form, stands out for its precise geometric movements, intricate hand gestures, and deep connection to spiritual storytelling.

Guru Kanaka Sudhakar, an experienced Bharatnatyam artist, mentor, choreographer, and advocate for holistic health through dance, highlights a dancer's breathing techniques in her book, *Indian Classical Dances: The Healing Powers*.

Sudhakar, known for her research on the therapeutic benefits of Indian classical dance forms, emphasises how controlled breathing enhances a dancer's performance and contributes to physical and emotional well-being.

'In classical dancing, there are three speeds in which the steps or a long chain of steps is performed. Between these steps within the same item, there is a period of relaxation when the dancer walks back gracefully or stands for a few seconds, waiting for the next beat to start. There is also the period of relaxation when she shows the *bhava* or performs the expressive part of the item in which she depicts the song's words differently. Here, the dancer rests after vigorous dancing. So, what the dancer is trained to do is to hold her breath for short intervals when doing the very fast steps till she either slows down or finishes the *theermana* (a final, conclusive gesture or phrase marking the end of a piece.)'

Pratihar means detaching oneself from distractions that hinder learning, while *dharana* involves adopting the art as one's sole purpose. *Dhyan* is immersing oneself in the practice, akin to Buddha's meditation.

Shovana recalls how her mother would correct her footwork as a child, stressing that it should never be jerky but naturally produce a rhythm, a *sangeet* or music. This teaching was about immersing oneself so thoroughly in the dance that the music arises independently, allowing *dhyan* (meditation) to manifest. It was a state where one begins to hear the music not just externally but from within—tuning into the melody of their surroundings or soul.

Next comes *samadhi*, a state where the ego dissolves, and the individual ceases to exist as a separate entity, allowing the art to take complete control. *Kala ke sath ekakkar* (becoming one with art) is a process of self-elevation, where one attains inner harmony. Only when there is peace within can one experience true peace with the world around them. In this state, nothing can disturb the tranquillity that has been achieved.

Kathak, in its entirety, encompasses more than just a single word. Even in *abhinaya* (expression), a term like *atariya* can be portrayed in multiple ways: as a *seedhi* (staircase), a *kotha* (brothel), or as referring to one's *maang* (hair parting) adorned with *sindoor* (vermilion) or earrings. It intricately blends *avidha* (literal meaning), *lakshana* (symbolic meaning), and *vyanjana* (metaphor), creating layers of depth and nuance in its expression.

Is there a specific body type required to be a dancer?

Shovana reflects on the traditional notions of feminine beauty often found in sacred texts, which suggest that a dancer should be tall, stunning, and slim, embodying the qualities of *komalangi* or *kamini*. However, she stresses that the true essence of a dancer lies in respecting and nurturing their body. While physical fitness is essential, excess weight or an underdeveloped physique can present challenges. Maintaining good posture, an active weight, and high energy is crucial. Ultimately, there is no single perfect body type for a dancer.

Sharon is in awe of Shovana's contagious energy and relentless drive. With so many performances on her schedule, it's hard to keep up, yet when you think she might take a break, she returns with fresh, captivating creations. Shovana brings scenes from Indian epics to life, adding her unique touch every time. She manages everything—from selecting texts to choosing artists for music and sound edits—almost single-handedly. She has an incredible ability to stage pieces with perfect details that make them shine. Sharon finds it challenging to memorise long monologues (like her twenty-two-minute text as Gandhari from *Andha Yug*) and is impressed by Shovana's skill. Having worked with her for years, Sharon admires her brilliance, multi-talented nature, and self-driven commitment to deliver excellent results consistently.

Shovana acknowledges that appearance plays a significant role in the visual arts but emphasises that the true essence of dance goes beyond physical beauty. On stage, a dancer fitting conventional beauty standards may initially draw attention. Still, as the performance progresses, the artistry of a dancer who doesn't conform to traditional ideals can captivate and shift the focus. The essence of dance transcends mere appearance, highlighting how the art form and the aesthetics elevate the dancer's beauty.

Historically, idealised depictions of female dancers in the *puranas*, poetry, and sculptures have set unrealistic standards of perfection, not always achievable.

Shovana challenges us to consider: what if men were subject to the same societal pressures to look masculine and beautiful?

She recalls a story from a friend about a male dancer with a large build and a prominent moustache. Initially, her friend questioned how he could be a dancer, but within moments, the dancer transformed into a graceful figure, captivating the audience with his nimbleness and artistry. It is not just appearance but the comfort and ease with one's body and movements that genuinely matter, allowing the dancer's aesthetics and expressions to shine through.

She remembers meeting a dusky-complexioned woman from Madhya Pradesh with striking features that captivated her—a reminder that beauty transcends traditional standards. *Kavi* Surdas himself celebrated the beauty of Krishna's *shyam rang* or dusky complexion.

'If a dancer is skilled, their artistry will captivate the audience. One could be a great rhythmic, *abhinayapurn* or a *shringarik* dancer—what truly counts is how their inner being resonates with their art. If dancers don't genuinely feel their character, their performance may seem shallow and won't touch the viewers. This is where the difference between a craftsperson and an artist comes in. While anyone can learn technical skills, art is something deeper. Artists breathe life into their work, a process known as *Pran Pratishtha*, making their performance not just a display of skill but a heartfelt expression.'

The question—'Can only females be classical dancers?' touches upon a more profound, sensitive issue that reflects society's historical attempts to confine art within restrictive boundaries. Over time, societal norms have often dictated who can participate in specific art forms based on gender, body weight, age, physical appearance, and other arbitrary attributes. This perspective not only undermines the universality of art but also stifles the creative potential of countless individuals.

Classical dance, a profound and expressive form of storytelling, transcends gender and physical characteristics. Yet, traditional views have sometimes labelled dance as a feminine pursuit, discouraging men from engaging in it or limiting their roles to specific archetypes. Similarly, ideals of beauty and youth have been imposed on dancers, sidelining talented individuals who do not fit these narrow moulds.

However, history and contemporary practice show that classical dance is enriched by diversity. Male dancers and performers breaking stereotypes of age or appearance have proven that passion and dedication are the true hallmarks of artistry.

Art thrives on individuality and expression, not conformity, and society must continue to challenge outdated norms that restrict its flow. Recognising and celebrating the diversity of artists ensures that the transformative power of art remains inclusive and boundless.

Guru Vijay Shanker, an experienced Kuchipudi and Kathakali exponent, has spent over four decades promoting Indian classical dance through performances, recitals, and lecture demonstrations. His work aims to foster national integration and global peace, emphasising that while each dance style has its unique expression, the underlying philosophy—the *shastram*—remains universal.

Guru Vijay discusses the bias men face in classical dance, sharing his struggle. Coming from a military family, his father was initially shocked by Vijay's desire to pursue dance, which was seen as a female-dominated art form. After some hesitation, his father allowed him to learn Kathakali, a physically demanding dance performed only by men. Later, Vijay's interest shifted to Kuchipudi. Despite facing stereotypes at every turn, he followed his heart.

Shri Siddhendra Yogi, a renowned reformer of Kuchipudi, introduced the tradition of using Brahmin boys for dance, as many Kuchipudi stories are based on the Bhagavad Gita and on Krishna's life. The belief was that only boys could maintain the dance's spiritual purity, reinforcing the gender bias that classical dance, especially devotional forms like Kuchipudi, was best suited for male performers. This tradition, while rooted in spirituality, also reflected the gender biases of its time.

Historically, Indian society viewed dance as a female domain, with little interest in male dancers. However, this perception has shifted, and male performers are increasingly celebrated. Anita Ratnam, a renowned Bharatnatyam dancer and choreographer, led a troupe of male dancers on a US tour, where their performances were met with enthusiastic audiences often filling the venues. This reflects the growing recognition of male dancers in Indian classical arts and the international appreciation for diverse artistic expressions.

'Is there a certain age to learn dance?' Shovana is often asked this question. 'I have a student who started Kathak later in life and is now fifty, eager to perform solo. She worries this might be her last chance, so I support her every step, even teaching her online.

'Then there's Anupama, who made incredible strides at forty-five. It proves there's no age limit for dance if you approach it passionately!' Shovana jokes, 'I can be a stern taskmaster, though. If they don't get it, I tell them they're just doing an item number. Classes sometimes stretch from six in the morning until ten at night—but they know their reputation, and mine, are on the line!'

As artists grow older, their relationship with their craft naturally evolves. The ageing process brings challenges and opportunities, and with it comes the chance to reinterpret the art they once mastered in new and meaningful ways.

'Of course, I know our bodies lose some of their whirlwind energy as we age—I'm not spinning in *chakkars* like I used to! But for me, ageing gracefully means finding purpose in everything I do. I love diving into old archives, pulling out sparks of creativity from the past. Each story has its lesson, and I aim to breathe fresh life into it. Variety is the spice of life, and my art is no different—it keeps things exciting and vibrant. Every performance should speak to the traditions that shaped it and to today's audience. By reinterpreting the past, I keep my art dynamic and connect more deeply with those who experience it.'

Listening to Shovana speak, Manjari interrups with a question of her own—'Do artists age?'

'Physically, perhaps, but at heart, they remain youthful, driven by a passion that transcends time. Their art evolves, pouring experiences and emotions into something more vibrant each year. Shovana Narayan, at age seventy-four, continues to command the stage with the same vigour, presenting characters and emotions with remarkable intensity. Her graceful, yet robust movements defy age, and it's her mental and emotional resilience that truly captivates.'

Shovana doesn't just perform; she channels her life's challenges into her art, using it as catharsis to heal and transcend pain. The stage becomes her sanctuary to transform personal struggles into universal beauty.

'Art is always alive and ever-changing. If it had become ossified, it would have faded away long ago. Instead, it has a vital essence—*prana* (life force). While art continuously evolves, it remains rooted in its core ethos and spirit. Like a river that flows from a single source, branching out into various tributaries, art has many paths but ultimately converges back into the ocean of collective experience,' maintains Shovana.

A great example is how we still find inspiration in ancient stories, even after many centuries. The Kathak community, for instance, has survived the passage of time, with roots tracing back to the *Adi Parv*, (a section in the Mahabharata), an important ancient text. This shows how, despite changes and challenges, the heart of Kathak and art itself continue to flourish, blending tradition with the ongoing journey of human expression.

Shovana quotes an ancient Prakrit verse as an inscription, related to the history of Kathak:

'Maggasirasuddhapakkhe nakkhhate varanaseeye nayareeye uttarpuratthime diseebhage gangaye mahanadeeye tate savvo kathako bhingarnatenam teese stuti kayam yehi raya adinaho bhavenam passayi.'

(During the month of Magha, on the bright half (Shukla Paksha) of the lunar calendar, at a particular star, northwest of Varanasi, on the banks of the Ganges, the shringar dance performed by Kathaks in praise of Lord Adinatha.)

Pratibimb
Reflections

Shivah Shaktya Yukto Yadi Bhavati Shaktah Prabhavitum,
Na Chedevam Devo Na Khalu Kushalah Spanditumapi.

(When Shiva is united with Shakti, he becomes capable of creation and action. Without Shakti, even Shiva lacks the power to move or act.)

In Indian philosophy, Lord Shiva, the cosmic dancer of destruction, is inseparable from Shakti, his feminine counterpart. Without Shakti, Shiva becomes *Shava*—a lifeless entity.

Shivah Shaktya Vihinah Shava Iva Prakirtitah.

Similarly, *Tandava* (representing vigour and destruction) is powerless without *Lasya* (symbolising grace and creation). Together, they manifest the perfect balance of energies necessary to sustain the universe.

Tāṇḍavaṁ Lāsyasametaṁ Yadā Syāt Sṛṣṭisthitipralayakāraṇamekam/
Śaktiśivāviva Bhedaṁ Vinā Tad Viśvaṁ Dhatte Samatāmadhunā Ca//

(When Tandava unites with Lasya, they become the single cause of creation, preservation, and dissolution. Just as Shiva and Shakti are inseparable, this harmony sustains the universe's balance.)

Strength without compassion is hollow, and grace without purpose is inert, urging you to cultivate both in harmony.

Shovana Narayan has masterfully woven these cosmic concepts into her dance productions, creating performances that resonate deeply in the present day.

Through pieces like *Ardh Narishwar*, which celebrates the Hijra community as divine embodiments of the Ardh Narishwar concept, *Roop Vidroop*, a poignant portrayal of an acid attack survivor, and *Toota Ye Vishvas Kyon*, a searing exploration of a daughter violated by her father, Shovana transforms mythology into a powerful medium for social reflection. Her productions highlight the struggles of women and marginalised groups and channel the energies of Tandava and Lasya to empower, heal, and inspire. By doing so, she redefines classical dance as a tool for societal change, making ancient wisdom relevant to contemporary challenges.

Politician Meira Kumar reflects: 'I deeply admire women, especially those who have achieved great heights. Whether I know them personally or not, their struggles and accomplishments inspire me. First, the fact that Shovana is a woman is itself a compliment. Second, she has earned significant recognition for her work. Not everyone receives the acknowledgment they merit.'

Meira Kumar, herself, defies expectations. As the first woman Speaker of the Lok Sabha, one might envision a bold, fiery, and loud leader, yet she wields her influence through intellect, grace, and quiet determination. A seasoned diplomat and politician, she has shaped change with a steadfast commitment to justice. From introducing British audiences to Indian art and culture during her tenure in London to overseeing the transition of Parliament to its new premises, her leadership has left an indelible mark. A vocal advocate for women's rights, she has consistently condemned injustice and championed issues affecting women. Her strength lies not in volume but in the depth of her convictions.

'It fills my heart with warmth to speak of someone as dear to me as Shovana. I have known her for many years, and when I reflect on my life, I think about the people who have truly enriched it. That list is quite short, and Shovana is undoubtedly on the list.

'I have warm memories of Shovana visiting our home with her younger sister, Ranjana. Shovana must have been around ten or eleven, dressed in pretty frocks, accompanying her parents. My father, Babu Jagjivan Ram ji—fondly known as *Babuji* and the former Deputy Prime Minister of India—had a special place in his heart for young girls, cherishing them as daughters. He adored Shovana and Ranjana; their family never missed his birthday celebrations.

'I still remember the joy of seeing these little girls, their presence lighting up the occasion. I was fortunate to be raised in a family where girls were deeply treasured. My father would personally feed Shovana and Ranjana cake, a gesture filled with warmth and affection. As guests arrived with garlands and bouquets to wish him, he would lovingly place them around their necks—again, a beautiful gesture reflecting his love for them.'

Meira Kumar fondly recalls watching Shovana grow up and transition into college. She vividly remembers when Shovana won a United Nations beauty contest, with her photograph appearing in *The Illustrated Weekly*. Meira delighted in seeing her shine and sensed even then that Shovana had a remarkable aura hinting at a future filled with outstanding achievements.

During 1977-78, Meira was posted in London as part of the foreign service, overseeing press and cultural affairs. At the time, many Indian performing artists struggled to gain international exposure, as India, still a developing economy, had strict limitations on foreign exchange. Those travelling abroad faced financial constraints.

Despite these challenges, efforts were made to bring Indian artists to the UK, and Meira played a key role in facilitating this. A non-governmental organisation (NGO) in the arts sector helped select performers, and Shovana was chosen. She confidently performed at the prestigious Victoria and Albert Hall, earning admiration from the British audience. Shovana visited the UK twice during Meira's tenure, leaving a lasting impression with her artistry.

'This was my first opportunity to witness her perform, which was truly special. I watched her blossom as an artist and a confident young woman ready to embrace the world. Over the years, I stayed in touch with her and her family, and every time I attended her performances, the auditoriums were packed with an audience that adored her artistry.

'When I became the Speaker of the Lok Sabha, I had the privilege of hosting speakers from various countries. Visiting dignitaries would often travel to cities like Delhi, Mumbai, or Bengaluru but wouldn't get to experience India's rich cultural heritage. I wanted to change that by introducing them to our arts, dance, and traditions.

'Before each formal dinner, I would invite the guests an hour early to enjoy a performance by renowned Indian artistes. I invited Shovana to present Kathak on one such occasion, and she graciously accepted. Her performance represented our cultural legacy beautifully, leaving a beautiful impression on our esteemed guests.'

Meira sees Shovana as a remarkable embodiment of the finest qualities in a woman and takes great pride in her achievements. She admires the thought-provoking themes Shovana chooses for her dance performances, as they often carry meaningful messages.

'Shovana has not only excelled in her journey but has also contributed immensely to Kathak. Through her art, she has conveyed powerful messages addressing societal issues. She continues to evolve and inspire with each new theme she explores.'

Meira firmly rejects the notion of *karma* and the transmigration of the soul, as she believes it leads to passive acceptance.

'I do not subscribe to these theories as they condition you to be willing victims, discouraging you from questioning or rebelling. The so-called *kartavya bodh* is, in a way, a trap that binds you to submission. Such beliefs enable oppression, absolving those who perpetrate injustice, of any guilt. One must stand up and rebel for the right causes—Shovana always does so.'

Meira describes Shovana as a true dreamer and, with her gentle yet profound insight, draws a subtle distinction between dreams and ambition:

'Shovana has never ceased to dream—for without dreams; her dance would lose its soul. There is wisdom and talent, and then there is hard work. But hard work without wisdom is futile, just as wisdom and talent without dedication amount to nothing. Yet even these three—wisdom, talent, and hard work—are meaningless without a dream.

'When one dreams for oneself, it is ambition. But when one dreams for the upliftment of the lowest of the low, it becomes a dream. Too often, we mistake our aspirations for dreams, yet they are merely pursuits of the self. In its purest form, a dream transcends personal gain—it is a vision for something greater than oneself,' Meira states.

Art uniquely elevates humanity, working quietly on the minds and hearts of those who experience it.

'Shovana Narayan's performances are a perfect example of how art can inspire and bring about change. Her ballets go beyond entertainment, carrying deep and meaningful messages that leave a lasting impact. Through her work, she blends passion, education, and creativity, thus creating a powerful combination that speaks to the audience on a deeper level,' observes Anuradha Goel, chairperson, PHD Family Welfare Foundation and past president of FICCI Ladies' Organisation.

Shovana, through her work and spirit, embodies this more extensive idea of empowerment—one that moves beyond individual achievement to transforming communities, one woman at a time.

True empowerment, as Anuradha sees it, lies in giving women the tools to succeed and helping them believe they deserve to thrive. Anuradha exemplifies this spirit through her journey. After completing her Senior Cambridge, she pursued higher studies in Canada and later graduated from Hindu College. Her upbringing was shaped by her father's career as a diplomat in the Indian Foreign Service, which took her to Holland for a period before she eventually returned to India.

For the past five decades, Anuradha has dedicated herself to welfare work, and she has known Shovana Narayan for over fifteen years. While their paths had crossed earlier, their friendship deepened as they began collaborating on initiatives within the PHD Chamber of Commerce Family Welfare Foundation.

'My entry into this field was purely coincidental. My child

was born at St Stephen's hospital. Dr Karan Singh, the Health Minister, encouraged hospitals to set up welfare units. My gynaecologist, also the hospital's director, suggested I start one. I was intrigued but hesitant, explaining that I was only twenty-two and had just given birth to my first child. The doctor replied, "The work will grow with the child." And that's exactly what happened.'

Anuradha's journey unfolded step by step, beginning with her formation of a welfare unit for needy patients. She took the initiative to start the Parent-Teacher Association (PTA) at Modern school in Vasant Vihar. This gradually led her to get involved with Shri Ram Bhartiya Kala Kendra, where she played a pivotal role as the chair during the FICCI Ladies' Silver Jubilee celebrations.

Serving as president of the FICCI Ladies' Organisation, Anuradha decided to honour twenty-five remarkable women from various fields across India. She approached Shovana Narayan, requesting her to accept an award in the creativity category, particularly following her outstanding work in the Commonwealth Games.

Assuming the role of chair at the PHD Family Welfare Foundation, she invited Shovana to join the Board, and they have collaborated ever since. Together, they are part of the Women and Child Development Committee, which conducts numerous women-empowerment programmes and presents awards to exceptional women.

One notable initiative they launched is the *Astitva Samman*, which recognises organisations that promote women's welfare, including women-friendly corporations, NGOs, government organisations, and Micro, Small and Medium Enterprises (MSMEs). Shovana serves as a jury member for this award. Following her suggestion, they also introduced awards for tenth, eleventh, and twelfth-grade students across India who have made socially valuable innovations. The jury consists of four secretaries from the Government of India—three retired and one currently serving—all women.

In 2023, they honoured Kirloskar as a corporation for its women-led factory in Coimbatore. They recognised an NGO that operates a hospital for women and a school for boys and girls in the remote hills of Uttarakhand. Shovana and Anuradha have united their efforts to make a meaningful difference in the lives of women and children.

Shovana invited Anuradha to join the Board at Asavari, an organisation hosting music and dance festivals. Their friendship and collaboration have flourished, growing beyond personal camaraderie into a professional alliance that uplifts their careers.

This culture of mutual empowerment did not stop there. Not only did Anuradha welcome the opportunity, but Jyotsna Suri also extended a similar gesture by inviting Shovana to join the board of independent directors for The Lalit Suri Hospitality Group. Recognising Shovana's wisdom, leadership, and vast experience, Jyotsna saw her as an invaluable resource whose presence strengthened the team and provided unwavering support.

'She is a Padma Shri awardee, and her dedication and hard work have earned her numerous accolades over the years. I am proud to have her on our board as an independent director. She is highly engaged in all proceedings, bringing valuable insights and contributing meaningful ideas to our discussions. Her commitment to the board is truly commendable. Our association has remained strong, and I sincerely hope it continues,' Jyotsna expresses.

It has been an extraordinary alliance—three accomplished women lifting countless others, transforming personal achievements into a shared legacy of success.

While Jyotsna served as the president of FICCI, Shovana played a pivotal role in shaping its cultural landscape, spearheading the culture committee with vision and dedication.

'My role in FICCI has been distinct from hers. While I was the president, Shovana has been an integral part of the culture committee, contributing significantly to its vision and initiatives. Her presence has brought immense value, enriching the committee with her deep understanding of the arts and passion for cultural preservation. One of her defining qualities is her wholehearted dedication to everything she undertakes. Whether it is her role as a dancer, a mentor, or a cultural ambassador, she commits herself entirely to ensuring that her contributions are meaningful and impactful.' Jyotsna reflects that her involvement in FICCI has been no exception—she has infused the culture committee with her expertise, elevating its stature and broadening its influence.

This cycle of women championing one another reflects the immense power of female solidarity. When women create spaces for each other, they elevate their careers and set the foundation for deeper, more meaningful collaborations.

True empowerment is not just about personal success—it's about lifting others as you rise. Shovana exemplifies this through her leadership, allowing her students to flourish while remaining open to suggestions and always learning and evolving as a teacher. She has nurtured a space where growth is shared, not confined.

'She defines what it means to be an empowered woman—balancing kindness, integrity, and excellence in two demanding professions. Mastering both bureaucracy and dance, she never compromised one for the other. She made her own choices—both in her career and personal life—and honoured each role with dedication, growing stronger with every step. To me, true empowerment lies in sustaining oneself while uplifting others. The instinct to help is inherent in most women (and men), but she used it first to strengthen herself and then extend that support to others, beginning with her students. She has gone out of her way to mentor them, and every student she nurtures and sends out into the world is an extension of her empowerment. She doesn't just shine on her own; she spreads her wings and shares her success with others, always intending to uplift and support them,' says Jyotsna.

For Anuradha, women's empowerment is about creating a ripple effect. It's about teaching skills that enable women to become self-sufficient while educating them on critical aspects of life. Through the PHD Family Welfare Foundation, which operates twenty-six development units across India, including in tribal areas, they have imparted skills and raised awareness on topics like gender sensitivity and self-defence.

In one striking example, during a gender sensitivity programme, they discussed how chromosomes determine a child's sex. A mother-in-law who had always blamed her daughter-in-law for not having a son touched her daughter-in-law's feet after the session, realising the truth for the first time. This small but profound moment symbolised breaking deep-seated beliefs and fostering understanding and compassion.

Anuradha remarks that Shovana Narayan embodies many facets beyond her identity as a performing artiste. A true artist is, first and foremost, a human being, attuned to the pulse of their times and actively engaged in addressing the challenges that hinder a nation's growth. Shovana has consistently highlighted pressing societal issues through her thought-provoking performances, offering subtle yet powerful reflections and pathways for change.

One such performance was *Roop Vidroop*—a stirring performance that delved into the complexities of love, societal pressures, and the enduring scars of trauma. Through evocative dance and poignant storytelling, Shovana portrayed a young woman's journey from radiant love to devastating betrayal, culminating in an acid attack. The narrative unfolded with profound symbolism—a swing representing innocence, vibrant colours dimming under the weight of family honour, and a mirror reflecting the struggle for self-acceptance.

The harrowing act of violence, depicted with haunting realism, left the audience breathless, while the dancer's portrayal of resilience and empowerment offered a powerful commentary on inner strength. Using a rose as a symbol of rebirth emphasised that beauty transcends physical appearance, resonating deeply with the audience. Complemented by Rama Pandey's poetic script and narration, the performance left an indelible mark, reflecting societal flaws and celebrating the human spirit's capacity for hope and transformation.

The performance also posed an intriguing challenge: how does one convey such profound themes in a way that resonates with a modern audience accustomed to fast-paced narratives and fleeting attention spans?

Could symbolism and poetic narration bridge this gap effectively or would its brevity overshadow the depth of the message?

Balancing artistic expression with audience engagement is no small feat, raising the question of how an artiste crafts performances that remain both impactful and accessible.

Shovana understands that. To adapt, she keeps her performances concise without losing their depth or purpose. Each production is carefully crafted to engage and influence the audience's thoughts and emotions, subtly working to shift their mindset.

While Anuradha values the adaptation of musical compositions to suit contemporary audience attention spans and expectations, Pavan Varma holds a contrasting perspective, reminiscing about an era when musical concerts would span entire nights. The audiences cherished the immersive experience.

'The era of those enchanting *mahfils*, where a raga would unfold throughout the night, and the audience would be completely absorbed, is long gone. Today, audiences often crave the fast-paced *drut*, the crescendo, the claps, and the rhythm of the tabla, rather than a slow, meditative *vilambit* raga. Classical dances, too, would once stretch through the night. In certain forms, such as Bharatnatyam, there is a gradual build-up, with seven specific steps to evoke the mood of the rasa.'

These traditions are not recent; they trace back to ancient times.

'Musicians and artists' roles have changed, with audience expectations now set at a different standard. As an artist, however, to my mind, you are not expected to lower yourself to the common denominator. It is unfortunate,' Pavan observes.

The essence is that any adaptation or deviation from the traditional form or spirit of art to align with the audience's preferences demands the discerning expertise of a true maestro. Shovana exemplifies such an artist who possesses the insight and ability to gauge the audience's pulse while making thoughtful adjustments to her content, all without compromising the sanctity of her art.

'A thing of beauty is a joy forever. Her performances are beautiful, not just in their execution but in how they resonate long after the final act. She demonstrates that true mastery comes from loving and being dedicated to what you do. Her tireless commitment and joy in her work shine through, making her art enjoyable and transformative.'

Anuradha sees Shovana as a person brimming with patience, enthusiasm, and an unwavering drive to make the most of every moment.

'I cherish Shovana as both a friend and a colleague. Her ever-smiling and warm demeanour radiates positivity, infusing any space she enters with fresh energy. She's the heart of every gathering, making everyone feel valued by her presence. During the COVID pandemic, Shovana's disciple in Vietnam, Anupama, performed a programme centred on Draupadi. Partway through the performance, Shovana was invited on stage, and her dance, full of joyful freedom, was truly mesmerising. The calibre of disciples she nurtures speaks volumes about her excellence as a guru. Over the years, I have witnessed many of her captivating performances. Recently, before her seventy-fourth birthday, her students paid tribute to her by presenting every aspect of Kathak she had taught them—intricate footwork, expressive abhinaya, or emotive bhav. Each element reflected the precision and perfection she imparts to her art.'

Lifelines

Ah, that day still makes me chuckle—imagine me lying there in a hospital bed, surrounded by an army of doctors and nurses, all fussing over me like I was a porcelain doll about to shatter. 'Complete bed rest,' they said, wagging fingers at me as if they had any clue who they were dealing with. Bed rest? For me? My mind never rests, let alone my body!

I lay there nodding solemnly, putting on my best obedient face, all the while plotting my great escape. They hovered around like jailers guarding a high-security prisoner, completely unaware of the rebellion brewing in my head. I mean, come on, how could they think I'd miss a performance, especially one my dear Lithuanian disciple, Kristina Dolinina, had worked so hard to organise? I had made a commitment, and nothing—not tubes, not needles, not even their dire warnings—was going to stop me.

So, with the stealth of a seasoned escape artist, I waited for the right moment. The nurses stepped out for a minute, and the doctors were probably busy writing yet another list of don'ts for me. I swung into action. With the tube still sticking out of my wrist (a minor detail, really), I slid out of that bed, swapped the hospital gown for my stage outfit, and made my getaway.

When I finally stood under the lights of the stage that evening, I couldn't help but grin. The tube dangling from my wrist felt like a badge of honour—a tiny souvenir from my escapade. I could almost picture the doctors back at the hospital, scratching their heads, wondering how I'd managed to slip past them. But that's me—always dancing to my own rhythm, doctors' orders be damned. Life doesn't wait, and neither do I!

Shovana Narayan's life is a whirlwind of dance, awards, and constant motion, but behind the scenes, there's a dynamic duo that makes it all possible: Manohar and Ganesh, her house helps, audience, cooks, photographers, advisors, clowns, and managers, all rolled into two.

If Shovana's life were a performance, these two would be the unsung heroes, seamlessly shifting between roles with impeccable timing. Need a quick snack between rehearsals? They're your chefs. Want to capture the perfect moment? They've got the camera ready. Feeling overwhelmed by the chaos? They're right there with a dose of humour and sage advice.

From managing her schedule to making her laugh after a long day, Manohar and Ganesh are the two pillars who make sure Shovana's world keeps spinning smoothly, even if it means stepping in as her most loyal—and occasionally mischievous—supporting cast.

Are they unsung?

No. Because Shovana makes sure they get their share of credit—not just personally or in the presence of friends and acquaintances, but also on stage. Backstage, they manage countless details that the public never sees, and each time, she ensures they receive the appreciation they deserve from an audience that not only knows their names but will always feel their impact.

'One of the defining aspects of growing up in our household was the deep relationships we shared with our house helps. Many people casually refer to their house helps as family, but in Mamma's case, it truly resonates. She has stood by them through their most challenging times, offering unwavering support, and they, in turn, have reciprocated with equal loyalty and devotion.

Ganesh's older brother, Dinesh, was one of the closest people in my life, and his tragic passing left a deep void. Mamma has always supported his family, ensuring they were cared for. Then there's Manohar, who has been with us for decades. Mamma first met him during her Bharat Sanchar Nigam Limited (BSNL) days when he worked as staff. She saw beyond the surface, forming a meaningful bond with him—just one example of how she has walked through life, connecting with people on a profound level. Together, they've laughed, cried, and shared every aspect of our lives. Mamma has always looked out for their well-being, and they've responded with complete dedication. Ganesh is the saint of our family,' Ishan adds.

Perkha beautifully says, 'This is where the village theory comes in. How could Ishan live in Vienna without constantly worrying about his parents in India? That's because Manohar and Ganesh are like the other sons of the house. Just as Ishan has had many mothers, Shovana Mamma has had many sons.'

Ishan echoes this sentiment with deep emotion, 'They are my brothers. There's no doubt, no reservations, no trust issues. Ganesh is our family's finance minister—he controls everything. They are truly our lifelines, in every sense of the word.'

Manohar Mandal hails from Bihar. He first came to Delhi in 1998 and found contract work at the BSNL office in 2000 as a fourth-class employee. Shovana was also posted in BSNL, serving as the Joint Director General in the audit department. Manohar would often wonder why so many important people came to see her. When his curiosity finally got the better of him, he tried to find out if she had some other role outside her official duties. That's when he discovered she was a highly celebrated dancer and had received numerous awards.

'My contract ended, and then Didi asked if I wanted to work for her. She provided me with a place to live and a job. I've been with her ever since. I have learned so much from her. She's so energetic! *Jab kabhi hum bimar bhi ho jate hain, toh unhe dekhkar energy aa jati hai.* (Whenever I feel sick, one look at Didi makes me energetic). Sometimes, she works until 3 am, and then again, you can hear the tap of her feet rehearsing at 4 am! She even takes online classes in the morning after her rehearsal,' shares Manohar. '*Shuru shuru mein bada ajeeb lagta tha humko jab Didi achanak car mein bhi taali bajate rahte the, ungaliyon par kuch ginte rahte the* (Initially, it felt strange seeing her clapping in the car and counting something on her fingers),' Manohar laughs. '*Tab baad mein samajh aaya ki gadi mein baithakar Didi tukde aur padhant banati rahti hain.'* (Eventually, I realised she was composing *tukde* and *padhant* while sitting in the car.)

'*Didi maa jaisi nahi, ma hi hai,*' (Didi is not like my mother. She is my mother) adds Ganesh, the other lifeline of the home. 'This house is more like a guest house—always full of visitors. *Didi ko dekhkar mein hamesha urjawaan rahta hun* (I always feel energetic seeing her). We all got COVID except for Didi and Herbert sir during the COVID period. *Hamari sankhya jyada thi, toh hum aaram se movement kar rahe the aur Didi aur sir kamre mein band kar diye gaye the.* (We were moving around freely despite being more in number, while Didi and Herbert sir were confined to their room),' Ganesh laughs.

'Ganesh joined in 2009. Didi treats both me and Ganesh like family. We have a lot of fun at home. We even have a room that serves as an auditorium where we would do all sorts of activities. Lockdown *mein bhi Didi ne kisi ko chain se baithne nahi diya.* (Didi did not let anyone sit idle even during the lockdown). I enjoy the activities we do with Didi, especially stage shows, because, in my childhood, I participated in cultural events in the village. I had opted for music as one of my school subjects, not realising how useful it would become. *Sangeet vo cheez hai ki agar sar mein dard bhi ho ya koi bhi pareshani ho toh sangeet sunkar dimag relax ho jata hai. Sangeet ki jeevan mein kya ahamiyat hai, ab pata chala hai.* (Music is something that cures headaches and relaxes the mind during stressful times. Now I have come to understand how important music is in life.)

'We first lived at Pandara Road, then moved to Khel Gaon, and after 2020, we shifted to the current farm at Pushpanjali, Vrijvasan. I manage the fieldwork, and Ganesh oversees the house. I also help manage the dance classes. We manage most of the backstage activities. Didi gives us due recognition publicly. I have been with Didi for twenty-four years and have learned everything—except Kathak!' Manohar jokes.

'*Bhagvan ki kripa hai ki Didi kabhi thakti nahi hain. Ek baar Didi ki tabiyat kharab thi aur humne unhe Privat Hospital mein bharti karaya tha. Ek din mein milne gaya toh pata chala ki mareez glucose ki bottle hatwa kar meeting attend karne ke liye gaya hai. Meeting bhi kya tha—dance class! Didi kaam ke chakkar mein doctors ko bhi chakma dekar bhag jati hain. Ek baar toh maine dekha ki hospital ke bed par kisi tarah laptop ooncha karke latka rakha tha! Didi ka hospital room kitabon ki library bhi ban gaya tha. Yeh hain hamari Didi.* (Thank God, Didi never gets tired. Once, Didi fell sick, and we admitted her to Privat Hospital.

When I went to visit her, I learned she had removed her IV drip and left to attend umm—actually, a dance performance!

In her dedication to work, Didi even manages to outwit the doctors. I once saw her balancing a laptop above her hospital bed somehow! The hospital room even became her library.)'

Kathak Lok

After one of her performances in Gaya, a reporter approached Shovana and asked, 'Will you visit the Kathak villages?' Intrigued, she asked him to explain, and he told her about two nearby villages named Kathak. Her curiosity was piqued. The following morning, she took a taxi to see one for herself and was amazed when she saw a sign reading 'Kathak.'

'When I returned to Delhi, I shared my discovery, but no one believed me,' Shovana recalls. 'Years later, I decided to dig into India's census records, and there it was—six or more villages named Kathak! I was thrilled and immediately approached the Secretary, seeking permission to investigate the link between these villages and the dance form Kathak.'

The book *Kathak Lok* began as a simple idea—a plan to document the history of the Kathak villages—but it grew into a more profound journey later when Shovana met Geetika Kalha. Shovana initially wanted to record her findings about these villages' ties to Kathak, but she had no idea that a chance encounter would bring her the perfect collaborator as well.

Geetika Kalha, an accomplished IAS officer with over thirty

years of experience, has made remarkable contributions to preserving and promoting cultural heritage in northwest India. With a background in history and expertise in rural tourism, museums, and cultural interpretation, she has dedicated her career to conserving buildings, museums, and monuments.

As the first appointee for Punjab, overseeing five states from Jammu and Kashmir to Rajasthan, Geetika's role was pivotal in elevating regional art and culture. Her work involved identifying local, often lesser-known artists and guiding them in presenting their art on national platforms. She crafted events and exhibitions to highlight regional aesthetics.

'It so happened that we found ourselves on the same flight. I had recently retired, while Shovana had already left her official duties. We were both invited to Khajuraho, where a performing arts museum was planned. Shovana was going there as a performing artiste, and I was involved in setting up museums. During the flight, she began sharing her discoveries about certain villages linked to Kathak, piecing together bits of information she had come across,' Geetika shares.

'After we attended the meeting in Khajuraho, we flew back together and had a long conversation about the performing arts, especially Kathak. Shovana suggested we visit these villages to uncover more about Kathak's roots. It felt like an adventure waiting to happen, and with my recent retirement, I was intrigued. Shovana would delve into the history and artistic aspects of Kathak, while I, drawing on my experience as a former IAS officer familiar with village work, would handle the inquiries—speaking with the *patwaris*, examining land records, and engaging with local communities, areas where my expertise lay. With the promise of our combined skills, I agreed. But after that, I didn't hear from her for an entire year,' she resumes.

'Then, a year later, Shovana called with the exciting news—she had secured the government's approval. She asked if I was still interested, and I agreed wholeheartedly. Retirement had left me with ample time and curiosity. I was thrilled by the chance to dive into this journey.'

'Geetika set up all the necessary meetings with village authorities, enabling us to access land records and delve deeper. Our first question in each village was why they were named Kathak,' Shovana shares.

'Our journey felt like a treasure hunt from a mystery tale—one key would open a door, only to reveal another door and a new key to find. We took cabs and travelled from one village to the next, asking questions to the *sarpanchs* and villagers. That's when the idea of writing a book first struck Shovana, and she proposed we collaborate. Although I hadn't written before, I enjoy new challenges, so I agreed,' adds Geetika.

This marked the beginning of *Kathak Lok*, a shared journey of years of research and discovery between two unlikely collaborators, brought together by a single, serendipitous conversation.

The idea of collaborating on a book brought Shovana and Geetika even closer, weaving their lives together through shared discoveries and late-night conversations. While they also used FaceTime and other means to work remotely, nothing compared to their focus when meeting to write and edit in person. Geetika was in a constant state of learning, while Shovana—though deeply immersed in dance—found herself uncovering new aspects of the art she had practised her entire life.

What began as simple documentation transformed into an exploration. Shovana would frequently stay at Geetika's home in Chandigarh, immersing herself in the collaborative process, while Geetika would travel to Delhi to work with Shovana in her environment. Their visits weren't just about work; these became opportunities to learn from each other, building a deep friendship as they uncovered the history of Kathak. The back-and-forth between cities kept them connected, strengthening their partnership as they pieced together their book, chapter by chapter.

'Initially, we knew of seven villages named Kathak, but as one discovery led to another, we eventually identified at least sixteen. With my background in history, this unfolding journey into the unknown was thrilling and intriguing. We visited each of these villages, and even in one place that wasn't named Kathak, the local district commissioner gathered all the artists to meet with us. One artist mentioned a village named Ishvarpur, where this art form had been practised for generations. Digging into British-era records, we found references indicating that this village, like others, had been granted as a *jagir* (land gift) to Kathaks,' Geetika explains.

The two were perfectly in sync throughout their long-term research work. They travelled extensively, never fussing about where they stayed or what they ate. A simple plate of *dal-chawal* was all they needed—no need for fancy meals. Their journey was filled with exploration, from visiting temples to watching Kathak performances.

'Our shared discipline was a huge asset as we worked on the book. We set deadlines for each chapter and made sure to stick to them. I truly admire Geetika's incredible work ethic. We wrote everything together—sharing notes, editing each other's work, and discussing every word, sentence, and paragraph,' Shovana recalls wistfully.

'Even when we weren't writing, Shovana remained disciplined. She would wake up early at my place to teach her disciples online, always mindful of every minute. We had a blast, sharing jokes and laughter along the way. People often ask how we managed to get along so well. I always say, the key is being able to laugh together. We laughed much, always finding something to laugh about. Without that shared joy and curiosity, the journey would have felt like a chore. I used to joke that I was the 'non-dance' person in this duo and insisted that the book shouldn't be too technical. It had to be accessible, even for someone like me who didn't know much about dance. Shovana would try to explain something to me, and I'd stop her with, "Excuse me, I don't get it." She'd struggle for a while, then throw her hands up and say, "Alright, I'll just dance it for you!" Honestly, I think she's performed more for me than she has on any stage. Whenever I couldn't grasp a technical detail, she'd stand up and dance it out, saying, "Now you can write about it!" It was hilarious—and much fun!' Geetika has a hearty laugh here.

Throughout the in-depth research, the two encountered revelation after revelation about the origins of Kathak, ultimately reshaping how the world viewed the dance form. They dove into the Upanishads, along with historical records, and traced Kathak's origins back to the *Samaveda*, establishing it as one of India's oldest dance forms.

The research would challenge and expand the story of Kathak's origins, showing it as a classical art form grounded in temple traditions and practised by Brahmins long before it was associated with royal courts. Their findings, supported by ancient scriptures and inscriptions, created a paradigm shift in India's understanding of Kathak.

This groundbreaking work has led most Kathak artists in India to adopt a new narrative when explaining its roots. The book was launched by Dr Karan Singh, former Minister of Education of India.

Dr Karan Singh's seventy-five-year public life spans intellectual, spiritual, cultural, and political realms. An avid supporter of dance, music, and the arts, he served forty years in Parliament and authored twenty books, mainly on Vedanta, which he lectures on, worldwide. Known for distilling deep spiritual values into simple language, he credits Shiva as his guiding force at ninety-three. He is widely known as a patron of art. His museum in Jammu houses Pahadi paintings and 20,000 books.

'I have known Shovana Narayan for half a century, first seeing her perform in the prime of her youth. What struck me was her unique combination of beauty and intellect—a rare blend. Here was a remarkable artist who was also an intellectual and a senior government officer, seamlessly balancing both roles. Her talent and versatility are truly exceptional.'

Dr Karan Singh candidly shares that he once held a bias against Kathak, mistakenly viewing it as a lewd art tied to brothels. Reading *Kathak Lok* transformed his perspective entirely.

'I initially perceived Kathak as a court dance, but deeper study revealed its rich history, including its connections to temple traditions—a fact illuminated through the research of Shovana Narayan and Geetika Kalha. This discovery transformed my understanding of the art form's depth. My first encounter with classical dance was in 1954, during a visit to Madras, where I witnessed Vyjayanthi Mala perform Bharatnatyam at the Madras Music Festival. The experience was unforgettable, and it impressed upon me the power of dance to represent India's cultural heritage.'

Dr Karan Singh emphasises the importance of government and private sector support, including Corporate Social Responsibility (CSR) initiatives, in promoting the arts, as they play a pivotal role in shaping young minds and bridging cultural divides.

As authors, Shovana Narayan and Geetika Kalha were

committed to finding reliable sources to support everything they wanted to establish. Their journey, step by step, through the complexities of religion, performing arts, Upanishads, and Vedas, allowed them to explore the rich history of India, which strengthened their partnership. The result of this deep dive into history is a book that reflects 7,000 kilometres of travel across north India, and five years of dedicated fieldwork, investigation, and research. The mission was to uncover the origin of Kathak villages and understand what Kathak and Kathak Lok truly represented. Travelling, witnessing Kathak performances in temples, meeting maharajas, dancers, scholars, and *swamis*, the authors uncovered layers of history. Slowly, bit by bit, the facts emerged, revealing a clearer and more accurate picture of the dance form's origins.

Their research uncovered little-known facts about the pre-Christian roots of Kathak and its role in preserving and propagating dharma over the centuries, continuing as a living tradition today. In the end, *Kathak Lok* became more about the people—the Brahmin Kathaks—who practised it, rather than just the dance form itself.

As they met these Kathaks, they were surprised to find that these were Brahmins who performed songs and dances from the Ramayana and the Mahabharata, using these stories to teach and entertain the community without using modern media. This storytelling tradition helped spread the epics across the country. However, the challenge lay in proving that Kathaks were originally Brahmins, as this would shift the narrative from Kathak being primarily a Mughal court dance to a temple art form rooted in Brahmin traditions.

The word Kathak comes from the Sanskrit term *katha*, which means story, but it's not just any story. It's a story about gods, often drawn from ancient scriptures. The literal meaning of *Kathak* can be broken down into two parts: *Ka* refers to *Bhagvan* (the Almighty), and *Tha* means *sthapit karna* (to establish). This can be done through a story, action, song, or dance. So, *katha* is always a spiritual discourse, not just a casual tale. The person who performed this katha became known as a Kathak.

In ancient India, only Brahmins, as the interpreters of sacred texts, were authorised to perform katha because they were seen as the messengers of God. There were three primary ways of teaching, or *updesha*. The first was *samit updesh*, taught through the Vedas, which were not to be questioned but accepted and internalised. Only Brahmins could learn and teach these sacred teachings. The second type was *subriddh samit updesh*, where the word *subriddh* means friend. This kind of teaching allowed for questions and discussions. The conversation between Krishna and Arjuna in the Bhagavad Gita falls in this category. This form of teaching could be delivered by a Brahmin or a high-caste individual.

The third type was *kanta samit updesh*. The word kanta means beloved or beautiful, and this method of teaching is done with the same affection and praise you would give to a beloved. It's often expressed through poetry, song, or dance. This category includes the playful banter between Radha and Krishna, as well as the light-hearted exchanges between Krishna and the *gopis*. This is the way most of us are introduced to our mythology, through thc joy of music and dance, which also contains a lot of *shringar rasa* (the emotion of love and beauty).

Many of our religious teachings are transmitted through music, with Sanskrit *shlokas* often sung in rhythmic patterns. This method of storytelling, known as narrative theology, is also practised in churches, where the Christian faith is conveyed through songs and chants that tell the stories and teachings of the Bible.

By the time Shovana and Geetika began working on their second book, *Indian Mythology through Classical Dance*, they were already in perfect sync. This made the process much easier the second time around.

'Shovana is often referred to as a dancing diva, but she doesn't let the title define her. She carries it with neither pride nor arrogance. Fearless and bold, she never shies away from addressing current issues or standing firm in her convictions. Her ability to speak her mind with clarity while remaining considerate of others sets her apart. She strikes a rare balance between being honest and mindful of people's feelings,' Geetika states.

'Shovana has written extensively and approached her work with remarkable creativity. Her most transformative book, *Kathak Lok*, stands out for its in-depth research, offering a groundbreaking perspective on Kathak. Unlike previous writings on dance, which were often theoretical, Shovana's work is rooted in facts. She explored court records, travelled to villages, and even brought traditional Kathak performers and musicians to the stage, showcasing an older, lesser-known style of Kathak performed by men—very different from what we see today,' says Sharon Lowen.

Pavan Varma, a prolific writer with a vast repertoire across diverse subjects, has contributed several blurbs to Shovana's literary works. As a friend, he strikes a perfect balance—unafraid to offer constructive criticism where necessary while generously praising her intellectual contributions. He profoundly admires her relentless pursuit of communication and expression, which she channels through various mediums, including dance, discourse, narration, and writing.

He says, 'Shovana is an accomplished author in her field, with numerous books showcasing her deep knowledge as both a scholar and a classical dancer. Her profound understanding of classical dance, especially Kathak, is evident in her writings. As the saying goes, *Sahitya, sangeet, aur poori ek sanskritik parampara ka jab jod hota hai, tab ek nritya upajata hai*. (When literature, music, and the entire cultural tradition unite, dance is born.) Shovana perfectly fits in the context.'

Anuttar
The Unanswered

Kamani Auditorium, New Delhi
9 March 2025

I
Ardhanarishvara

The curtain rises. The stage is adorned with golden marigolds, mango leaves, and vibrant silk drapes. A sacred fire (*havan*) burns in a copper vessel at the centre. The groom and bride sit in front of it, draped in finery, their faces radiant with joy. Their mother, a graceful woman in her late sixties, stands beside them, performing the ritual of warding off the evil eye with a brass plate of camphor and red chilies.

Soft music of bells and chants fills the air. Dancers twirl gracefully around the couple, celebrating the auspicious occasion.

Suddenly, the beats of *dhols* rise, and a group of transgenders make a grand, colourful entry. Dressed in bright saris adorned with heavy jewellery, they clap rhythmically, their kohl-lined eyes sparkling. Their laughter fills the air as they bless the couple with exuberant gestures.

The mother smiles warmly, stepping forward to offer gifts—silk, bangles, and money. The transgenders accept with gratitude; their hands raised in blessing.

Among the dancers celebrating, a few women begin playfully teasing the transgenders. They swirl around them, pulling lightly at their saris, imitating their movements with exaggerated gestures. The laughter is sharp, edged with mockery. The transgenders pause, their joy flickering, their bodies stiffening as discomfort seeps in.

The mother's face darkens. She steps forward, her presence commanding. The laughter ceases. The teasing women shrink away, sensing the shift in the air.

She turns to the transgenders; her expression filled with understanding. A deep silence settles as she removes her dupatta, draping it over the shoulders of one among them. The transgender looks at her, eyes wide, as if recognising a forgotten truth.

Slowly, the mother places their *bindi* on her forehead and dupatta on her shoulders. She adjusts her bangles, allowing the identity to flow from one to the other as if dissolving the boundary that has kept them apart.

The transformation unfolds in stillness. The onlookers murmur. The same women who had laughed now whisper among themselves, their amusement turning into bewilderment, then discomfort. The mother stands, her gaze unwavering. But then, the weight of their stares presses upon her. Her hands tremble. She steps back, faltering. The reality of her defiance crashes down. The whispers grow, swelling into silent judgement.

The stage darkens. A single spotlight illuminates a towering idol of Lord Shiva, *Ardhanarishvara*—half-male, half-female. The mother turns toward it, her form small yet unyielding before the divine presence.

The flames of the *havan* flicker, casting eerie shadows. A question lingers in the air, unspoken yet thunderous: If Shiva can exist as both male and female, worshipped and revered, why must humans who embody the same duality be ridiculed?

The idol remains silent. The weight of centuries presses into the stillness. The transgenders step forward, placing their hands gently on the mother's shoulders. She exhales, her shame dissipating. Her spine straightens. Her hands remain folded, but now in resolve, not submission.

Lights fade. Curtain falls.

***

II
Shakuni—The Dice of Fate

The scene opens in the grand court of Gandhar, bathed in the golden hues of twilight. Courtiers stand in clusters, murmurs filling the vast hall as King Subal reclines on his ornate throne. A guard rushes in, his breath laboured, whispering urgent words into the king's ears. The king stiffens, his face darkening with disbelief.

The atmosphere thickens as the news spreads—Bhishma *Pitamaha*, the formidable warrior of Hastinapur, has entered Gandhar's borders with his army. The court erupts into anxious chatter, eyes darting toward the king. Shakuni, the young prince, steps forward, his expression a mask of quiet fury as he goes to pick up Bhishma *Pitamah*.

The imposing figure of Bhishma enters, exuding authority, his broad frame draped in pristine white, shimmering under the sunlight. Only the silver of his hair betrays his age; his presence defies time. The silence in the court is deafening as he speaks with an air of unshaken authority. He brings forth a proposal—Gandhari, the princess of Gandhar, is to be wed to Dhritarashtra, the blind prince of Hastinapur. If denied, the mighty army of Hastinapur will descend upon Gandhar, leaving behind nothing but smouldering ruins, widowed women, and orphaned children.

A wave of horror ripples through the court. Shakuni clenches his fists, his nails digging into his palms. His eyes burn with helpless rage as he looks toward his father, who sits frozen, trapped between filial love and devastation.

Before Shakuni can process his thoughts, the rustling of silken fabric is heard as Gandhari steps forward, her ethereal beauty marred by the sorrow in her eyes.

A stillness overtakes the scene as she speaks—not in fear, but in resolute acceptance. She chooses marriage over war, pledging herself to the blind prince. And then, with an unwavering hand, she picks up a strip of cloth and binds it over her eyes, vowing never to witness the world again. Shakuni, her cherished brother, stands frozen in silent shock. He averts his gaze, his face cloaked in sorrow.

As the reality of her sacrifice dawns, Shakuni is transported into a memory—a childhood moment of innocence and dreams. Like temple bells, a young Gandhari's laughter twirls in the palace garden. Her tiny hands grasp her brother's as she asks in treble tones, 'Will my prince come one day, riding a white stallion?' The image of her joy shatters against the cruelty of fate. The audience watches, many moved to tears, as Shakuni, known for his wit and deception, now becomes a vision of delicate sorrow, his expressions weaving an unspoken tale.

The scene shifts—the wedding—is an opulent affair, yet a quiet lament lingers beneath the grandeur. Shakuni, his heart weighed with anguish, watches his sister walk away into a destiny she did not choose. His fingers twitch, his mind calculating—revenge will be his, not through war, but through the slow unravelling of Hastinapur's legacy.

Years pass. The court of Hastinapur now thrums with tension. The fateful game of *chausar* unfolds. Shakuni, now a master of cunning, sits with his sharp gaze fixed on the Pandavas. One by one, they fall, losing land, wealth, and dignity. The dice roll, bearing the whispers of a brother's pain, a kingdom's vengeance. With each throw, history is rewritten, fate twisted into a noose.

The climax is a deafening silence as Draupadi is dragged into the court. The air is thick with unshed tears, trembling rage, and unspoken prayers. Her sari, a cascade of crimson and gold, is pulled, unravelling endlessly under Dushasana's merciless grasp. The court watches, breathless, as she closes her eyes, surrendering to the divine. The fabric does not end; it multiplies, an endless river of dignity shielded by Krishna's unseen hands.

The moment lingers. Draupadi stands, head high, eyes burning with unyielding defiance. The court is frozen—time itself holds its breath.

The sound of thunderous claps erupts. The audience is mesmerised, their eyes brimming, their hearts echoing the weight of history. The curtain falls on a stage steeped in emotion, leaving an aftertaste of sorrow, resolve, and unanswered questions.

***

III
Toota Ye Vishwas Kyun

The stage is dimly lit, bathed in pale blue and soft gold hues, casting an ethereal glow. A young girl stands centre stage, her arms wrapped around herself, her body trembling. Shadows flicker across her face, her eyes darting, haunted by invisible spectres of a recent past too dark to name. Every sound, every movement around her, seems to press against her like an unrelenting force.

A group of friends her age bursts onto the stage, dancing and laughing, their movements free and joyous. Their feet tap against the floor rhythmically, and their arms stretch toward the girl, beckoning her to join. They twirl around her, weaving a circle, oblivious to the horror etched on her face. A friend tugs at her hand; another playfully nudges her shoulder. The girl shudders, recoiling as though burned. Her breath hitches, her fingers clawing at her own skin as if trying to erase something unseen.

The friends pause, confused. Their laughter falters, eyes filling with questions. One steps forward, concern lining their voice. 'Why won't she play?' Other turns to her mother, who has been watching from a distance, worry deepening in her gaze.

The mother approaches, her voice laced with warmth, calling out to her daughter with sweet, familiar names—*Chanda*, *Jigar ka tukda*. Her voice is a melody of love meant to soothe and heal. The girl hesitates, her body still taut, then—slowly—she moves. One step. Then another. And then, in a single motion, she collapses into her mother's embrace, burying herself in the warmth of the only touch that does not scar.

The mother strokes her hair, whispering reassurances. But beneath her calm exterior, a tempest brews. She feels the girl's heartbeat against her chest, rapid, uneven, frightened. And then, a whisper—a broken, fragile confession. The girl's lips tremble as she utters words that splinter the mother's world apart. The words crawl into her mother's ears like a curse, sending a violent shudder through her body. The mother recoils, her hands trembling, her breath catching in her throat. Her eyes widen in disbelief, darting between her daughter's face and the storm raging in her mind. This cannot be. This must not be. The father—her husband—could not have…she stiffens. The air between them thickens. Disbelief, horror, agony—each emotion flits across her face in quick succession. This cannot be. How could this be? Her hands tremble as she cups her daughter's face, searching for answers in teary eyes that cannot lie.

The girl flinches at her mother's hesitation, mistaking her shock for disgust. She withdraws, her world collapsing yet again. The audience watches, their faces reflecting unease, some clutching their seats, others lowering their gaze, unable to meet the stage's devastating truth. They are witnessing a battle unseen—one mother's war against the silence, one daughter's struggle to reclaim herself. The inner chaos consumes her. Questions claw at her mind. Would anyone believe this? What will society say? How can a father commit such an act? Should she seek justice? Should she silence herself? Should she shush her daughter's voice? Should she confront the guilty, interrogate hard, or seek a confession?

She battles her demons in an agonising struggle, and then—she wins. She rises, reborn in resolve. She will save her child, no matter the cost. The audience watches, the weight of silence pressing upon them, their eyes glistening with tears, breaths bated.

Her mind is made up, and she searches for her daughter, calling her with the sweetest of names, her voice laced with newfound strength. The friends return, their laughter filling the air once more. They look for their friend. The mother calls out, but before the anticipated reunion, the stage undergoes a sudden transformation.

Male dancers clad in all-black, their faces hidden behind eerie masks, emerge onto the stage. They encircle the mother, their movements predatory, their laughter sharp and mocking. Their voices drip with scorn, taunting her choices, ridiculing her resolve. The mother recoils, her strength momentarily faltering. She withdraws, shrinking under their shadowy presence, sinking onto the stage as the torment of society closes in around her.

The audience leans forward; breath hitched. Some shift uncomfortably in their seats as if the judgement cast upon the mother also extends to them. Others wipe away silent tears, witnessing the weight of her isolation.

But then—like a phoenix rising from her ashes—she emerges again, her resolve burning brighter. She stands tall, eyes ablaze, fists clenched. No longer a mere mother but a force of reckoning. She will name the pain. She will fight. She will avenge if need be. The masked figures retreat into the darkness as her unyielding presence fills the stage.

But when the audience anticipates a hopeful ending

of courageous resolve, an unforeseen tragedy shatters their expectations—the daughter is shown hanging.

The curtain falls.

A heavy silence engulfs the air, thick and suffocating.

The audience exhales, then erupts—thunderous applause crashing through the hall.

The questions posed in all three dance productions remain unanswered—*Anuttar*.

Nritya-Tatva
The Substance of Dance

'I turn,
endlessly caught in this whirl,
the pirouette of desire,
the bhanvar,
where each step leads me back to where I started.
Is this the dance of life—
forever bound to circles,
with no end, no release?'

'The whirl is not your prison,
but the rhythm of existence
not meant to escape,
but to be embraced.
The music plays on,
and you, like the dance,
are both fleeting and eternal.'

'What is this fragile art that I create,
When I know all will fade, and time won't wait?

My limbs tremble, my heart beats in fear,
For what is born must vanish, disappear.'

'In the endless cycle, there is no end—
What seems like death is where life begins.

The dance, the art—these are not bound,
They live on forever, beyond all sound.'

'What of my name when time moves on?
Will my dance be remembered, my light long gone?
If I vanish like dust, like the wind's soft breath,
What meaning remains in the face of death?'

'Your name may fade, but the dance shall remain,
It will echo through time, through joy, through pain.
Art is a seed sown in eternity's ground,
It lives, it grows, though silence surrounds.'